WHAT OTHERS SAY ABOU

I have not read anything that has so stirred my heart, informed my mind and engaged my imagination in a long time. With great courage, determined honesty and a disarming humility, Steve Cox explores the issues du jour that threatens the unity of our church. He is unafraid to re-examine his own tradition and presumptions while demonstrating an utter determination to be faithful to the One who speaks through the written Word and is most fully revealed in Jesus Christ. Through the lens of his own personal journey (father of a gay son) as well as his professional journey (ordained in the Church of England) this book will inspire all who struggle to hold together their own doctrinal conviction, pastoral practice, and institutional loyalty. But this book also needs a health warning: it may seriously challenge your pride and extend your horizons, as God's grace works ever more deeply to reform us into the likeness of our Lord Jesus Christ. I urge you to read, mark and learn from every chapter... already having just completed it I want to ponder it again!

Rt Revd Dr Jo Bailey Wells, Bishop of Dorking

At this time there are two issues which I hear church leaders wrestling with more than any other. Firstly, how do we encourage deeper discipleship amongst Christians? Secondly, how do we engage fruitfully with issues that divide us – often issues of sexual ethics? Steve's book addresses both in a thorough, challenging and fundamentally Jesus-centred way. He focuses not on the answers but on how to conduct ourselves through our disagreements in a Christlike way. You could not read this book properly and fail to be changed by the challenges it poses to every Christian. If we embrace its principles as a church, our witness in society will be enhanced.

I believe that the church needs this book and I hope it is published soon.

Revd Alan Hulme
(formerly Director of Mission,
Diocese of Guildford, currently vicar of St Matthew
& St Oswald's with Overslade, Rugby)

NAVIGATING BY THE SON

Finding Our Way in an Unfamiliar Landscape

Stephen Cox

Matador
9 Priory Business Park,
Wistow Road, Kibworth Beauchamp,
Leicestershire. LE8 0RX
Tel: 0116 279 2299
Email: books@troubador.co.uk
Web: www.troubador.co.uk/matador
Twitter: @matadorbooks

ISBN 978 1800462 335

British Library Cataloguing in Publication Data.
A catalogue record for this book is available from the British Library.

Printed and bound in Great Britain by 4edge Limited
Typeset in 10pt Minion Pro by Troubador Publishing Ltd, Leicester, UK

Matador is an imprint of Troubador Publishing Ltd

To Johnny,
for actually being the kind of father I aspired to be,
and to James,
whose faithfulness and integrity sent me on a journey of discovery.

TABLE OF CONTENTS

PREFACE

The Bible tells us to love our neighbours, and also to love our
enemies; probably because they are generally the same people.

(G. K. CHESTERTON)

1 John 2:5   'This is how we know we are in him: Whoever claims
to live in him must live as Jesus did.'

A BRAWL BETWEEN MONKS

The newspapers reported that 'Israeli riot police have rushed into one
of Christianity's holiest churches and arrested two clergymen after an
argument between monks erupted into a brawl next to the site of Jesus'
tomb. Dozens of worshippers traded kicks and punches, knocking down
tapestries and toppling decorations at the site in Arab East Jerusalem.
"We were keeping resistance so that the procession could not pass
through... and establish a right that they don't have", a young Greek
Orthodox monk with a cut next to his left eye told *Associated Press*.

The monk, who gave his name as Serafim, said he sustained the
wound when an Armenian punched him from behind and broke his
glasses.

After the brawl, the church was crowded with Israeli riot police
holding assault rifles, standing beside Golgotha, where Jesus is believed
to have been crucified, and the long smooth stone marking the place
where tradition holds his body was laid out.

1

The feud is only one of a bewildering array of rivalries among churchmen in the Holy Sepulchre.'[1]

After the event each side, supported by their respective bishops, blamed the other.

There are so many things wrong with this that it is hard to know where to begin. The monstrous sinfulness of the brawl eclipses any perceived wrong complained of by either side. To brawl over perceived slights in defence of Jesus is absurd. He never stood on his dignity. It is so counter-productive to Christian life and witness, to everything for which the Church of the Holy Sepulchre claims to stand that the offences that gave rise to the brawl pale into trivial insignificance in comparison.

'To their loss they are crucifying the Son of God all over again and subjecting him to public disgrace.'[2]

The accounts of the brawl reminded me uncomfortably of relations and disputes current within the Church of England and the Anglican Communion. That may sound absurd. When have members of General Synod, or bishops at the Lambeth Conference, resorted to a 'punch up'? However, I believe that the way that we are handling many of the issues that divide Anglicans today, not least the issue of homosexuality, has the potential to betray Jesus Christ just as profoundly. There is at times the same lack of proportion. I believe God often looks on with greater concern at how we conduct our disputes, and how we treat those with whom we disagree, than at which side of the various debates we stand on. Jesus spoke a great deal about love, in particular about how we treat our enemies, and about how we exercise power. All too often the response of Christians to a perceived sin or error is a sin in itself.

This is not to say that questions of Scripture, doctrine, church order and ethics do not matter, or that there is no truth to be struggled for.

---

1   *The Times* 10/11/2008

But we can so easily end up straining out a gnat and swallowing a camel.[3]

It is possible to claim to possess the truth in a *manner* that effectively denies Jesus. We tend to do this when we lose sight of the fact that the truth *is* Jesus, not the many shibboleths we choose to surround Him with. Jesus is the greatest gift in the world. He came to offer reconciliation, grace, forgiveness for sinners, and a life for others that refused to stand on its rights, even when crucified. Jesus never said "Don't you know who I am? You can't do that to me". When we model hard-hearted separation, division, unforgiveness, ungrace, self-righteousness, or fear (often manifesting as self-protectiveness) in our church disputes, we are no longer recognisably His. We may be thoroughly biblical, we may have every argument on our side in the dispute in question, but the world will no longer be listening, and neither, I suspect, will God.

(POST) TRUTH IN AN AGE OF ANGER AND IDENTITY POLITICS

We live in an age characterised by identity politics and various flavours of nationalism, with a resultant epidemic of scapegoating of minorities or of anything or anyone perceived to be 'other'. The air seems thick with contempt and disdain. We live in an era of Trump, the breakdown of trust in politicians, the rise of the far right, increasing division over Brexit and a noticeable epidemic of anger in the public sphere. Do Christians and churches have anything compelling to say, or are we destined to be an echo chamber for the divisions and contempt around us? Is it an answer just to seek the middle ground and to try to be nice? How does this sit with a Saviour who said,

"'Do you think I came to bring peace on earth? No, I tell you, but division. From now on there will be five in one family divided against each other, three against two and two against three. They will be divided, father against son and son against father, mother against daughter and

---

3   Matthew 23:24

daughter against mother, mother-in-law against daughter-in-law and daughter-in-law against mother-in-law.'"[4]?

How do we stand for truth in an age that sometimes defines itself as 'Post-Truth'? How do we contend for truth without being contentious, stand for truth without being arrogant or judgmental?

What does it mean to be a follower of one who claimed to be 'the way, the truth and the life' in an age where truth seems to be devalued, and many who claim to know the truth seem to have the potential to become dictators?

Arguably what the world needs most from Christians is not a community that never argues, but a community that takes truth seriously enough to argue, whilst disagreeing well. The world needs better examples of dealing with difference, disagreement and resentment. This is what Christian graces like forgiveness, reconciliation, honesty and forbearance are all about.

The recent history of the church contains some notable examples of bad practice, particularly in the Church of England's debates over female bishops and over homosexuality. However, there are increasingly some signs of good Christlike practice emerging, particularly the way that the decision over women bishops was eventually taken,[5] after some years of growing distrust and increasing polarisation, and a change in the tone of the homosexuality debate since a process of shared conversations[6] was established. These give me more hope now than when I commenced this book.

'WHO ARE THE LEPERS, THE GENTILES OR THE UNCLEAN, FOR US?'

Jesus eschewed contempt. Those held in contempt by others (such as

---

4   Luke 12:51–53
5   See p.213ff
6   See p.167, 168

lepers, Gentiles, and the religiously unclean) He seemed to treat with greater respect. Who are the lepers, the Gentiles, or the unclean for us? This is not an easy question for anyone to answer. Contempt is self-justifying and therefore hard to recognise. If such attitudes are ingrained in a culture, then they have become 'normal' and what is normal for us is hard to see as exceptionable. In wider society contempt is increasingly heard concerning refugees and immigrants.[7] In church when debate polarises, it seems to me that the tone of the Pharisees for the unclean echoes again in the debates about homosexuality, not in every conservative voice, but in too many for comfort. I was (and still am) disturbed that most gay Christians I have known, including those who are strictly celibate, do not find the church a safe place to take off the masks and let others know that they are gay. Surely a church that was a true reflection of Jesus would not be like that?

My Journey

About seventeen years ago I prayed what for me then was an almost unthinkable prayer. I paused for a long time before I prayed it. I couldn't imagine the sequence of events that would be necessary for God to lead me to see the issues differently, and I wanted to pray with full openness to allow God to work in me. I asked God to show me if I was wrong on the issue of homosexuality. I was not prepared for how painful and disturbing God's answer was to prove. I took a conservative position, and it seemed obvious to me then that this was the only biblical view and therefore the only legitimate Christian view.

A year or so later, my prayer began to be answered in a way I had not anticipated, when I discovered suddenly and unexpectedly that my devout and deeply Christian older son was gay. Three things were very clear, firstly that he had not chosen to be gay, secondly that his efforts, which had been long-lasting and persistent, to find 'healing'

---

7   Not at all the same thing but often conflated as if they were.

from homosexual orientation, had been to no avail, and thirdly that he loved God and was submitted to God in a way that won (and still wins) my admiration and respect. Over the next several years he moved to a position of believing that the expression of homosexual love was not necessarily un-Christian. Though we still do not totally agree over how to interpret the Bible on this issue, I was deeply changed by engaging with the questions raised. I found myself reading the Bible with a fresh urgency. In so doing I found myself reflecting more biblically on how we live together with profound and emotive disagreement, and on what God might be saying to us when we see Jesus and the fruits of his Spirit clearly manifested in those with whom we profoundly disagree. I have found that the scriptures have a great deal to say on the matter in ways that have enriched my discipleship and my love for Jesus Christ, and have opened up the Bible to speak afresh in all kinds of circumstances.

With John Stott, I believe that 'the real hallmark of the evangelical is not only a present submission to what he or she believes the scripture teaches, it is a prior commitment to be submissive to what we may subsequently learn to be the teaching of scripture – whatever scripture may be found to teach.'[8]

Occasionally when I hear believers speaking up for the authority of the Bible, they seem to be saying little more than 'I believe in the Bible because it agrees with me so completely'. Such a view is hardly a commitment to the authority of Scripture, however much it may pose as such a commitment.

AN OUTLINE OF THIS BOOK

This book is the result of my journey of exploration in making sense of what it means to be a fellow member of the body of Christ with my son whose biblical interpretation I still do not fully share, but whose discipleship and Christlike character I admire and learn from. It is not primarily about homosexuality. It is about being Christlike, and what that might mean in a church that is often seen as divided and party-spirited, much like the Judaism of Jesus' day. It is about where we find our identity. It is not primarily about my experience, or my son's, and is not an account of our story, but it is my reflection arising from our experience and the fresh perspectives thus opened up for me. It is a book about how we treat our 'enemies' within the family, about how we argue well, about grace and honesty and disagreement. It is about the ambition to be holy over the desire to be 'right'. It is about what it means in these circumstances to imitate Jesus Christ as an individual, and about whether an institutional church can or should attempt to be Christlike with any reasonable hope of success.

Of course, these reflections have, I believe, a good deal to say about how we now relate to same-sex attraction and those who are so attracted, so towards the end I shall return to this issue in an attempt to apply some of what I have learned, but I must stress again, that the book is about being Christlike in a divided and fractious church and society, and only secondarily about homosexuality.

Working this through has led me to insights and perceptions for which I think I will be grateful until my dying day and beyond. Jesus and the Bible have become vivid for me in fresh ways and my appetite for both has intensified.

Based upon my own experience I would suggest that, just as my son has become a source of spiritual renewal for me even though we do not agree on everything, so with a renewed and Christ-centred perspective gay people become not so much a problem as a reservoir of renewal for the church.

I feel a great diffidence in writing about being Christlike. I do not pretend to have mastered these things. To do that I would have to be perfectly like Jesus Christ. Among many things, I am far too temperamentally contentious and argumentative for that. For a long time I was reluctant to begin writing, fearing that my own flawed ability to respond in a Christlike manner disqualified me from saying anything.

As Clive James has written about 'pontificators', 'He, or she – in my case he – speaks with a special pontificating voice: integrated, judicious even in its doubts, purporting to contain the distilled wisdom of a lifetime's experience. Almost always, I suspect, this voice is at odds with the personality from which it emerges, and in my case the discrepancy is so glaring that even I can spot it.'[9]

However, I now see that a realistic fear of falling, standing as a fellow sinner, is the only stance from which to advocate anything in the kingdom of God. So... Lord have mercy... here goes.

---

9   http://news.bbc.co.uk/1/hi/magazine/7768021.stm, 5 December 2008

CHAPTER ONE

THE IMITATION OF CHRIST

"Don't the Bible say we must love everybody?"
"Oh, the Bible! To be sure, it says a great many things;
but then, nobody ever thinks of doing them."

(*UNCLE TOM'S CABIN*, HARRIET BEECHER STOWE)

LIVING IN THE MIDST OF ANGER

During the Brezhnev era at the height of the Cold War, Billy Graham visited Russia and met with government and church leaders. Conservatives back home reproached him for treating the Russians with such courtesy and respect. He should have taken a more prophetic role, they said, by condemning the abuses of human rights and religious liberty. One of his critics accused him of setting the Church back fifty years. Graham listened, lowered his head, and replied, "I am deeply ashamed. I have been trying very hard to set the Church back two thousand years".[10]

Within church and society anger is rife as trust breaks down, relational skills are at a greater premium and people without a shared framework of beliefs have little basis for constructive response to disputes or disagreements of principle, beyond lashing out, or retreating into apathy, disguised as tolerance. As the irritations grow,

---

10 *What's So Amazing About Grace?*, Philip Yancey, p.264 (Zondervan, 1997)

9

so apparently placid people can switch suddenly from apathy to blaming, scapegoating and vicious criticism, egged on by a capricious and cynical press.

Nick Hornby has portrayed it with wickedly sharp observation, 'There are people like that now, I've noticed, people who seem angry enough to call for the return of the death penalty or the repatriation of Afro-Caribbeans, but who won't, because, like just about everybody else in our particular postal district, they're liberals, so their anger has to come out through different holes. You can read them in the columns and the letters pages of our liberal newspapers every day, being angry about films they don't like or comedians they don't think are funny or women who wear headscarves. Sometimes I think life would be easier for David and me if he experienced a violent political conversion, and he could be angry about poofs and communists, instead of homeopaths and old people on buses and restaurant critics. It must be very unsatisfying to have such tiny outlets for his enormous torrent of rage.'[11]

In an age of Trump, Brexit, *les gilets jaunes*, and growing rage, David's fictional wife seems to have got her wish.

But in the church it is meant to be different.

'Don't have anything to do with foolish and stupid arguments, because you know they produce quarrels. And the Lord's servant must not be quarrelsome but must be kind to everyone, able to teach, not resentful. Opponents must be gently instructed, in the hope that God will grant them repentance leading them to a knowledge of the truth, and that they will come to their senses and escape from the trap of the Devil, who has taken them captive to do his will.'[12]

In practice, the church is often *not* different. Intra-family disputes, and civil wars, are notorious for their viciousness. Thus, letters to the church press regularly misrepresent the positions of those on the other side. Frequently the worst behaviour of our opponents is put forward

11   *How To Be Good*, Nick Hornby, p.36 (QPD/Penguin, 2001)
12   2 Timothy 2:23–26

as though it were typical. After a sermon on the subject of biblical obedience, I was approached by a fellow Christian who only wanted to talk about the American gay bishop, Gene Robinson, as an example of biblical disobedience (he has a same-sex partner). This was a convenient way of sidestepping any personal application of that morning's sermon. It became even more unhelpful when he went on to characterise the bishop as a rebel only interested in the flesh and in self-indulgence, someone who would impose any cost on the church so that he could have his own selfish way. Now I don't want to turn Bishop Robinson into a paragon of virtue; he's a sinner, no doubt, like the rest of us. I agree that aspects of his lifestyle have raised legitimate questions about his appointability as a bishop. However, is it not likely that, far from being a selfish libertine, Bishop Robinson has paid a heavy price for standing up for a position he believes in, on behalf of a constituency that he feels is rarely heard in the heart of the church? Is it not possible that he means it when he portrays his stand as one he sees as constrained by his understanding of the Gospel? I disagree with his position. I also believe that we all have not just a right, but a duty, to stand up for what we believe. But we do not have a right to traduce and slander in defence of our position. It is not Christlike to believe the worst of others, to use insult in place of argument, to present their positions unfairly, or to treat them as enemies, except (perhaps) as enemies whom we are also called to love.

LOVE YOUR ENEMIES

Because we are not Jesus, and therefore not perfect, we can never afford to place ourselves in a position where we cease to listen, and so imply that we have nothing to learn from our enemies. Perhaps it is especially our enemies from whom we have much to learn. 'Our enemies' opinion of us comes closer to the truth than our own.' (Francois La Rochefoucauld).[13] At its most basic, our enemies probably

---

13   Quoted in *How The Mind Works*, by Steven Pinker, p.423 (Penguin, 1998)

stand in a place from which we have not viewed the issue and can see a side of it we have not considered. Jesus could speak of sin and sinners with authority partly because He was 'a friend of sinners'. The Pharisees could not because they did not know them or their world. Purity taboos prohibited it.

But it goes deeper than that. If love, forgiveness of enemies, unity, and humility are major themes of Jesus' teaching, then surely Jesus has an agenda when He brings enemies across our path. That agenda *might* have more to do with our learning than with their defeat. This applies even when those enemies are not just personal enemies, but 'ideological enemies' who seem to stand against what we believe as Christians.

How to Argue for Truth: Disagreeing Without Being Disagreeable

This does not mean that truth does not matter.

When Balaam[14] was summoned by Balak, the pagan King of Moab, to put a curse on the Israelites, Balaam would not. Balak took Balaam to a succession of mountain peaks to view the hordes of Israel, in effect saying, 'try looking at it from this point of view'. Each time Balaam refused, saying "'Did I not tell you I must do whatever the Lord says?'"[15]

We are not only permitted to dispute vigorously, we are required to, if integrity and truth are to mean anything. In an age of 'fake news' if we promote reconciliation without regard to truth we will betray the one who is 'the way, the truth and the life', and in the long run stoke disillusionment and therefore more anger.

We are required at times to disagree, just not disagreeably. 'Dear friends, although I was very eager to write to you about the salvation we share, I felt compelled to write and urge you to contend for the faith

---

14   Numbers 22:1 – 24:25
15   Numbers 23:26

that was once for all entrusted to God's holy people.'[16] We will explore some Christian principles for how to disagree in Chapter 8.

Love does not demand we dissemble. Close friends tend to know what is on each other's minds, and do not necessarily have to agree in order to continue as friends.

During my first year as a curate I had a first-floor flat on a corner of two streets in Hackney. One day I heard the sound of two loudspeaker vans approaching, each campaigning for candidates in the forthcoming Greater London Council elections. Each loudspeaker was relaying the voice of a member of our team of churches. Jimmy was campaigning for the Conservatives (and was in fact the candidate), Brian for the Labour Party. They met just below my flat, where they each stopped, got out of their respective cars, shook hands, chatted amiably for a few minutes, then continued campaigning, each trying to persuade the Kingsmead Estate why their candidate would be better than the opposition. For those with the eyes and good fortune to see, this was a powerful act of Christian witness, and it in no way diminished the importance of the arguments of the respective manifestos. At a time of great political bitterness (Margaret Thatcher was in 10 Downing Street and Ken Livingstone at County Hall) that simple act of Christian fellowship, alongside a willingness to continue the contest, spoke volumes.

BROTHERS AND SISTERS WHO DISAGREE ARE STILL FAMILY

So when I heard of bishops who would not come to the 2008 Lambeth Conference in case they had to share Holy Communion with those with whom they disagreed,[17] I wondered what was going on. After all, in full awareness of the facts, Jesus shared communion with Judas moments before Judas went out to betray Him.

With regards to criticism of his methods and message from

---

16 Jude 1:3
17 This is still very much a live issue. For example, see *The Church of England Newspaper* 26/10/18, p.5 'Bishops Reach Out to Gafcon'.

fundamentalists who were unhappy about some with whom he was working, Billy Graham said, 'If a man accepts the deity of Christ and is living for Christ to the best of his knowledge, I intend to have fellowship with him in Christ. If this extreme type of fundamentalism was of God, it would have brought revival long ago. Instead, it has brought dissension, division, strife, and has produced dead and lifeless churches.'[18]

I have had the privilege of working with colleagues from Iran and Eritrea, who have been persecuted for their faith to the extent of lengthy imprisonment and torture, and who have seen their colleagues and church members killed in some numbers. They speak with sober realism about their tormentors but also with grace, forbearance and lack of rancour. Their lack of vitriol sometimes contrasts with the manner in which I encounter Christians in this country speaking or writing about their fellow Christians who happen to be on the other side of some contentious debate or other. How the Lord must weep over us.

What held Jimmy and Brian together as they canvassed for opposing parties was participation in the life of Jesus. We need to be very sure indeed of our ground before we conclude that someone who claims to be a fellow believer is no longer in Christ. 'Who are you to judge someone else's servant? To their own master, servants stand or fall. And they will stand, for the Lord is able to make them stand.'[19]

INCARNATING, NOT JUST DEFENDING THE TRUTH

Truth matters. Outright and blatant lies increasingly appear to reap rewards. Many commentators were aghast at how obvious and provable lies did not seem to dent support for Donald Trump in the US elections, or for Brexit in the UK referendum. Dishonesty, such as

---

18   *Just As I Am*, Billy Graham, p.251
19   Romans 14:4

lying to Parliament, that would have led to ministerial resignations in the past, passes with barely a whimper.[20]

Truth matters. Absence of truth corrodes trust, and eventually leads to bitter disillusion. It dissolves societies.

As Christians we believe that Jesus is 'the way, and the truth and the life'.[21] He *is* the truth. He doesn't just point to it. This means that in order to stand for truth we must do so in a way that reflects Him, imitating His character, therefore demonstrating integrity, compassion, respect, humility and boldness. If we claim to defend and define the truth of the Christian faith, but do so in ways that are not Christlike, we obscure the truth however accurate our verbal definitions. This is obvious when stated. It just does not seem to be so obvious in practice.

There is a fundamental difference between us and Jesus. He is the truth, and He is perfect. We are not the truth, neither do we possess the truth in full, nor do we reflect it fully. Thus we have to listen, to learn and to be corrected. We must be as suspicious of ourselves as we are of others, and as generous with others as we would be with ourselves. We can only, with integrity, contend for truth by pointing to Jesus. When Christian contends with Christian, each should be so concerned both to help the other reflect Jesus and to better to reflect Jesus themselves, that the sight is edifying to any onlooker. This might still involve robust contention, but the spirit is different. Once contenders start brawling (metaphorically, or literally), it is futile their trying to point to Jesus. He is nowhere to be seen.

Where Jesus is concerned the ends cannot justify the means. He is 'the way' as well as 'the truth and the life'. If our way does not reflect Jesus, to that extent we deny Him, however much we may feel we are contending in His cause.

---

20 An example has just happened as I write this. Greg Clark, the business secretary, has been caught out having promised a £61 million support package for Nissan, having told Parliament that no such pledge or payment had been made (*The Independent* 5/2/19).

21 John 14:6

GOOD NEWS AND FAKE NEWS

Jesus didn't come to offer a 'party manifesto'. Jerusalem was awash with them at the time. He didn't just come to tell, He came to embody, to demonstrate a way (*the* way) of being human. Words are cheap. The fact that God sent his son, not a message tells us something about the authenticity and depth of his love for us. The Word became flesh. Jesus came to demonstrate Kingdom life, and to invite men and women into a transforming participation in that life with Him. This participation leads to us incarnating His life, His attitudes, His treatment of friends and enemies alike, His attitude to self and suffering, His way of identifying with the poor and weak and the rich and powerful. It means seeing Him as our role model and receiving Him as our inner strength and inspiration. In particular it means letting Him transform some of the hidden things that drive us, that are so deeply ingrained in our nature, and so profoundly enfleshed in our culture that it is easy not even to notice that they exist, let alone realise that they are displeasing to Him.

There's a story of a man coming into a room full of his friends who are all puffing away on cigars and cigarettes. He can hardly breathe and complains, "Boy, it's smoky in here", to which one of his friends retorts, "How do you know? You've only just come in". It's hard to see those things that are characteristically wrong in our own culture. By culture I don't just refer to the secular, worldly culture 'out there'. All culture is fallen, even church culture. Every church subculture must have something of the Devil in it, simply because we are all fallen. Sometimes that sinfulness is an unconscious copying of the world around, sometimes, like the self-righteousness of the Pharisees, it is a reaction against the world around. Unless our agenda is set by Jesus it is bound to produce poison fruit. Jesus' kingdom should define our culture, Jesus' character shape our character, and we are to react solely to His leading and love, not react to the world, however zealously holy our reaction against the world might at first appear to be.[22]

---

22   Romans 10:2–4

This means modelling our life on Jesus' character and Jesus' values. It would be extremely odd if this left us basically the same as most other people in our culture who make no effort to imitate Jesus! We do not have everything invested in this life. We know that primarily we are citizens of the Kingdom of Heaven.

It seems to me that there is a strange lack of interest in Jesus' humanity in much of the church. His name is the password that gets us into heaven, but His name seems strangely divorced from the content of His life and character in much proclamation. He is the risen ascended Lord. He is part of the Trinity, He is a theological idea, but His character and the sharp particularity of His teaching seem to recede from us the closer we get to much preaching and teaching about Him. Could it be that we have taken Him for granted? Look at any hymn or song book and try to find songs that reflect Jesus' life on earth other than His birth, death and resurrection. You won't find many. Of course we worship Jesus in His exalted glory, we acknowledge Him as part of the Trinity, we know that we owe Him our hope of heaven, His birth, death and resurrection are wonderful, vital, central, but should this be to the near exclusion of His life and character as recorded in the Gospels?

I believe that only so can we explain the eighty per cent (by some accounts) of US evangelicals who supported Donald Trump in the 2016 presidential election. Only when Jesus becomes a symbol for a particular political or ethical programme, and His human life, His character and His personality are relatively ignored, can such things happen. That such a large proportion of professed believers could rally behind a man who assaulted and abused women, who is thin-skinned and defensive, and who has made a career out of revenge, who is money and power-obsessed, and is a proven inveterate liar, is truly shocking. Truth is meant to be incarnate and Jesus-shaped. It is far more than a matter for manifestos.

It is so easy to be more like the world than like Jesus without really noticing, even though we believe all the 'core doctrines' about Him. The prevailing culture easily shapes our reactions to, for example, power and its pursuit, to riches and poverty, to enemies and conflict, and to sin in ourselves and others. If we do not pay close attention to who Jesus really is, we will almost inevitably project onto God our own preferences of what we would like God to be.

We are called to meditate on the life and character of Jesus, and then, with the Holy Spirit's help, to imitate Him. We are called not just to be retailers of Jesus' teaching, but incarnaters of it. Otherwise we become mere arguers over words. 'The Word became flesh' but all too often, we have made it only word again. We are to both speak of God's forgiveness, and to demonstrate it. We are to preach on Jesus' self-emptying, and let it inform our every exercise of power, our ambition, our whole demeanour.

Ed Silvoso recounts that 'A pastor friend of mine was visited by a homosexual who was dying of AIDS. Without disclosing his illness, the homosexual invited the pastor to have lunch, and they went out to a restaurant. Halfway through their meal, the homosexual paused, looked the pastor in the eye and blurted out, "I am dying of AIDS", while tensely waiting for the pastor's reaction. With tear-filled eyes, the pastor reached across the table and touched the homosexual's arm while saying, "I am sorry. I am truly sorry". Later, the homosexual received Jesus. He explained his decision to the pastor: "Do you want to know why I decided to receive Jesus? When I told you I was dying of AIDS, I was watching your body language. I wondered if you would quickly lean back, away from my face, or if you would surreptitiously move your glass and your plate towards you. I was not listening to your words, but I was watching the language of your body. Instead of rejecting me, you reached out and touched me. Your eyes filled with tears. You empathised with me. You accepted me. Then and there, I decided that your God is the God I want to meet when I die."'[23]

---

23   *That None Should Perish,* Ed Silvoso, p.82 (Regal Books, 1994). Of course it is
      problematic to call someone 'a homosexual', because of the implication that this
      is all they are, that this word defines them. This kind of thinking is part of the
      problem in the church. However, I am speaking with the benefit, over the author
      at the time of writing, of over twenty years of hindsight.

CHRISTIAN INTEGRITY

So, what is involved in this Christlike consistency and integrity? Is it keeping the rules; don't kill, don't lie, don't cheat, don't steal, don't sleep with anyone other than your spouse? Well, it must involve those things, but so far we have only described a normal Pharisee. So we must go further. What is involved in going further? Is it just one more command that Jesus adds, 'Be nice'? Is that what this book is about?

Jesus wasn't exactly renowned for keeping the rules. Dietrich Bonhoeffer arguably broke the first rule above, 'don't kill', by being implicated in a plot to assassinate Hitler, yet many regard him as one of the greatest examples of Christian consistency ever. Why?

We need to imitate Jesus in acting as though we do not have everything invested in this life. Our lifestyles reflect our values, and if we have set our hopes on 'an inheritance that can never perish, spoil or fade... kept in heaven for you',[24] then our lifestyles will be shaped by that; our impact on the environment, our sexual behaviour, our attitudes to money, to ambition, to power, will be different from those around us. This is one reason Bonhoeffer's example rings out with such conviction. He lived as though he did not have everything invested in this life. While in Tegel Prison awaiting execution he wrote 'I don't just want to live, but to do the most I can with my life. Since this must now happen through my death, I have made friends with it also. On this ride between death and the Devil, death is a noble companion.'[25] He knew that living as Jesus lived might in some measure mean dying as Jesus died. We will explore this more in Chapter 4.

BEING SUSPICIOUS OF OURSELVES

We should not underestimate our ability to resist Jesus' way of being and doing. If we stay on the surface we might think it's easy. 'Don't

---

24   1 Peter 1:4
25   *Dietrich Bonhoeffer*, Eberhard Bethge, p.832 (Fount, 1977)

steal', 'Don't murder'. Well, it's easy to know whether we have murdered or not, isn't it? But Jesus said,

"'You have heard that it was said to the people long ago, 'You shall not murder, and anyone who murders will be subject to judgment. But I tell you that anyone who is angry with a brother or sister will be subject to judgment.' "[26]

Ah! Perhaps it's not so easy after all. It's so easy to be 'moral' in an angry way. Perhaps it is not so long a road from Christlike indignation over the fate of the unborn, via contempt and anger, to the bombing of an abortion clinic. It's so easy to develop a religious zeal that lacks the heart of God's righteousness which is Christ (Romans 10:[2-4]). Perhaps the monks of the Holy Sepulchre[27] are not so far from us. We have an almost infinite capacity to deceive ourselves, and the wise person knows that fact, even if they often do not recognise the particular deceptions. 'There's one way to find out if a man is honest: ask him; if he says yes, you know he's crooked.' (Mark Twain)

'The heart is deceitful above all things
and beyond cure.
Who can understand it?' [28]

'THOSE SINNERS', OR 'WE SINNERS'?

This understanding of our inbuilt bias to sin is central to an ability to love our enemy. If we are suspicious of ourselves because we are aware of our inbuilt bias, our tendency to stray from Jesus, then those we are in dispute with become our fellow sinners, not *those* sinners over there. Even Jesus, who committed no sin,[29] stood in solidarity with us sinners at His baptism.[30] Once, moreover, we know that we are beloved

---

26 Matthew 5:21–22
27 See p.1
28 Jeremiah 17:9
29 1 Peter 2:22
30 Matthew 3:13–15

and forgiven sinners, it will not be so easy to hold *those* sinners in contempt. This knowledge is the difference between a friendly family argument and a civil war. As Philip Yancey said after reading the bile and hate-filled letters sent to his gay friend by people claiming to be Christians, 'Grace dies when it becomes us versus them'.[31]

Alexander Solzhenitsyn wrote, 'If only there were evil people somewhere insidiously committing evil deeds and it were necessary only to separate them from the rest of us and destroy them. But the dividing line between good and evil cuts through the heart of every human being…'[32]

'Us and Them' in an Era of Identity Politics

The identification of ourselves with good, and those out there with evil, is the direct road to religious nationalism, to religious war, to persecution and The Inquisition, to self-righteousness and Pharisaism, to religious manipulation and schism, to the crucifixion of the Messiah. It is the profoundest possible betrayal of Jesus, however religious the language in which righteousness is claimed. When Sarah Palin argued at a rally in Ohio during the 2008 election, that "We understand how important it is that this team be elected. For one thing, we know who the bad guys are, OK?"[33] did she have a clue how profoundly at odds with her Christian faith such a statement was? Taken at face value it disqualified her from salvation by the one who said, "'I have not come to call the righteous, but sinners.'"[34]

It is equally true and equally important to understand that each one of us, including our worst enemies, is made in the image of God. No one can be written off, and no one is to be hated (including Sarah Palin).

---

31 *What's So Amazing About Grace?*, Philip Yancey, p.172 (Zondervan, 1997)
32 *The Gulag Archipelago*, Alexander Solzhenitsyn, Ch.1 (Harper Perennial, 2018)
33 CNN Politics.Com 12/10/08
34 Matthew 9:13

PROJECTING ONTO THE BIBLE?

To see things this way is not to be soft on sin. Rather it is to be hard-headed about where sin is located, here as well as there. The trouble with so many who make a spectator sport out of others' shortcomings by judging them, is that they do not take sin, or the fall, or Jesus' remedy for them nearly seriously enough. They tend to limit sin to certain actions that they find offensive, and fail to notice the deeper corruption, the self-centredness that afflicts us all.

How can we achieve Jesus' way of seeing and loving when our hearts are so tricky, when self-deceit is ever present, when 'all have sinned and fall short of the glory of God'?[35] It is so easy to be converted to a pre-packaged set of Christian beliefs, and to mistake this for conversion to Jesus Christ. We like what the preacher said about Jesus, as it chimes with what we believe about family, or the poor, or politics, or whatever. It's all too easy to spend the rest of our lives campaigning on these issues with a passionate but proud and unloving intensity, thinking that we are disciples, but in fact being mere ideologues. Whom are we serving, the living Lord Jesus to whom the Bible bears witness, or the Jesus who confirms our prejudices, who is a projection, an idol in our heads? The only way to be sure is to let the scriptures read us in depth every day. For this process to have integrity, we need to hear from more heads than our own and more cultures than our own. Diversity is one of God's gifts to His Church, among other reasons, because only with it can we take off our culturally tinted spectacles and see the Bible better (by seeing it from someone else's standpoint). More about this in Chapter 7.

As noted above, those Christians whom we are tempted to regard as 'enemies' might conceivably be our best teachers here.

BLESS THOSE WHO PERSECUTE YOU

How then should we respond when we feel our fellow Christians are

---

35   Romans 3:23

wrong, even damaging the cause of the Gospel, even, perhaps, trying to silence or drive us from the church?

We are not used to persecution or opposition in the West. Most of us have experienced opposition, mainly, if at all, only from other Christians. Only in recent years have militant atheists become strident, and the first hints of persecution, or at least unfair opposition, emerged. So unused to this are we that we don't know how to react. We tend to become indignant in defence of our rights, conveying the appearance that we are mainly concerned about ourselves, whereas Jesus told us to rejoice when persecuted.[36] There is an offence to the Gospel, and the Bible repeatedly tells us that it will bring us opposition. My clergy colleagues in my last parish reminded me that opposition is normal for Christians. One of them had spent a year in prison for his faith in Eritrea, another had been under siege in a Christian hospital in a Moslem part of Nigeria while a mob of over a thousand tried to burn it down. When we face opposition, which in England is not likely to amount, yet, to such persecution, are we surprised? Do we start taking it personally and react accordingly? Jesus said, "'You will be hated by everyone because of me'"[37] so it is fairly stupid to start taking it personally. We take it for Jesus Christ's sake, and therefore must react as He would react. 'When a soldier gets shot at, he doesn't get his feelings hurt. He isn't plagued by self-doubt. He doesn't wonder if this is the kind of work he is cut out for. He doesn't peer over the edge of his foxhole and shout back, "Was it something I said?". Getting shot at just goes with the territory. Don't take it personally.'[38]

It is for Jesus' sake, therefore, that we turn the other cheek and forgive, as Jesus commanded. If this is true when our opponents are non-Christians, surely it is every bit as applicable when the 'other side' are Christians. We must be eirenic, refuse to take it personally or to get personal. We must turn the other cheek, and be known for our love, not for our fierceness.

---

36   Matthew 5:11–12
37   Matthew 10:22
38   *Leadership* magazine, Fall '94, p.154

Causing Offence

However, we need to go one step further to ascertain whether it is the Gospel that is offensive, or us. It is usually hard for us to see the difference. It is all too easy to refuse to see our own offensive behaviour. We can hide behind the offensiveness of the Gospel, and even take a perverse delight in provoking offence. After all, it must prove how faithful we are being, right? However, the fact that some people will oppose us if we serve Jesus in no way guarantees that we are never offensive in ourselves by being in some way un-Christlike.

Learning to Live With Other Sinners

Often persecution, or more likely in Western culture, mere opposition or hostility, will come from within the church. The church is sick. Of course it is. It is made up of sinners like us. Therefore there is no reason for either judgmentalism or complacency.

Of course there will be tensions in churches. The church is called from every culture, every background, every taste and temperament. Just after my own conversion as an undergraduate, I joined a 'Beginners Group'. As I glanced around the room at my first meeting I thought there was no one there I could possibly get on with. I was a sort of middle-class hippy manqué, with hair over my shoulders and flared jeans. There was a skinhead, several very conformist-looking types in tweed jackets, side partings and polished black or brown shoes (these were great crimes in my immature and intolerant eyes), and an aristocratic 'rich kid' type whom I thought (until I got to know him) was rather spoiled and out of touch with the world. I thought there was no way I would fit in. As I got to know them several things happened. Firstly, some of those I had superficially judged became my good friends. Secondly, I discovered that none of them was as I first imagined them to be. There was so much more to them. Thirdly, the fact that we all had Jesus Christ in common (albeit only since very recently) gave us enough to make it both worthwhile and possible to stay together. Fourthly, as we got to know one another well, irritations arose, though not usually in the form or from the people I had anticipated at first meeting. However, the example of Jesus and the power of the Holy Spirit seemed to give us the ability and motivation to overcome these hurdles. At the end of two terms I was desperately sad that the group had come to its scheduled end.

Jesus Christ invites us to overcome barriers. There is no reason to set ourselves apart, either in proud judgment, or in despair. Once we belong to Jesus Christ we are a part of His 'body'. We are therefore fellow members and belong in relationship whether we like it or not.

As Phil Potter has said, 'Perhaps the greatest personal challenge in relationships is to love the people we don't naturally like and commit ourselves to being alongside them. Our natural tendency is to say, "Love your neighbour as yourself" – just choose your neighbourhood!'[39]

Once we belong to Jesus, our neighbourhood is no longer solely up to us. We must go where He sends us.

LOVE 'BEARS ALL THINGS, BELIEVES ALL THINGS, HOPES ALL THINGS, ENDURES ALL THINGS'

The rest of our church is part of the cross we have to bear, *and we are part of the cross that they have to bear*. Grace is the only answer; grace to believe in ourselves, grace to believe in the church, grace to believe in our enemies,[40] all because Jesus believes in us all. So ultimately it is by His grace that we believe in Jesus, because He believes in us (*us*, not just me). The biggest miracle is not that we believe in God but that He believes in us. Our faith is a response to that miracle, and is no great achievement on our part. Certainly it is nothing that gives us the right

---

39   *The Challenge of Cell Church* by Phil Potter, p.89 (Bible Reading Fellowship, 2001)

40   Yes, 'believe' in our enemies. Jesus must have believed in some redeemable potential, and must have recognised His image in even His worst enemies, to have died for them/us.

to stand over others in judgment. A large part of becoming Christlike is to learn to believe and hope as He does, when faced with sin and failure within ourselves, or in the church or the world. We are each to be one of those who 'bears all things, believes all things, hopes all things, endures all things.'[41]

'Love is patient, love is kind. It does not envy, it does not boast, it is not proud. It does not dishonour others, it is not self-seeking, it is not easily angered, it keeps no record of wrongs. Love does not delight in evil but rejoices with the truth. It always protects, always trusts, always hopes, always perseveres.'[42]

Can we be known as those who do not delight in evil, but without coming over as self-righteous, as those who believe in reform of the church, but know our own need of reformation just as much, who are passionate about holiness and also are known as those who rejoice rather than those who carp and cavil? Will we be those who always hope because our hope is kept for us in heaven, and who thus persevere, and are not therefore known as critical cynics, always on the verge of quitting?

THE JOURNEY SO FAR

Christians, and the church of which they are part, are called to be different, distinctive, Christlike.

We live in an age of mounting anger and increasing dishonesty. If the church is disputatious, bitter, angry or lacking integrity, it will not matter whether we win our arguments or lose them. We will have denied Jesus by who we are.

Truth matters. Absence of truth corrodes trust and all ability to live together. Therefore Christians will often have to contend for the truth, but we must contend as Jesus would have done. He called us to love our enemies, and if that command

---

41   1 Corinthians 13:6 RSV.
42   1 Corinthians 13:4–7 (NIV)

extends to those in the world who would persecute us, how much more must it apply to those brothers and sisters within the church with whom we disagree or of whom we may even disapprove.

We are not therefore called never to have disputes or arguments, but to be a community of people who know how to conduct arguments within the bonds of peace and mutual love, in imitation of Jesus Christ.

Until we are used to thinking of 'us sinners' rather than 'those sinners' we can hardly have the mind of Christ who identified with us sinners in His baptism.

In the first part of this book I will examine the example of Jesus Christ as it bears upon these things. In the latter part I will look at how that example might transform the way we handle some debates currently tearing the church apart, in particular, the debate about homosexuality in the Anglican Communion.

CHAPTER TWO

THE CHARACTER OF JESUS

'In Jesus, God found a way of relating to human
beings that did not involve fear.'

(*THE JESUS I NEVER KNEW*, PHILIP YANCEY P.35–36)

Mr Beaver of Aslan, '"Is he – quite safe?"... "Safe? Who said
anything about safe? Course he isn't safe. But he's good."'

(*THE LION, THE WITCH AND THE WARDROBE*, C.S. LEWIS)

THE RULE OF LOVE, OR THE LOVE OF RULES

Following Jesus involves more than just obeying His commands. He
led by the example of His whole life, not just by His words. 'The Word
became flesh.' Christians, by focusing on some of the commands and
downplaying the example, risk becoming rather like the Pharisees.

Law alone is not enough. 'Legalism fails miserably at the one thing
it is supposed to do: encourage obedience... In a demonstration of
this principle, some surveys show that people raised in teetotalling
denominations are three times as likely to become alcoholics.'[43]

John 1:17   'For the law was given through Moses; grace and
truth came through Jesus Christ.'

---

43   *What's So Amazing About Grace?* Philip Yancey, p.206 (Zondervan, 1997)

Was Jesus a legislator? He didn't come to abolish the law, but He didn't pin his hopes on it either. He knew that it was a blunt tool that was often misused by those engaged in power games and manipulation.

The New Testament was not written as legislation, though it is often read and construed as if it were. There are many things there that are disastrous taken as legislation. We should honour the Sabbath, but pernickety regulation has in the past come close to the Pharisaical.[44] Many of the important teachings of Jesus could not possibly be turned into legislation. For example, we should live for today and not be anxious or greedy.[45] How do you turn that into law? Or love of neighbour or enemy? And in those instances where law can be effective, it can still tend to limit goodness as well as evil by provoking us to try to think of all the exceptions, to do the minimum necessary to comply, while doing little to change our lifestyle and values.

When we rely upon laws and regulation, we also almost inevitably become radically inconsistent. Why are many Christians of my acquaintance who are fierce about sexual ethics, quite happy to shop on the Lord's day? Do the Ten Commandments not have something to say about both? I was recently harangued by a fellow Christian, who is a divorcee married to a divorcee, about how plain is the biblical teaching about homosexuality, and how can there be any leeway. Is Mark 10:11–12 not just as clear about divorce?

Of course, one could argue that the Christian Sunday is not the Jewish Sabbath, or that Jesus' attitude to the Sabbath mandates a fresh approach. We could examine the Markan teaching about divorce in the light of the so-called Matthean exception[46] 'except for sexual immorality' (though the word translated 'sexual immorality' is notoriously contested). These are respectable arguments. However, in pursuing them we are likely to miss the point of what Jesus was trying

---

44 Witness the complex array of permitted types and size of outlets allowed to open, and permitted goods for sale, prior to 1994.
45 Matthew 6:30–34
46 Matthew 19:9

to do, namely to go to the heart of the matter, to God's core intention, which points to issues and values too profound for legislation. One example is that the Sabbath was made for man, not man for the Sabbath.[47] This suggests that the Sabbath has a value being missed both by the legalists and by those who would set this teaching aside altogether. Again, whilst the law made provision for divorce, the important point is that God's intention is for married couples to enjoy a loving covenantal permanence.[48]

There was a person who wanted to hire a driver to take a loaded truck over a road running alongside a deep ravine. Several candidates interviewed said they were precision drivers who could steer the truck inches from the edge. But the one who got the job said they would be trying to steer as far away as possible.[49] Law, regulation and command inspire a powerful temptation to go as close to the edge as we can, to see what we can get away with.[50] This can create a certain minimum amount of order, but it can never create holiness. Law can forbid certain forms of exploitation, but it cannot compel generosity. It can forbid certain kinds of abuse, but cannot compel warmth and love.

If faith rests content with legalistic regulation, all joy goes out of the exercise of faith. Worship, love, generosity and compassion are relegated in favour of compliance, and our Heavenly Father takes on the aspect of a combined health and safety and best practice compliance officer. (Say what you like about the necessity of 'health and safety', those tick box forms have never yet inspired joy in me.)

As trust between people and communities breaks down, increasingly rules are brought in to fill the gap. As the idea of self-denial seems more and more strange to many, so legislation is relied on to impose certain socially desirable limits. One of the reasons politicians are held in so little esteem is because, in the absence of shared societal faith and values,

---

47   Mark 2:27
48   Mark 10:4–9
49   *Church of England Newspaper*, May 1993
50   Romans 7:8

politicians are looked to by the public to achieve by law all kinds of things that law cannot achieve or create (like 'respect'[51]). Of course laws are needed. They have their limited place. The passing of laws and the punishment of wrongdoing is a proper function of the state.[52] Christians are called to be in government just as they are called to be in steel making, but Jesus wasn't legislating any more than he was making steel.

Jesus maintained an enormous respect for the laws of God. He said, "'Do not think that I have come to abolish the Law or the Prophets; I have not come to abolish them but to fulfil them. For truly I tell you, until heaven and earth disappear, not the smallest letter, not the least stroke of a pen, will by any means disappear from the Law until everything is accomplished. Therefore anyone who sets aside one of the least of these commands and teaches others accordingly will be called least in the kingdom of heaven, but whoever practises and teaches these commands will be called great in the kingdom of heaven. For I tell you that unless your righteousness surpasses that of the Pharisees and the teachers of the law, you will certainly not enter the kingdom of heaven.'"[53]

Yet Jesus could seem cavalier to the point of disregard in an attempt to get to the heart of what the law means. Thus the Pharisees could say of Him, 'This man is not from God for he does not keep the Sabbath'.[54] Yet Jesus was not rejecting the Sabbath law, but valuing it as the joyous gift of God it is, over those who had turned it into a burden and forgotten that the Sabbath was made for man, not vice versa. Jesus does not take issue with those who showed zeal for the law per se, but with those who interpreted the law so as to negate its original intention, especially when they imposed their burdensome interpretations upon others. 'Jesus replied, "And you experts in the law, woe to you, because

---

51   In 2005 the press was full of the agenda of the Home Office's 'Respect Unit' under the so-called 'Respect Czar', Louise Casey. The idea was fairly soon abandoned.
52   Romans 13:1–5
53   Matthew 5:17–20
54   John 9:16

you load people down with burdens they can hardly carry, and you yourselves will not lift one finger to help them."[55]

Obeying God's revealed will might involve sacrifice, but such sacrifice was to be taken on willingly, not imposed by the morality police (more about this later). Jesus was looking for disciples who were willing learners, not just subjects who might be no more than sullen compliers. Only to such willing disciples would the liberty and joy inherent in God's law become apparent, only such could understand Jesus when he said, "'Take my yoke upon you and learn from me, for I am gentle and humble in heart, and you will find rest for your souls. For my yoke is easy and my burden is light.'"[56]

This does not mean that Jesus was always going for the soft option. He radically intensified the demands of the law in all kinds of ways by moving beyond the law to the intention of His Father that lay at its heart.

'You have heard that it was said to the people long ago, "You shall not murder, and anyone who murders will be subject to judgment." But I tell you that anyone who is angry with a brother or sister will be subject to judgment.

'You have heard that it was said, "You shall not commit adultery." But I tell you that anyone who looks at a woman lustfully has already committed adultery with her in his heart. If your right eye causes you to stumble, gouge it out and throw it away. It is better for you to lose one part of your body than for your whole body to be thrown into hell.'[57]

That this is in no sense legislation is readily apparent. If this were the Book of Leviticus we might just manage to believe that this was the prescribed penalty for adultery or lust. However, this is plainly not Jesus' intention. Nor, I believe, is it, as I once regarded it, merely rabbinic hyperbole. Jesus is describing the nature of the Kingdom of God, where the blessings of radical, freely-chosen obedience are such

---

55   Luke 11:46
56   Matthew 11:29–30
57   Matthew 5:21–22 & 27–29

that it literally would be worth tearing out one's own eye for. Nothing could be further from Jesus' intention than that a self-appointed (or church-appointed) thought police should go around threatening the angry or the lustful with terrible penalties if they do not conform. Jesus does not want conformity, the submission of fear, he wants holiness, the submission of love.

Jesus' vision is demanding and cannot be institutionally controlled. So institutions have a habit of abandoning it in favour of various forms of legalistic sin management. Let's face the truth, once two Christians gather you have the beginning of an institution. We would do well to heed Cardinal Newman's observation that "every organisation seemed to start with a prophet and end up with a policeman".[58] Therefore it is imperative that in all our institutional disputes, all our church life, all our life, we strive to stay Jesus-centred. The simple wristband motto, 'WWJD', 'What Would Jesus Do?', is the most profound and important behavioural question we can ask. There has been much criticism of this slogan of late, following its use by protesters against the banking system camped outside St Paul's Cathedral.[59] The criticism has focused on the naïvety of the question, as it gives no easy or clear answers in many instances. This misses the point. It shifts our frame of moral reference profoundly and radically. We must examine our actions, reactions and thought in the light of this question at all times. What a difference, for example, would be made to our disputes, were we to ask whether we were reflecting Jesus' character and approach, and were we manifesting the fruits of the spirit.[60] This marks the dividing line between true disciples of Christ and mere religious ideologues.

Dallas Willard in *The Divine Conspiracy*[61] criticises 'gospels of sin management'. His target is the tendency of the church to substitute

---

58   Quoted by George Carey in the Lambeth Conference 1998 Archives, http://www.lambethconference.org/1998/news/lc024.cfm
59   Winter 2011
60   Galatians 5:22–23
61   *The Divine Conspiracy*, Dallas Willard, Ch.2, 'Gospels of Sin Management' (Fount, 1998)

schemes for sin management for full-blooded, whole-hearted, Christ-centred discipleship. 'The only thing made essential on the right wing of theology is forgiveness of the individual's sins. On the left it is removal of social or structural evils. The current Gospel then becomes 'a gospel of sin management'. Transformation of life and character is no part of the redemptive message. Moment to moment human reality in its depth is not the arena of faith and eternal living.'[62]

Or, instead of whole life discipleship, 'sin management' can take the shape of a narrow legalism sometimes so narrow as to be the ecclesiastical equivalent of single issue politics.

These approaches fail by taking part of the truth as if it were the whole truth. Individual forgiveness is important, even essential, but it is not the whole Gospel. Many single moral issues are important, but they are not the whole Gospel. Politics and social justice are important, but they are not the whole Gospel. The only single element that can be said to be the whole Gospel is Jesus Himself, and all the partial Gospels seem to lose sight of Him somewhere along the way. Perhaps this is how we end up with Christians apparently defending the Gospel of Jesus Christ in ways that are manifestly so un-Christlike.

Once we reduce what we believe to a series of laws, or a set of propositions divorced from the living Lord Jesus Christ, we can easily become party zealots or cynics. We certainly will no longer be easily (mis)taken for the one who was nicknamed 'friend of sinners'.

WHO IS THIS MAN? ASPECTS OF JESUS' PERSONALITY

So what is the character of Jesus like? What are the aspects of His personality and character that would help us answer the question 'What would Jesus do?'?

Well, firstly, He wasn't too fussy about religious rules. He had a

---

62   *The Divine Conspiracy,* Dallas Willard, p.50 (Fount, 1998)

'reputation'! Everyone knew He was a Sabbath breaker,[63] a friend of sinners.[64] He would touch lepers[65] and enjoy their hospitality,[66] thus rendering Himself 'unclean'. He allowed His feet to be washed by a prostitute,[67] and chose a tax collector for a disciple.[68] To achieve a similar effect today He would have to be entertained by a notorious paedophile priest, choose an Al-Qaeda terrorist as a key aid, spend an evening at a convention of gay Christians and relax on the following day with the Beaufort Hunt.

He could get angry, especially over those who abused power or privilege[69] (so we had better not confuse the call to be Christlike in our disputes and arguments, with a call to be 'nice').

He valued the scriptures as the revealed will of God. He refers to what is 'written', that is the scripture, twenty-nine times in the first three Gospels. His attitude to scripture was summed up when, in the midst of the temptations, He replied to the Devil, "'It is written: 'Man shall not live on bread alone, but on every word that comes from the mouth of God.'""[70] Indeed, He replied to every one of the Devil's temptations by quoting from scripture. The scripture was authoritative to Jesus for life and salvation.

He was concerned above all for His Father's reputation,[71] and to that end sought to be wholly submitted to His Father's will.[72] In fact He was so submitted to His Father's will that He treated His own actions and identity as identical with His Father's.[73] For this He was accused of blasphemy.[74]

---

63 John 9:16.
64 Luke 7:34.
65 Matthew 8:1–3
66 Matthew 26:6
67 Luke 7:37–39
68 Mark 2:14
69 Matthew 23:13–36; John 2:14–17
70 Matthew 4:4
71 John 12:28
72 John 12:49; John 5:19
73 John 14:9–11
74 John 10:33

He was prayerful.[75] Solitary prayer, often in the early morning or late at night, seems to have been a regular habit with Jesus. He also assumed that His followers would pray too.[76] This seems to be an aspect of seeking to be wholly submitted to His Father's will. Prayer was the place of communication with and empowerment by His Father, and He took it for granted that anyone seeking to live for Him and for His Father would do the same.

We're beginning to get a picture of someone deeply devout, deeply in love with God, and not in the least religious.

He did not distinguish persons (Romans, lepers, Gentiles, Samaritans, poor, rich, guilty, etc., etc.). He said to a thief on the cross 'today you will be with me in paradise'.[77] He would happily sit and converse with a Samaritan woman[78] though it might scandalise others, and He would respond to the request of a synagogue ruler[79] or a Roman occupation officer[80] equally. He valued the poor,[81] and was suspicious of riches in a way that His contemporaries found mystifying, even shocking.[82] He valued those who knew they were guilty over those who thought they were acceptably respectable and righteous.[83] He chose both a tax collector[84] (an unclean outcast and a collaborator with the occupier) and someone with close connection to the High Priest[85] among His followers. He was born into a run-of-the-mill family; not desperately poor, His father was a skilled craftsman,[86] but not rich or influential either, and living as second-class citizens under Roman occupation. He took the risk of being conceived illegitimately[87] (being

---

75 Mark 1:35
76 Matthew 6:5
77 Luke 23:43
78 John 4:7-9
79 Mark 5:35–43
80 Matthew 8:5–13
81 Luke 21:2–4
82 Mark 10:17–25
83 Luke 18:10–14
84 Luke 5:27–28
85 John 18:16
86 Mark 6:3
87 Matthew 1:18–21

the only person in human history with a choice in the matter). He associated with outcasts, the powerless, those on the edge of society, the sick and the desperate.

'Today, theologians debate the aptness of the phrase "God's preferential option for the poor" as a way of describing God's concern for the underdog. Since God arranged the circumstances in which to be born on planet Earth – without power or wealth, without rights, without justice – His preferential options speak for themselves.'[88]

He possessed miraculous powers but was restrained in using them. He walked on water,[89] stilled a storm[90] and turned water into wine,[91] but as far as we know did these things only once. As Philip Yancey comments, 'What self-restraint!'[92]

He was truly humble. The night before His death He washed the feet of His disciples,[93] an action then considered so degrading that a master could not require it of a Jewish slave.[94]

When I lived and worked as a short-term mission volunteer with the church in Iran, one of the less pleasant jobs in the boys boarding hostel was assisting the warden (also a missionary from England) with cleaning out a number of large paraffin heaters ready for the next winter. It was a filthy job that involved scraping out huge quantities of encrusted soot, and it left us both looking like chimney sweeps (which we were, I guess). The warden in particular came in for some criticism (from other staff, parents of boys at the hostel and others) for doing something so beneath the dignity of his position. It occurred to me then that this is exactly the kind of thing Jesus would do, and exactly the sort of criticism He endured. 'Jesus never said "You cannot treat me like that. Don't you know that I am the Son of God?"'[95] It's been

---

88   *The Jesus I Never Knew*, Philip Yancey, p.38-39 (Marshall Pickering, 1995)

89   Matthew 14:25

90   Luke 8:24–25

91   John 2:1–11

92   *The Jesus I Never Knew*, Philip Yancey, p.180 (Marshall Pickering, 1995)

93   John 13:4–5

94   *The Jesus I Never Knew*, Philip Yancey, p.189 (Marshall Pickering, 1995)

95   *The Calvary Road*, Roy Hession, p.61 (CLC, 2002)

said that of all the things to do with one's dignity, the most stupid is to stand on it. Jesus never did that.

He was patient, and yet had much to be impatient about. The religious authorities lacked both integrity and insight in dealing with Him.[96] His own disciples regularly let Him down,[97] and were exceedingly slow to understand what He taught them.[98] His prayer times were interrupted.[99] He was often surrounded by crowds so that He struggled to get time alone to teach His disciples, let alone to rest.[100] He was so hard pressed that His family even began to worry for His mental health.[101] He was surrounded by people trying to get Him to serve *their* agenda,[102] the very thing He longed to free them from. Yet He was renowned for being gracious. He remained the man for others.

HE IS BRILLIANT

Sometimes in thinking about Jesus, especially if we have grown up in a Christian culture, or been a Christian a long time, we can miss the obvious through over familiarity. We can get so used to thinking of Jesus as 'the standard' that we come to regard Him as 'standard'. It's the same process by which 'normal' has come to mean 'ordinary'.

Among all His other attributes Jesus was brilliant. He had a great mind (had a high IQ) and was 'emotionally intelligent' (had a high EQ). Over and again He stunned people with the perceptiveness and authority of His answers. He taught about God with insight, knowledge and wit in a way that captivated crowds, and left them convinced that this man knew what He was talking about.[103] When the religious

---

96   E.g. Mark 12:13
97   E.g. Luke 9:46–50
98   E.g. Mark 8:17–21
99   Mark 1:35–37
100   Mark 6:31; Mark 9:30–31
101   Mark 3:20-21
102   Luke 12:13–14; John 6:26–27
103   Matthew 7:28–29

authorities tried to trap Him, He was always one step ahead, answering brilliantly, wittily and devastatingly.[104] He experienced the full range of human emotions, including fear and anxiety (in the garden of Gethsemane for example[105]), and frustration, even irritation (for example, with His disciples),[106] but was not ruled by such emotions. He was not panicked by them into rash actions. He did not cease to love, and remained submitted to His Father. One cannot imagine Him ever panicking, though He clearly knew what it was to be disappointed and apprehensive. He never lacked courage, though He clearly knew what it was to be afraid.

He was fully human and fully God, yet a more integrated personality would be impossible to find. He bestrode the Jewish and Gentile worlds, crossed gender divides, mixed with the rich and the poorest outcast, yet seemed to know entirely who He was. He was, it seems, thoroughly comfortable in His own skin.

He knew how to still storms, control unclean spirits and violent demoniacs, cut short the usual time and several of the ingredients required for making wine, and still came up with something that amazed by its quality. It has been argued that Jewish wine of the first century was probably nothing like what we know now. Production and storage methods would have left a fairly rough and acidic beverage for modern tastes, probably tainted from the animal skins used for storage. Then Jesus came along and produced something akin to Châteauneuf-du-Pape. No wonder the Gospels tell us repeatedly (thirty-three times) that people were 'amazed' by Him. Could it be that we have become too familiar with Jesus? 'In His case, quite frankly, presumed familiarity has led to unfamiliarity, unfamiliarity has led to contempt and contempt has led to profound ignorance.'[107]

Centuries before Freud, and psychoanalysis, He knew what made

---

104 Luke 20:19–26
105 Matthew 26:36–46
106 Luke 9:41; Matthew 16:8–11
107 *The Divine Conspiracy*, Dallas Willard, p.1 (Fount, 1998)

people tick. He knew what was in a person.[108] He told Peter in advance how He would react under pressure,[109] and knew in advance exactly what Judas would do.[110] Yet for all these abilities, He never tried to control or manipulate anyone.

I think that sometimes we take Jesus' abilities for granted. We might be tempted to think that as He was the Son of God, He must have come hardwired with all of this information and wisdom. If we think this way we seriously underestimate Him.

Firstly, His wisdom, His brilliance, were hard won. He didn't know everything. If you think He did, bear in mind that it wasn't only the crowds who were amazed at Jesus. He was amazed at *them* also. In His home town, 'He was amazed at their lack of faith.'[111] Amazement implies, among other things, surprise, and you cannot be surprised if you know everything in advance. This should not surprise us. The Gospels tell us that 'Jesus grew in wisdom and stature, and in favor with God and man.'[112] Being human clearly involved learning and developing like the rest of us.

Secondly, that learning and development continued into adult life. In a puzzling passage from Matthew, when a Gentile woman came to Jesus seeking healing for her daughter, Jesus at first refused to respond.

'Leaving that place, Jesus withdrew to the region of Tyre and Sidon. A Canaanite woman from that vicinity came to him, crying out, "Lord, Son of David, have mercy on me! My daughter is demon-possessed and suffering terribly."

Jesus did not answer a word. So his disciples came to him and urged him, "Send her away, for she keeps crying out after us."

He answered, "I was sent only to the lost sheep of Israel."

The woman came and knelt before him. "Lord, help me!" she said.

---

108   John 2:25
109   Luke 22:31–34
110   John 13:18–30
111   Mark 6:6 (see also Luke 7:9)
112   Luke 2:52

He replied, "It is not right to take the children's bread and toss it to the dogs."

"Yes it is, Lord," she said. "Even the dogs eat the crumbs that fall from their master's table."

Then Jesus said to her, "Woman, you have great faith! Your request is granted." And her daughter was healed at that moment.[113]

Was Jesus inherently racist? Did He not care? The explanation that makes most sense to me is that this was a learning experience for Him. In this encounter He was working out the implications of His mission beyond the borders of Israel. I'm aware that this might present problems for some for whom Jesus' perfection means He must have been omniscient at all times. But let me ask this: If Jesus was fully human, and if the Gospels make clear that this involved growing in wisdom as well as stature, what sense does it make to maintain that Jesus ceased the normal lifelong process of learning and growing in wisdom at some arbitrary early age? Wisdom does not normally stop growing when stature is complete.

Thirdly, if Jesus was fully human, then He took upon Himself fallen human nature like the rest of us. Any other conclusion means that His battle in the wilderness with the tempter was a sham, and that He had an undeclared hidden advantage that renders His example to the rest of us meaningless and impossible to follow. It renders the call to 'walk as He walked'[114] akin to an invitation to race against an athletics drug cheat. In saying He shared our fallen human nature I do not mean that He sinned. The scriptures are clear that He did not.[115] I mean that the battle against sin was a real battle, that He had to fight against a real propensity to sin like the rest of us, that each fresh temptation had to be faced, evaluated, prayed over and strength from His Father sought to overcome it.

This is why we can confidently say, 'For we do not have a high priest who is unable to feel sympathy for our weaknesses, but we have

---

113   Matthew 15:21–28
114   1 John 2:6
115   Hebrews 4:15

one who has been tempted in every way, just as we are – yet he did not sin.'[116]

He has really been there, done that, and got the T-shirt.

I find many reluctant to run with this conclusion in case it somehow diminishes Jesus.

It has long been so. My wife's family has a long history of involvement in the Catholic Apostolic Church, a mixture of catholic ritual and charismatic revivalism, which took root in the early part of the nineteenth century. Edward Irving was one of its founders (the movement was sometimes, but misleadingly, called 'Irvingites'). He was expelled from the Church of Scotland in 1833[117] for maintaining that Jesus Christ took upon Himself fallen human nature, which Irving termed 'sinful human nature' (though stressing that Jesus committed no sin). The process that ended in conviction for heresy and deposition from the ministry was begun originally by an Anglican minister, Rev. Henry Cole. He expressed his horror of Irving's teaching thus, 'What I felt at hearing such awful blasphemy against the person of the Son of God, declaimed with accompanying vehement gesticulations... I cannot describe... "This, sir," I observed, "is, to me, a most awful doctrine indeed!"'[118] I suspect that today, without ever having examined the issue, many would instinctively side with Henry Cole.[119] But is this biblical? Only, surely, if we do not give the phrase 'tempted in every way, just as we are'[120] its full weight.

Why stress these things? Why emphasise that Jesus had to learn and grow like the rest of us, that He inherited our fallen nature, and thus had a serious struggle to resist sin? Because I think there is a widespread tendency to discount Jesus' achievement and to neglect Him as an

---

116 Hebrews 4:15
117 *The Life of Edward Irving. The Fore-Runner of The Charismatic Movement*, Arnold Dallimore, Chapter 19 (Banner of Truth, 1983)
118 *The Life of Edward Irving. The Fore-Runner of The Charismatic Movement*, Arnold Dallimore, p.78–9 (Banner of Truth, 1983)
119 Indeed Arnold Dallimore, in the book cited above, takes exactly this view.
120 Hebrews 4:15

example to be imitated, because, it is believed, it all came too easily to Him (it didn't); and because it was all handed to Him on a plate (it wasn't). This obscures to us what a masterpiece of humanity He made of His life. It also tends to lead us to discount the possibility of emulating Him. He is Jesus, so it's all right for Him to behave like that, but He can't expect it of us (but He does). If He is fundamentally different from us in His humanity then whatever discipleship is, it can't be the imitation of Christ, but this is precisely what it is meant to be. I suspect that it is mistaken belief in this area that led to the situation discovered by a Europe-wide survey of 21,000 people by 'The Bertelsmann Stiftung Foundation', which found that of those who called themselves 'religious' over half said that their faith had no bearing on their politics or sexual behaviour.[121] Jesus' example and our lives have been de-coupled.

Jesus' life was a real and amazing achievement. It shone with a compelling brilliance that won allegiance because He made sense of life as no one before, or since. If we cannot appreciate this ourselves, or help others to appreciate it, we will give them little reason to follow Him. Few of our contemporaries have grown up close enough to faith to accept it without compelling reason, and this generation does not respond to appeals to authority. Authority has to be earned. But Jesus has earned it, many times over, if we have but eyes to see.

Dallas Willard writes:

'The life and words that Jesus brought into the world came in the form of information and reality. He and his early associates overwhelmed the ancient world because they brought into it a stream of life at its deepest, along with the best information possible on the most important matters.

'Jesus himself was thought of as someone to admire and respect, someone you thought highly of and considered to be a person of great ability. Worship of him included this – not, as today, ruled it out. This attitude was naturally conveyed in such New Testament names and

---

121   *Church Times* 10/10/08

phrases as "the Prince of life", "the Lord of glory", "abundant life"; "the inexhaustible riches of Christ" and so on. Today these phrases are emptied of most intellectual and practical content.

'It is the failure to understand Jesus and his words as reality and as vital information about life, that explains why, today, we do not routinely teach those who profess allegiance to him how to do what he said was best.'[122]

Willard continues; 'Jesus is Lord' can mean little in practice for anyone who has to hesitate before saying, 'Jesus is smart.'[123]

As I mentioned in Chapter 1, how far we have drifted from such an appreciation of Jesus is tellingly revealed by our worship. I combed through the first twenty-five hymns and songs in a well-known modern song and hymn book and found just one song that referred to anything after Jesus' nativity and before his crucifixion.[124] During a recent seven-week sabbatical worshipping in a variety of churches, I encountered only one line of one hymn that referred to the same period. So much public worship completely ignores the largest part of Jesus' life, focusing on His birth, death and resurrection, and His ascended power. Now, all of these things are vitally, hugely, important, but surely not to the point of obscuring the rest of His human life and example so completely. Did God go to such trouble and risk to become incarnate only for us to forget all about it again?

HE IS UNPREDICTABLE – AND YET HE IS CONSISTENT

And yet, how can one stay interested in Jesus for a lifetime? The four Gospels can be read in about seven to ten hours. We soon become

---

122 *The Divine Conspiracy*, Dallas Willard, p.2 (Fount, 1998). I owe a large debt to Willard in this section. Since reading and re-reading what he has to say about the character of Jesus I have found my worship and prayer renewed and my journey of discipleship reinvigorated.

123 *The Divine Conspiracy*, Dallas Willard, p.108–9 (Fount, 1998)

124 It was an alphabetically (not thematically) arranged song book, so this finding was not a quirk of the way the material was organised.

familiar with them. I have been reading the Gospels several times a year for over four decades. Do I not get bored? Frankly, on the whole, no. Occasionally I do, I get distracted, or I do not read with my full attention, or I feel I already know what the passage has to say to me. But on the whole the Gospels, like the rest of the Bible, speak freshly again, and again. In fact, I know it speaks more freshly to me now than it did when I started reading it seriously upon my conversion in 1972. It really is a living book through which Jesus speaks to us. Every time I read it, I discover fresh things about myself, about the world around me and about Jesus. The last thing I would now say about Jesus is that He is predictable. He is not one of those irritating people to whom one can say, "Oh! I just knew you would say that". His life and teaching draw me deeper, shed new light on old and new issues, and help me understand myself and others in fresh ways, year after year.

Philip Yancey says,

'In many respects I would find an un-resurrected Jesus easier to accept. Easter makes him dangerous. Because of Easter I have to listen to his extravagant claims and can no longer pick and choose from his sayings. Moreover, Easter means he must be loose out there somewhere. Like the disciples, I never know where Jesus might turn up, how he might speak to me, what he might ask of me. As Frederick Buechner says, Easter means "we can never nail him down, not even if the nails we use are real and the thing we nail him to is a cross".'[125]

No wonder Mr Beaver could not say he was safe.[126] He's untamed, and 'he must be loose out there somewhere.'

JESUS DID NOT COERCE, HE INVITED

But Mr Beaver also said that He was good. Therefore there is no need to fear Him. The consistent teaching of the Bible is that if we are going to fear anyone, it had better be God, who is ultimately 'in charge'. "'I tell

---

125 *The Jesus I Never Knew*, Philip Yancey, p.223–224 (Marshall Pickering, 1995)

126 *The Lion, The Witch and The Wardrobe*, C. S. Lewis, Ch 8

you, my friends, do not be afraid of those who kill the body and after that can do no more. But I will show you whom you should fear: fear him who, after your body has been killed, has authority to throw you into hell. Yes, I tell you, fear him.'"[127]

Having explained that there is no one worth fearing other than God, Jesus points out that actually His character means we need not fear Him either unless we reject that love and choose to fear.

"'Are not five sparrows sold for two pennies? Yet not one of them is forgotten by God. Indeed, the very hairs of your head are all numbered. Don't be afraid; you are worth more than many sparrows.'"[128]

'Perfect love drives out fear.'[129] This is the process summed up by John Newton in the hymn 'Amazing Grace'; *''Twas grace that taught my heart to fear, And grace my fears relieved.'*

There are few things that post-modern people fear as much as coercion and the resultant loss of autonomy. And 'religion is coercive, right?' Say the word 'religion' today and what are the images that come into the minds of many people: the Taleban and Islamic State, the Northern Ireland conflict, the burning of witches, religious wars, the persecution of gay people, miserable enforced Sundays, killjoy clergy? Well, the religious authorities of Jesus' day were strict and coercive – and Jesus hated what they did.[130]

Jesus did not coerce obedience. He invited it. I cannot stress this enough. When the rich young ruler came to Him, Jesus challenged the young man to give away his wealth, but He did not try to manipulate him, cajole him or coerce him. When he refused the invitation, Jesus let him walk away, though He 'loved him'.[131]

The essence and climax of Jesus' non-coercive mission is of course the cross (this is the focus of Chapter 4). He did not try to crush rebellious humanity but to woo. He refused to strike back but forgave.

---

127   Luke 12:4–5
128   Luke 12:4–7
129   1 John 4:18
130   Luke 11:46
131   Mark 10:17–23

This was of a piece with His whole life. Mohammad led armies, Jesus chose the life of a wandering preacher. He would not even use His startling insights into human character[132] or His miraculous powers to manipulate obedience,[133] but relied upon a straightforward demonstration and explanation of the truth.

This was grasped at an early stage in the history of the church, though too often forgotten later.

In the 'Letter to Diognetus' written in the early part of the third century, the author shows that they have a firm hold on the significance of the cross for our understanding of the power of God. Responding to the question of why God sent His Son to the world, the author replies: 'to rule by tyranny, fear and terror? Far from it! He sent him out of kindness and gentleness, like a king sending his son who is himself a king. He sent him as God; he sent him as man to men. He willed to save man by persuasion, not by compulsion, for compulsion is not God's way of working.'[134]

A significant strand of the Old Testament saw God's law not so much as restriction, but as God's lovingly offered gracious gift.

'What other nation is so great as to have their gods near them the way the Lord our God is near us whenever we pray to him? And what other nation is so great as to have such righteous decrees and laws as this body of laws I am setting before you today?'[135]

Once we see 'the law', or God's plan and intention, as a gracious gift, it becomes something to be shared rather than imposed, and those without it become those to be pitied, rather than those to be angry with.

It could not have been otherwise. Jesus' teaching had at its heart the love of God and neighbour. Love cannot be compelled, only received, on the one side, and freely offered on the other. A concomitant of love, also at the heart of Jesus' teaching, was the challenge to deny ourselves

---

132   See p.39, 40
133   Matthew 4:1–10
134   Quoted in *The Power of God and the gods of Power,* Daniel L. Migliore, p.60–61 (Westminster John Knox, 2008)
135   Deuteronomy 4:7–8

and take up our cross (more on this in Chapter 4).[136] This is about an attitude of mind that loves God and neighbour instead of putting ourselves first, and trusts God enough to cope with the consequences, even if they either feel like a kind of death, or actually do lead to our death. This is about faith, hope, love and security. In living it, Jesus modelled a joyful freedom and lack of fear that is deeply attractive. Needless to say, this too cannot be compelled.

Dallas Willard warns against the mentality that always has to straighten others out.[137] He opened my eyes to the true meaning of the first twelve verses of Matthew Chapter 7, beginning, 'Do not judge or you too will be judged', and containing the proverbial warning, 'Why do you look at the speck of sawdust in your brother's eye and pay no attention to the plank in your own eye?' '(Matthew) deals with the deadly way in which we try to "manage" or "control" those closest to us by blaming and condemning them and by forcing upon them our wonderful solutions to their problems... Disaster awaits – greater or smaller, sooner or later.' The problems are outlined in v. 1–6 (do not judge) and the solutions in v. 7–12 (ask, seek, knock). The solution is not condemning, or demanding, it is asking, simply asking. Few can resist a pleasant request, and if they do resist, there is the asking of prayer.

I have closely witnessed this condemning, demanding way of 'pastoring', and of making disciples, at least three times. Each time the minister involved became more and more exhausted as the people being 'helped' needed more and more intensive input to 'keep them on the straight and narrow'. All the energy had to come from the person who really wanted the change, the pastor. Each time the minister found it very exhausting to do the work of God. 'It was Emperor Hirohito of Japan, the last divinised ruler of Japan, who said, "You cannot imagine the extra work I had when I was a god". The church needs clergy who can laugh at themselves, not take their work too seriously.'[138]

---

136 Matthew 16:24
137 *The Divine Conspiracy*, Dallas Willard, p.238 (Fount, 1998)
138 *Being Human, Being Church*, Robert Warren, p.180 (Marshall Pickering, 1995)

It's hard to do this if we are playing God.

On each of these three occasions, after initial results, this bullying, controlling approach quickly led to collapse as people became weary, disenchanted or discouraged, as did the minister. I should know. The first of the three times, I was that minister. Mercifully, three times in quick succession, the Lord said to me through others, "You love them and I'll change them". It was one of the most liberating messages I've ever heard in my life.

Jesus wants to see us change because He loves us, but He does not coerce, manipulate or twist arms. He is heartbreakingly patient. Jesus readily admitted that the law of God allowed divorce 'for your hardness of heart' but made clear there was a better way that was God's true intention, namely that marriage should be permanent, and that remarriage amounted to adultery. His followers demurred at this, imagining, no doubt, a harsh application of legal penalty.

'The disciples said to him, "If this is the situation between a husband and wife, it is better not to marry."

Jesus replied, "Not everyone can accept this word, but only those to whom it has been given. For there are eunuchs who were born that way, and there are eunuchs who have been made eunuchs by others – and there are those who choose to live like eunuchs for the sake of the kingdom of heaven. The one who can accept this should accept it."'[139]

Clearly, this was an invitation, not a threat. A serious invitation – Jesus is saying that divorce is not in the plan and intention of God – but it is not a threat.

Grace in Action: Christian Pregnancy Counselling

How we understand Jesus here, as issuing an invitation or as coercing, has important consequences for how we treat others and how we serve in His name.

---

139   Matthew 19:10–12

At a meeting of local clergy I had the privilege of listening to Celia Wyatt of 'Choices', a Christian pregnancy counselling centre in North London. I was struck by her love for her clients, the utterly non-judgmental and compassionate way she described them, without in any way compromising her concern about abortion and its consequences. Her attitude reminded me powerfully of Jesus in its moral seriousness and in its empathy with sinners and victims. Her approach was totally devoid of manipulation and coercion and respected the integrity and moral responsibility of her clients. This of course did not make Celia Wyatt morally neutral any more than the same approach made Jesus morally neutral. However, she and others involved in Christian pregnancy counselling have repeatedly been accused, by some Christians, of moral indifference and relativism. Yet Celia writes, 'Counselling such women over the last five years has persuaded me – as if I needed it – that abortion is *never* a good solution to an unplanned pregnancy.'[140]

Exemplifying such attacks is *What is Going on in Christian Crisis Pregnancy Counselling?* by Dr E. S. Williams.[141] Dr Williams believes that the approach of Christian Pregnancy Counselling Centres such as Choices, and others sponsored by the Christian charity 'CARE', is essentially the same as that offered by pro-choice organisations such as Marie Stopes clinics. 'The advice provided by CARE's network of pregnancy counselling centres exhibits all the essential characteristics of pro-choice dogma. Like pro-choice, CARE's counselling promises a pregnant woman to help her find out what she wants to do about her pregnancy.' He goes on to accuse such centres and 'CARE' of 'departing from the faith once and for all entrusted to the saints' and of 'promoting abortion'.[142] This is clearly a monstrous slander to anyone who knows

---

140 Celia Wyatt in *Triple Helix*, the magazine of The Christian Medical Fellowship (Winter '07 edition), p.16
141 *What is Going on in Christian Crisis Pregnancy Counselling?*, Dr E. S. Williams (Sutton: Belmont House Publishing, 2005)
142 http://www.belmonthouse.co.uk/CARE/care_and_abortion.htm#_ednref2 and E. S. Williams (op. cit.) p.45

the work of those involved or the people involved in it. He criticises the non-judgmental approach, apparently quite unable to perceive the difference between a 'non-judgmental' and a 'values free' approach. He says, 'The Bible is the most judgmental book in the world and Jesus is judgmental'.[143] Apparently he believes that what women tempted to an abortion need is someone to tell them that it is wrong. All my pastoral experience tells me that in the absence of a trusting relationship between the person tempted and the adviser, such advice is ineffective, and even in the presence of such a relationship it is so much better if the counselee can be led to such a conclusion for themselves. If *they* can see it, then this opens the door to real repentance, forgiveness and a relationship with their Saviour, something that a mere telling off rarely if ever achieves. In a conversation with me, Celia stressed that in being listened to and helped to reflect on the options and their consequences, much suppressed guilt, shame and grief is brought to the surface, and facing this begins a process of taking responsibility for action in a way that can lead to repentance and forgiveness.

She says, 'Like God we respect her moral decision; our hearts are pained if she makes the wrong choice; and we are there when the consequences of her choice overwhelm her'.[144] Which of these two approaches sounds more like that of Jesus? Which is more likely to attract the soubriquet 'friend of sinners'?[145] Which approach is 'full of grace *and* truth'?[146]

'Choices' has also faced much suspicion from the secular establishment, who fear a judgmental or manipulative 'Christian' agenda. Gradually they have won confidence and receive referrals from doctors and health centres, and a rapidly increasing number of invitations to go into schools where they can bring a Christian perspective into sex and relationships education. How tragic then,

---

143   Williams (op. cit.) p.59
144   Wyatt (op. cit.)
145   Matthew 11:19
146   John 1:14

that such an approach is most viciously attacked, from a supposedly Christian perspective, by those who cannot get their heads around the fact that Jesus was non-coercive and commanded us to be non-judgmental. Once again, an effective work in Jesus' name, with Jesus at its heart, is attacked by the religious 'thought police'. But then, this is exactly what happened to Jesus.

MEEKNESS

'In Dorothy Sayer's play *The Man Born to Be King*, King Herod tells the Magi, "You cannot rule men by love. When you find your king, tell him so. Only three things will govern a people – fear and greed and the promise of security." King Herod understood the management principles Satan operates by, the same ones Jesus declined in the wilderness.'[147]

Jesus was powerful. We read that straight after the temptations in the wilderness[148] 'Jesus returned to Galilee in the power of the Spirit'.

That power was manifested immediately in all kinds of ways: in power over unclean spirits,[149] in authority to teach,[150] to forgive sins,[151] in power to heal[152] and to work miracles.[153]

But this power emerged after His encounter with the Devil in the wilderness, where He refused to use such power in selfish ways, but only in submission to God. 'Luke's narrative leaves us with little room to evade the conclusion that this power from God was unleashed because he refused to exercise it in a selfish, spectacular or secular manner.'[154]

This refusal to use power in ungodly ways, or for His own ends,

---

147   *The Jesus I Never Knew*, Philip Yancey, p.74 (Marshall Pickering, 1995)
148   Luke 4:1–13
149   Luke 4:41; Luke 4:36
150   Luke 4:32
151   Luke 5:24
152   Luke 5:17
153   Luke 5:1–10
154   *Jesus and Power*, David Prior, p.54 (Hodder and Stoughton, 1987)

was radical, not just ruling out coercion and revenge, but manipulation also (for example, using even generosity in a calculated way to earn favours was not His way).[155]

Jesus' whole attitude to power and its exercise was *meek*. Meekness, as a concept, has had a bad press. It provokes slightly subversive jokes, like the two pieces of graffiti, 'The meek will inherit the earth, if it's all right with the rest of you,' and the cynical, 'The meek will inherit the earth, but not the mineral rights.' In the world's eyes, the meek are seen as the disregarded losers.

Victorian Sunday school pictures of 'gentle Jesus, meek and mild' spring to mind, with overtones of the insipid, as if Jesus was not quite man enough, and in fact was rather a wimp. If we think like this, we have misunderstood the concept of meekness radically. It is a word more associated with bulls and oxen, plough horses and war horses, than with frightened rabbits.

The word 'meek', *'praus'* in Greek, is variously translated in the New Testament as 'meek' 'gentle' or 'humble'.[156] 'It was originally used of a horse, or some other animal, which had been broken in, tamed and was now useful to its owner... Meekness therefore means power under control.'[157] Once we understand this, the quotation at the head of this chapter from C. S. Lewis makes more sense, '"Is he – quite safe?"... "Safe?... Who said anything about safe? Course he isn't safe. But he's good."'[158] He is safe like an animal that could kill with one toss of its horns, but chooses not to: 'power under control'.

This meaning of meek, of a beast yoked to a plough, powerful, with its power at the disposal of a purpose, is clearly what Jesus has in mind when he says: '"Take my yoke upon you and learn from me, for I am gentle and humble in heart (meek), and you will find rest for your souls. For my yoke is easy and my burden is light."'[159]

---

155   Luke 14:12–14
156   *Jesus and Power*, David Prior, p.186 (Hodder and Stoughton, 1987)
157   *Jesus and Power*, David Prior, p.60 & 61 (Hodder and Stoughton, 1987)
158   *The Lion, The Witch & The Wardrobe*, C. S. Lewis, p.75 (Puffin, 1973)
159   Matthew 11:29–30

This comes immediately after Jesus makes one of the most startling and all-embracing of His claims to power, "'All things have been committed to me by my Father. No one knows the Son except the Father, and no one knows the Father except the Son and those to whom the Son chooses to reveal him'."[160]

His power is only exercised in total submission to his Father. This is the secret and source of His power.

"'For I did not speak on my own, but the Father who sent me commanded me to say all that I have spoken. I know that his command leads to eternal life. So whatever I say is just what the Father has told me to say'."[161]

'Jesus gave them this answer: "Very truly I tell you, the Son can do nothing by himself; he can do only what he sees his Father doing."' [162]

It is submitted power, power under control. This is why the Lord could say to the apostle Paul, "'My grace is sufficient for you, for my power is made perfect in weakness.'" [163]

Jesus' meekness is apparent in both the fact and the circumstances of His birth. He made himself dependent upon a teenage couple for His sustenance, was born into an occupied country under a vicious puppet king. The creator of the universe made Himself vulnerable for a purpose.

His meekness is apparent throughout His teaching, which expects us to be like Him, refusing to throw our weight around. 'If someone slaps you on one cheek, turn to them the other also.'[164]

His meekness is apparent in His life, particularly in His full submission to His Father's purpose, perhaps most clearly exemplified in His prayer in the Garden of Gethsemane. "'My Father, if it is possible, may this cup be taken from me. Yet not as I will, but as you will'." [165]

---

160 Matthew 11:27
161 John 12:49–50
162 John 5:19
163 2 Corinthians 12:9
164 Luke 6:29
165 Matthew 26:39

Surely it is most of all apparent in His death. "'Put your sword back in its place,' Jesus said to Peter, "for all who draw the sword will die by the sword. Do you think I cannot call on my Father, and he will at once put at my disposal more than twelve legions of angels? But how then would the Scriptures be fulfilled that say it must happen in this way?"'[166]

Possibly the greatest mystery of all, is that this meekness was not a disguise. It was not something that the creator of the universe had to adopt just to avoid scaring the living daylights out of the rest of us. It revealed the true nature of God: humble, meek, almighty and all loving.

'The Messiah who showed up, however, wore a different kind of glory, the glory of humility. "God is great", the cry of the Moslems, is a truth which needed no supernatural being to teach men,' writes Father Neville Figgis. 'That God is little, that is the truth which Jesus taught man.'[167]

Such meekness has a winsome quality wherein lies some of its power. In some French bibles the word meek is translated '*debonnaire*'. It is hard not to say of Jesus, however suspicious we are of power, that we like His style.

JESUS AND POWER

Many of the idols we seek are shortcuts to power. Most instances of 'bad religion' are the result of a non-Christlike approach to power, whether the suicide bomber or the bullying prelate. 'The Living God is not a projection of our will to power or our deep-seated desire to dominate others. While majestically strong, the living God shows that strength most awesomely in the humility of a servant Lord… We need to know the difference between the power of the living God and the

---

166 Matthew 26:52–54
167 *The Jesus I Never Knew*, Philip Yancey, p.34–35 (Marshall Pickering, 1995)

distorted images of divine power that haunt our lives.'[168] Once we find ourselves exercising power, even in defence of the Gospel, in ways reminiscent of the idolatrous powers, Jesus, 'the power of God',[169] is rendered invisible.

Surely this is at least part of what Jesus meant by saying that we must become as little children.[170] We must become as those who have no weight to throw around. How can the church of God be this way when it relies upon power and privilege? Rumour has it that a priest in the early Middle Ages was being shown around the Vatican. The guide, referring to the riches on display, proudly said, "Well, we can no longer say 'silver and gold have I none'," to which the priest replied, "No, and neither it seems can we say 'in the name of Jesus Christ of Nazareth rise up and walk.'"[171] Maybe the loss of the final trappings of establishment are necessary before real renewal can happen in the Church of England?

My Power Is Made Perfect in Weakness

When Christians dispute in a way that does not reflect the meekness of Jesus, they *cannot* win the day for Jesus. They may win the argument, they may win a power struggle, they may win over popular opinion, but Jesus never wins. In the service of Jesus, the end never justifies the means. If it did, then Jesus should have given way to the tempter in the wilderness. To justify the means by the end, as when Peter wielded the sword to defend Jesus, is, at root, a failure of faith. It is trusting our judgment over Jesus', our pragmatically achievable results over His providential rule, our own self-validation over His eventual vindication. The latter will survive at the end, the former will not. It will be burnt up like straw.[172]

---

168   *The Power of God and the gods of Power*, Daniel L. Migliore, p.15&16 (Westminster John Knox, 2008)
169   1 Corinthians 1:24
170   Mark 10:13–16
171   Acts 3:6
172   1 Corinthians 3:10–15

Choosing our own way to advance Jesus' cause can lead to some grotesque spectacles. 'On 1 September (1644), at Tippermuir near Perth, they (an Irish Catholic army) met and defeated an army of Covenanters carrying a banner, *"Jesus and no quarter"*.'[173]

There is a power in the meekness of Christ that the bluster and threats of naked power does not understand.

'In 603, Augustine summoned the leaders of the British Church to a conference at a place on the borders of Wessex which in Bede's time was still called "Augustine's Oak". There he invited them to accept his brand of Christianity – or else. For its part, the British delegation, which contained a large contingent from the monastery at Bancornaburg (Bangor), had consulted a wise hermit on the way to a conference. "If Augustine is meek and lowly of heart", they were advised, "it shows that he bears the yoke of Christ and offers it to you. But if he is haughty and unbending, then he is not of God, and you should not listen to him." When Augustine did not even bother to rise and greet them, they had their answer. The conference ended with Augustine issuing threats.'[174]

SOME CAVEATS AND EXCEPTIONS: WHEN IS INVITATION NOT ENOUGH?

However, there are some occasions when Jesus seems to 'come on strong' and at least one where He is definitely coercive. Do these not provide some justification for those who would seek to be enforcement officers for Christ?

The 'woes' of Matthew 23 are a pretty powerful denunciation. No 'gentle Jesus meek and mild' here. '"Woe to you, teachers of the law and Pharisees, you hypocrites!… You travel over land and sea to win a single convert, and when you have succeeded, you make them twice as much a child of hell as you are… Woe to you, blind guides!… You

---

173   *The Isles*, Norman Davies, p.588 (Macmillan, 1999)
174   *The Isles*, Norman Davies, p.199 (Macmillan, 1999)

blind fools!… You are like whitewashed tombs, which look beautiful on the outside but on the inside are full of the bones of the dead and everything unclean. In the same way, on the outside you appear to people as righteous but on the inside you are full of hypocrisy and wickedness… You snakes! You brood of vipers! How will you escape being condemned to hell?"'

Is this meek? Does this not undo much of my argument so far? Well, 'yes' and 'no'. Yes, it is meek, and no, it is of a piece with my argument so far. Jesus' heart went out to the ordinary people, 'When he saw the crowds, he had compassion on them, because they were harassed and helpless, like sheep without a shepherd.'[175] The law had been given, remember, as God's good gift, and was a cause for rejoicing. By their constant manipulation of God's laws into endless petty rules and restrictions, the Pharisees had made many ordinary people's lives a guilt-ridden misery. They condemned and they criticised, but they showed no mercy. "'The teachers of the law and the Pharisees sit in Moses' seat. So you must be careful to do everything they tell you. But do not do what they do, for they do not practise what they preach. They tie up heavy cumbersome loads and put them on other people's shoulders, but they themselves are not willing to lift a finger to move them.'"[176]

To people under such loads Jesus said, "'Come to me, all you who are weary and burdened, and I will give you rest. Take my yoke upon you and learn from me, for I am gentle and humble in heart, and you will find rest for your souls. For my yoke is easy and my burden is light.'"[177]

To those who imposed such loads he said: "Woe unto you!"

David Prior comments, 'Nobody could possibly have perfectly kept "the tradition of the elders", neither the Pharisees nor even their scribes. The regulations governing the Sabbath provide a good example. The law (or Torah) said a man must not do any work on the

---

175 Matthew 9:36
176 Matthew 23:4
177 Matthew 11:28

Sabbath; the traditions (the Halakah) laid down how many paces a man might walk, how heavy a burden he might carry. In fact, thirty-nine basic actions which constituted work were laid down as forbidden on the Sabbath. For example, it was forbidden to go on a journey, to till a farm, to light a fire, to ride a beast, to strike, catch or kill an animal or a bird, to fast or to make war.

'In such ways the great principles of the law were broken up into thousands of petty rules and regulations. 'By the time [these] scribal interpretation[s] of the Law [were] finished, it took more than fifty volumes to hold the mass of regulations which resulted.'[178] This was the burden the Pharisee earnestly undertook to carry – and zealously sought to impose on others. They had managed to turn religion into an intolerable burden. William Barclay[179] has posed some searching questions for modern examples of Pharisaism: 'Does it make [religion] a joy or a depression? Is a man helped by his religion or is he haunted by it? Does it carry him, or has he to carry it?'[180]

If meekness is power under control, in this case God's control, and bent to God's purpose, then it makes sense that the one place Jesus would 'take the gloves off' would be with those who were oppressing the people in the name of God, who were using power in God's name, but not under God's control. Jesus condemned those who traded in condemnation. He put down those who were exalting themselves at the expense of others. These were people who, in the name of God, were exploiting their position of power to their own advantage, at the expense of others less powerful than themselves. Even their piety was for reputation and appearance, rather than directed at God. 'Everything they do is done for people to see.'[181] They were hypocrites, not 'honest sinners'.

---

178 *The Daily Study Bible: The Gospel of Matthew*, p.282 (St Andrew Press, 1976) quoted in *Jesus and Power*, David Prior
179 *The Daily Study Bible: The Gospel of Matthew*, p.285 (St Andrew Press, 1976) quoted in *Jesus and Power*, David Prior
180 *Jesus and Power*, David Prior, p.127–8 (Hodder and Stoughton, 1987)
181 Matthew 23:5

This explains Jesus' one 'violent' act, the cleansing of the temple. 'So he made a whip out of cords, and drove all from the temple courts, both sheep and cattle; he scattered the coins of the money changers and overturned their tables.'[182] The authorities were making an exorbitant profit by insisting that all money was changed into special coinage to pay the temple tax, and by selling the animals for sacrifice, and all this in the 'Court of the Gentiles', which was intended to be a place of prayer for all nations. 'A certain charge was legitimate. But the temple money changers had a monopoly and often charged exorbitant rates. The enormous wealth of the temple is illustrated by the fact that the Roman, Crassus, is said to have taken from it a sum equal to about two and a half million pounds sterling (1971 prices).'[183]

The word 'violent' is probably an exaggeration. This was one man among many, vastly outnumbered, and using what is probably better translated as 'a whip of rushes' than a whip of cords, more of a fly whisk than a whip. 'It is clear, that it was not so much the physical force as the moral power He employed that emptied the courts.'[184]

Jesus was fundamentally non-coercive, and the one exception, quite logically and consistently, was towards those who used their power in God's name, to coerce, oppress and cheat others. This was His purpose, 'to set the oppressed free'[185], and His power was controlled and bent to this purpose. This is meekness, not weakness. One is reminded of the same mistake Hitler made concerning Great Britain. He mistook a nation that was, at that time, fundamentally peace-loving, for a weak nation that would never fight, not even to restrain greater violence and injustice. There is a world of difference between meekness and weakness, but they are easily confused.

When the weak were harmed by the strong, Jesus could be

---

182 John 2:15
183 *The Gospel According To John*, Leon Morris, p.193 (Marshall, Morgan and Scott, 1972)
184 *The Gospel According To John*, Leon Morris, p.194 (Marshall, Morgan and Scott, 1972)
185 Luke 4:18

fierce, but any who today would use this as an excuse for speaking disparagingly of their fellow Christians, or of supposed 'sinners', or in order to enforce Christian behaviour, rather than to invite others into it, will run the risk that Jesus will one day say, "'I don't know you or where you come from. Away from me, all you evildoers!'"[186]

THE JOURNEY SO FAR

In Jesus Christ the Word became flesh. God spoke through His whole life, not just His words.

Jesus was remarkable, but overfamiliarity with Him can make that hard to discern. People followed Him because He was compelling, not because He was coercive. They were drawn to Him because He made sense of life, and regularly we are told that all kinds of people were 'amazed' at Him.

He did not arrive hardwired to achieve this masterpiece of a human life. The Gospels make it clear that He had to learn and develop and face very real temptations. The fact that He did not sin does not mean that He could not have sinned. Failure to appreciate this can make Jesus' example seem remote, out of reach and unrealistic for us to aspire to. But aspire to it is exactly what we are meant to do.

He came to lead us into holiness. He did not come to legislate for us, knowing that law was often abused, and was insufficient to create true godliness. Jesus was interested in holiness not mere compliance.

Unlike compliance, holiness cannot be coerced, so Jesus' characteristic way of relating to us was by inviting, not by threatening, manipulating or coercing.

He could have coerced, but His power was under control.

---

186   Luke 13:27

This is the meaning of meekness. He does not throw His weight around.

When Christians dispute in a way that does not reflect the meekness of their Saviour, they cannot win the day for Jesus Christ.

Chapter Three

The Character of Jesus and a Couple of Dodgy Characters (the character of our age and our own character)

'Then Jesus came to them and said, "All authority in heaven and on earth has been given to me – And surely I am with you always, to the very end of the age." '

(Matthew 28:18-20)

If Jesus is God incarnate, we should expect the implications of His coming to reverberate throughout history, to shape how we understand everything, from the ages before Him, to the ages to come. His deeds, His teaching and His character should be the lens through which everything is understood, and the example which every individual life and collective culture should attempt to emulate. As far as possible Jesus should shape our understanding of culture, not culture shape our understanding of Jesus.[187]

In this chapter we will pause from exploring the character and example of Jesus directly, in order to do some initial exploring of what difference such knowledge of Jesus might make to our understanding of our own culture, of ourselves and the role of the Bible in shaping this understanding.

---

187   Though God who became incarnate must be expressed in the local flesh of each individual culture. That is a different matter.

THE CHARACTER OF OUR AGE: JESUS CHRIST
AND POST-MODERNISM

Our age has often been described as 'Post-modern'. 'Post-modern' has many different meanings. Philosophically it is suspicious of ideologies, truth claims and grand theories. Some seem to be saying that there is no such thing as truth, only a point of view, or an interpretation. In many ways this is a reaction against intellectual traditions stemming from the enlightenment, sometimes referred to as the 'modernist'[188] project. These are widely held to reflect a white, male, colonialist and privileged point of view. According to much post-modern philosophy truth claims are largely power plays and an attempt to control others. The resultant suspicion of theories and dogma has been given considerable fuel by the twentieth-century experience of Nazism and Soviet Communism.

One can see echoes of post-modern philosophy in many contemporary attitudes. Scepticism and fear of religion, interest in what works rather than in theories (pragmatism), distrust of institutions and extreme individualism, and a fairly radical subjectivism (the idea that something can be true for me but not for you, or vice versa) are all part of the same picture. Common to them all is an attempt to preserve the liberty of the individual, to retain autonomy and resist coercion.

A 'post-modern' approach to truth lies behind many of the battles of the Trump presidency in the USA, and Brexit in the UK, with their suspicion of experts, complaints of fake news, claims to alternative truths and alternative facts, and the regular replacement of reasoned debate with anger and assertion.

Suspicion of truth claims can lead to a cavalier approach to truth. Speaking of the Brexit referendum campaign, Ryan Coetzee[189] believes

---

188 'Modern' and 'post-modern' do not in this sense refer to periods of time, as in contemporary and post-contemporary, but rather to a collection of cultural and philosophical assumptions.
189 Director of Strategy for 'Stronger In'

the campaign was hurt by a breakdown of trust between rulers and the ruled, and a flourishing of conspiracy theories: "Britain got caught up in something that is sweeping the West, and that involves distrust to the point of paranoia. It involves growing fear of the other, whether that person is foreign or black or whatever it might be. It involves a turning away from reason, evidence, logic – those ideas that have built what is called the West over the past 500 years. What the Leave campaign did was they turbocharged that lack of trust." Craig Oliver[190] believes, "We were up against a campaign that was prepared to mislead on an industrial scale."[191]

Many have criticised post-modern approaches to philosophy as leading to absurdity. If there is no such thing as truth, all research, thinking, and criticism falls down. Therefore, many now argue that post-modernism has hit its highwater mark as a philosophy, and is past its prime, though culturally it is probably still on the rise. Whether it ever was a philosophy, or merely an extreme habit of scepticism, is open to question. However, surely the so-called post-modernists were onto something. Surely truth claims have in fact been used as power plays repeatedly, and those who control or influence the organs of thought and information have been the privileged and powerful.[192] Thus the popular fear of truth claims, and of organisations claiming to make them, has a life of its own and will not (and maybe should not) disappear too easily.

However, there can be little doubt that some of the fruits of these cultural trends are distinctly un-Christlike. The rejection of overarching truth is fundamentally at odds with belief in one true God who made all things. The extreme suspicion of truth claims corrodes

---

190   Director of Communications for David Cameron
191   *All Out War: The Full Story of Brexit*, Tim Shipman, p.585 (Collins, 2016)
192   Donald Trump's repeated references to 'fake news' are part of this same struggle, as are the various arguments raging about the influence of unregulated social media on elections and referenda. Are the social media a democratisation of politics and opinion-shaping, or a gateway to manipulation by shadowy powers at home or overseas? Or both?

shared values and trust, dissolves community and inexorably leads to radical individualism. No wonder the idea of our shared humanity is being sidelined, and racism and scapegoating of minority groups are on the rise. The diminution of belief in reason reduces confidence in and willingness to participate in debate and negotiation, leading to the substitution of assertion, anger and even violence. Lack of confidence that there can even be such a thing as truth feeds directly into a greater willingness to lie, and a greater openness to be taken in by lies. While much of the church has been taken up with gender issues, unnoticed by many, the fundamentals of a culture built upon belief in one God have been dismantled.

On the back of this ride in the false prophets. People like Viktor Orbán, prime minister of Hungary, with his appeal to religious nationalism, 'Christian Hungary' over against Moslem immigrants, or Donald Trump, who by some accounts scored eighty per cent support from conservative evangelicals[193] in the last election. One look at their characters should reveal a glaring disparity between them and the character of Jesus Christ. How could some US Christians lose the plot to this extent? So yet again the alternative to a post-modern view of the world seems to be (populist) authoritarianism, and the old fears of truth claims are further stoked, as many fail to see that politicians like Trump, Orbán and many others are the bastard offspring of post-modern values.

Many have described our culture as having travelled from being 'post-modern' to 'post-truth'. But, as Elvis Presley reputedly said "Truth is like the sun. You can shut it out for a time, but it ain't goin' away".

So, what does Jesus have to say to our transitioning culture?

THE TRUTH NAILED DOWN

As we have seen, the idea of objective and ultimate truth threatens many in our culture who fear coercion in the name of that truth. It

---

193   This does not mean the same as 'conservative evangelical' in the UK.

has often been a short road from saying 'I have the truth' to saying, 'You must obey me'. This short journey is perhaps best summed up by the official Soviet newspaper, *Pravda*, meaning 'truth', and its link with Soviet coercion, including thought control. Does 'I have the truth' mean 'I have the right to be obeyed and the right to judge'? Jesus repeatedly and in all kinds of ways made it clear that it does not. 'Crucified truth threatens no one and coerces no one. Its power lies in its powerlessness.'[194] The world looks at Christians, and too easily concludes that if Christians can treat each other the way that we sometimes do when we disagree, what chance would the rest of the world have if we ever again attained power. Would we really eschew enforced conformity?

After a century in which powerful idolatrous political creeds (Fascism and Communism) have trampled on individuals' lives and rights in the name of secular ideology, the stage could have been set for a worldwide return to Christ, as the one who, more than any other, is trustworthy with power. In some parts of the world I believe that this is exactly what is happening. However, Christians have not, on the whole, convinced our Western part of the world that they are sufficiently Christlike to be trusted with truth claims, and certainly not with power. Only when we have the humility to realise that we cannot be trusted with power will we sufficiently be able to reflect the one whose power is made perfect in weakness, and 'who, being in very nature God, did not consider equality with God something to be used to his own advantage; rather he made himself nothing.'[195]

Of course, in the current cultural climate of suspicion about truth claims, Christians are often unfairly accused of intolerance. It is not intolerant per se to have strong and clear convictions. It only becomes intolerant when we display contempt for other's opinions or try to suppress or coerce them.

There is a sense, of course, in which Christians have asked for it.

---

194   Roy Clements at The National Association of Evangelicals, 1997
195   Philippians 2:6

How often have Christians been 'the meek' and the mild until they have attained power? Speaking of a (Pre-Reformation) Christian tradition of scholarship without coercion, in which the world (science) and the word were held in dialogue, J. Andrew Kirk says:

'From within, the tradition was vandalised by a particularly devastating will-to-power. The gigantic conflict between the forces of the Reformation and the Counter-Reformation were still playing themselves out. The "territorial tragedy" of Christianity encountered its nadir in the Thirty Years' War, when the non-violent compulsion of truth and the authority of conscience were substituted by the coercive force and authoritarianism of the religious state. This absolutism was also mobilised against the incipient findings of scientific discovery. [They] failed to perceive the nature of genuine Christian freedom.'[196]

We have never lived down the Thirty Years' War, which gave to religion an aura of intolerance. Even those (many) who have never heard of it are affected by its legacy which has given religion a reputation for being the causer of wars. Just when the twentieth century provided ample evidence (in Russia and Germany and elsewhere) that secular regimes and creeds also cause wars, and that perhaps the problem was humanity's will to power rather than religion, along came the Northern Irish troubles and then Al-Qaeda and ISIS to confirm the old prejudice.

One Christian foray into the field of coercion was when the fringe group 'Christian Voice' and its director Stephen Green decided to oppose the musical *Jerry Springer, The Opera* for blasphemy, in 2004 and 2005. There is a debate to be had about whether *Jerry Springer, The Opera* is or is not blasphemous. I have not seen it, and don't propose to go into that debate now. Let's just assume for the moment that it is blasphemous. What then?

Stephen Green claimed that the purpose of demonstrations at the Cambridge Theatre was to 'explain to theatre-goers why the show is

---

196   J. Andrew Kirk, in *Tolerance and Truth*, p.161 (Rutherford House 2007)

offensive *to us*'.[197] Well, who really cares? People are being offended all the time. Some were offended by the stance taken by 'Christian Voice'. That should not shut up 'Christian Voice', any more than Stephen Green's offence should close the musical. Surely the important issue is whether God was offended, and if so, what to do about it. To be fair, 'Christian Voice' was concerned about this too, but the fact remained that they also stressed their *own* offence. It is of little moment whether Christian Voice, or I, or anyone else is offended. Once we go down that road it is open to anyone to play the victim card in order to silence expression they do not like. There is an epidemic of this at the moment, as exemplified by the 'no platforming' movement in British universities.

From a Christian perspective the important issue is blasphemy against God, the honour of God, and the danger people put themselves in if they mock, reject or ignore God. How would Jesus react to such issues? How did he react? And how did 'Christian Voice' react?

Well, 'Christian Voice' published the private phone numbers of BBC staff on their website, which led to those staff and their families receiving abusive and threatening phone calls (including threats of violence). They also instituted unsuccessful legal proceedings against the BBC for blasphemy. This of course was a coercive act and intended to be so.

How does such a response stand next to the example of one who, when crucified, never said "Don't you know who I am? You can't do that to me", who came not to call the righteous, but sinners to repentance? The right response *might* have been to demonstrate outside the theatre, but only to lovingly warn the blasphemers and to testify to the world concerning God's true nature. It is notoriously difficult to demonstrate positively and lovingly. Street demonstrations in our culture tend to be confrontational and negative, against sin, not for sinners. And contrary to the alleged blasphemy going on inside the theatre, attempting to

---

197   Christian Voice website: http://www.christianvoice.org.uk/springer.html (Italics mine)

bear witness to the true nature of our God and Saviour, Jesus Christ, by using coercive methods that were un-Christlike, is inherently self-defeating (possibly itself blasphemous).

Such responses tend to lead to all Christians being lumped together, in the popular imagination, with the Moslems who rioted and committed acts of violence over the Danish cartoons of Mohammad, or with the murderer of Theo van Gogh, a Dutch artist, who was killed for making a film exposing the abuse of Moslem women. To be fair, Stephen Green specifically renounced the use of violence by Christians in response to some of the abusive phone calls made to BBC staff. However, his whole approach and strategy was (and I believe was designed to be) intimidatory and coercive, so the public perception of him as of the same ilk as Islamist radicals had some basis. This impression was further reinforced by 'Christian Voice's' appeal to the example of Sikh and Moslem radicals to motivate Christians to take action. The 'Christian Voice' website said, 'The story broke just a week after 400 Sikhs felt strongly enough about the play *Behzti* (Dishonour), which depicted sex abuse and murder in a Sikh temple, to protest outside (and inside) the Birmingham Repertory Theatre, and to close the show. God sent a challenge to Christians to look at the willingness of Sikhs to stand up for their religion.'[198]

Yet *The Times* reported at the time, 'The violence that forced the cancellation of a controversial Sikh play was caused by militant extremists who aligned themselves to the protest, organisers claimed yesterday.

The Sikh community fears that its reputation has been tarnished by the trouble at the Birmingham Repertory Theatre, which led to the play *Behzti* (Dishonour) being abandoned.

The Times has learnt that members of the Sikh Federation were among the demonstrators on Saturday night. The group was formed in the aftermath of the banning of the International Sikh Youth

---

198   http://www.christianvoice.org.uk/springer.html

Federation under the Terrorism Act 2000. The ISYF is committed to the creation of an independent Sikh state in India and, according to the Foreign Office, has been involved in assassinations, bombings and kidnappings, mainly directed against Indian officials and interests.'[199]

Christian indignation can contain the seeds of much destructiveness.

It seems strange that an organisation claiming to be a 'Christian Voice' should take such people, rather than Jesus Christ, as their role model. I fear this is one of the many results of ceasing to regard Jesus as a credible human example that we noted in Chapter 2.

Every time Christians resort to the use of naked power and coercion they confirm widely-held fears that, because of our strong convictions, we must, of necessity, be dictatorial. Simultaneously, while not intending to, we bear false witness to Jesus, who showed how possession of the truth and non-coercion belong together in the economy of God.

Thus, those Christians who complained to the Advertising Standards Authority, in an attempt to ban an atheistic bus advert, which read 'There's probably no God. Now stop worrying and enjoy your life', did immense harm to our Christian witness. They both reduced our plausibility in this culture and behaved in an un-Christlike way. They simultaneously conveyed the impression that our case cannot stand up to argument, and that we are not in favour of free speech or liberty of thought.[200] How much better to welcome the opportunity for debate, to use the advert to take the case for Christ to the community around us. *The Church Times* published a wonderful cartoon, picturing a man at a bus stop outside a church, in the pouring rain, next to a church noticeboard which read, 'There's probably no bus, so come to

---

199 *The Times*, 22/12/04

200 A Christian bus driver who refused to take his bus out with this advert upon it, I would put in a different category. He was not imposing his will upon anyone. As a man risking his job he was in a position of manifest weakness, and of only very limited power. He was much closer to the position of Jesus whose clash with authority led him to the cross.

church and enjoy yourself for a bit'.[201] With permission we were able to reproduce this on our church poster board in order to advertise the launch of a new evening service.

The post-modernist position, as we have noted, seems to be that there can be no such thing as truth, only a point of view. All truth claims are merely attempts to control other people's thinking and to exercise power, usually in support of sectional interests.

This is often how 'truth claims' (ideologies) *have* tended to be used. But they do not *have* to be so used. Jesus who said 'I am the way, the truth and the life' did not so employ truth. The Christian answer must be to reflect the non-coercive nature of Jesus, and His delight in diversity[202] The more it is true that there are neither racial, cultural, gender, nor class divisions in the church of God, the less can we be seen as representing sectional interests. The more Jesus' weapon of choice is seen as being his own cross, the more it will be realised that 'crucified truth threatens no one'. He is authoritative but not authoritarian. He doesn't throw His weight around. Jesus seems to be the ideal hero for post-modern people who fear abuse of truth claims. He is the best conceivable antidote for the post-modern fear of religious coercion. However, this will all remain invisible to most unless the church, the body of Christ, can abandon its modernist ways with coercion, ideology and power games.

THE SPIRIT OF GOD OR THE SPIRIT OF THE AGE?

Some might claim that what I am arguing is a selling-out to the spirit of our age, that by arguing for abandonment of coercion, I am saying that anything goes, that relativism rules, that there is no truth, or if there is, we cannot know it, and so must just tolerate everything and anybody.

This soft-headed approach to truth has been sharply caricatured.

---

201 *Church Times*, 16/1/09
202 See p.138ff

'Instead of having "answers" on a math test, they should just call them "impressions" and if you got a different "impression", so what? Can't we all be brothers?'[203]

Jesus' non-coercive strength in weakness can be mistaken for the 'anything goes', 'my truth is as good as your truth' culture that rules in some circles today. But they are radically different. The latter wouldn't go to the cross for anything, though it might kill if it thought you intolerant.

The Spirit of the Age rejects coercion (in theory), so does Jesus (in practice). The Spirit of the Age says there is no such thing as truth. Jesus says, 'I am the way and the truth and the life'.[204] The truth is personal, and therefore relational. The truth is Jesus, not an ideology, and Jesus is 'gentle and humble of heart'.[205] Because Jesus is the truth, truth cannot be co-opted by any sectional or personal interest without facing His judgment. This is not a selling-out to the Spirit of the Age, but rather Jesus answering the questions and fears of this age, just as He has been the answer to the questions of every other age.

This should not surprise us. The 'Enlightenment' from which the modern expression of many of our liberal principles sprang, was in part a reaction to coercive religion, and, in particular, the Thirty Years' War. But it also sprang from Christian principles, and from a return to Christian roots in the Gospels. 'The principle of religious freedom does not stand solely on secular grounds. It has a basis also in the Christian understanding of the God of the gospel. Recall the declaration in the third-century *Epistle to Diognetus*...: "Compulsion is not God's way of working." Christians are to bear fearless witness to the truth of the gospel in all times and places, but they may not use coercion of any form to enforce this witness. The post-Constantinian church attempted at times to justify compulsion in matters of faith.

---

203   Jack Handy, 'Deep Thoughts', quoted in *The Undertaking*, Thomas Lynch, p.171 (Jonathan Cape, 1997)
204   John 14:6
205   Matthew 11:29

Those attempts were serious departures from the witness of the New Testament to the crucified Lord.'[206]

In an age that is hungry for 'spirituality', and suspicious of religion, no one more successfully defuses the dangers of 'religion' than Jesus. At the same time, no one offers a more powerful and coherent 'spirituality' than Jesus.

JESUS' PERSONALITY AND OURS

What do we find when we examine our own personalities and temperaments through the lens that is Jesus?

Someone puts a hand on our shoulder, do we feel our personal space has been violated, or do we feel 'I have someone here who's on my side'? Our personality will affect how we perceive and how we react (as also will our culture). Do we instinctively see a risk as an opportunity or a threat? Do we regard 'big picture' people as idle and impractical dreamers leaving the real work to us detail people, or do we rail at those 'detail' people with their 'small minds', 'nit-picking' and inability to see the big picture? Whether we perceive a constructive critic as a threat, or a useful ally, will also be strongly influenced by our personality type. Whether we get on best in a crowd, and are strong on fellowship, or thrive in silence and solitude, and take to silent prayer like a duck to water, is probably not a measure of how holy we are, but of our personality type and our degree of extroversion or introversion.

Our personality type is likely to affect our theology. It may strongly influence whether we go for the cut and dried or the unquantifiable (clear doctrine or mystery), those Bible passages concerning judgment or concerning mercy, straining at gnats or only camels. We most of us tend to pick scriptures that favour our own predisposition, and we tend to interpret individual scriptures to suit our own disposition and prior beliefs. We will explore this a little more in Chapter 7.

---

206 *The Power of God and the gods of Power*, Daniel L. Migliore, p.128
(Westminster John Knox, 2008)

Take 2 Thessalonians 3:14–15: 'Take special note of anyone who does not obey our instruction in this letter. Do not associate with them, in order that they may feel ashamed. Yet do not regard them as an enemy, but warn them as you would a fellow believer.' Inevitably some will find their attention easily drawn to 'Do not associate with them, in order that they may feel ashamed' and others to 'Yet do not regard them as an enemy, but warn them as you would a fellow believer'. If we are not to misread scripture, we need to understand our own preferences and personalities, lest they mislead or blind us. I am *not* saying we must change our personalities. That would be to deny our God-given gifts. 'Traits, easily measured by psychologists, are aptitudes which are part of what we inherit and develop because of our genetic potential. Our faith in Christ, and his grace working in us, enables us to use them in new ways. But to try to change our basic personalities, rather than accepting them as part of what we are given, seems to me to lead to endless problems. It is to look for magic, not the miraculous changes that grace brings. It is like looking for spiritual cosmetic surgery, or a brain transplant.'[207]

Rather we need to understand ourselves sufficiently to know when we are really being biblical, and when we are simply reading our own preferences into the Bible. I often (not always, but often) marvel at how theological debate and difference, supposedly based upon the Bible, seems uncannily to mirror the personality types and preferences of the protagonists.[208] More is going on here than meets the eye.

We can easily find ourselves in a self-reinforcing echo chamber where like opinions reinforce like opinions in ever deepening bigotry. *The Independent* recently carried a report of the significantly increasing numbers believing in a 'flat Earth'. Researchers investigating this put the phenomenon down almost entirely to the use of YouTube.

---

207 *Genius and Grace*, Dr Gaius Davies, p.19 (Hodder and Stoughton, 1992). Dr Davies is a psychiatrist, who, in this book, examines nine well-known figures from Christian history to show how God works with and uses a diversity of personality types.

208 See p.162ff

"'It comes down to the way that the algorithms work," said Dr Landrum. "Under normal circumstances that might not be problematic. But it means that if someone's looking up conspiracy videos, it's going to suggest more conspiracies."

This creates the impression among viewers that there is an enormous amount of evidence for the flat-Earth theory.[209]

If we do not join Jesus in crossing beyond the boundaries of our own instinctively chosen social circle, we can find ourselves experiencing a similar phenomenon as familiar and congenial opinions keep echoing back to us.

There is a story about the biblical scholar T.R. Glover. 'Two Oxford dons were talking together: "Have you read Glover's autobiography?" "I didn't know he had written one." "Oh yes. It's him to the life. Only for some reason he's called it *Jesus of Nazareth*."'[210]

As far as we are able, we need to let Jesus' personality, not ours, be the lens through which we read. Whenever we sense dissonance between what we are saying, doing, and believing, and the character and teaching of Jesus this should sound alarm bells, and send us to solid thought, prayer and fresh Bible study. Whenever we find ourselves interpreting the Bible in a way that feels uncomfortable when set alongside Jesus, we need to take a fresh look. 'Karl Barth warns of "the irremediable danger of consulting Holy Scripture apart from the centre", that is apart from Jesus Christ. If scripture is read apart from Him, Barth contends, "the Scripture principle will not stand very long".'[211]

Jesus is The Word of God. The Bible is The Word of God in a secondary and derivative sense as that which bears witness to The Word incarnate. The Word of God written is always to be read through the lens of The Word of God incarnate. So, Jesus was able to say, "'...

---

209   *The Independent*, 18/2/19
210   *Good News for a Suffering World*, Philip King, p.126 (Monarch, 1996)
211   *The Power of God and the gods of Power*, Daniel L. Migliore, p.121 (Westminster John Knox, 2008) referring to Church Dogmatics IV/1, Karl Barth.

nor does His word dwell in you, for you do not believe the one He sent. You study the Scriptures diligently because you think that in them you have eternal life. These are the very Scriptures that testify about me, yet you refuse to come to me to have life".[212] When you think about it, this was a massive claim to authority on Jesus' part.

If we do not read all Scripture through the lens that is Jesus, we will inevitably colour our vision with the tinted spectacles of our own personality, culture and world view, which may not be as Christlike as we thought.

This should alert us to a necessary humility in approaching others with whom we disagree and in asserting our own opinions, a humility that Jesus modelled for us. It should also alert us to the value of those who differ from us. If our understanding is likely to be coloured by the lenses of the personality and cultural spectacles we wear, and by our own vested interests, this is not a counsel of despair, as though truth cannot be attained, and all is relative. It means that, to see the truth, we need each other, and especially we need those who are followers of Jesus while being radically different from us. More about this in Chapter 7.

So if an excess of prophetic zeal leads us to want to exclude, silence, traduce or hate our opponents, perhaps we should meditate on the fact that Jesus rebuked his disciples when they wanted to call down fire on the heads of those who opposed them (Luke 9:54, 55). When we are tempted, in an excess of zeal that outstrips love, to try to bully other people into life changes that we know will be good for them, perhaps we need to recollect how Jesus never coerced, never manipulated, and perhaps we should reflect that, while Jesus undoubtedly has an agenda of transformation for them, it might *not* include making them more like us.

In practice our distorted understandings of ourselves and our distorted understandings of God interact. It has been brilliantly

212   John 5:38–40

described in a passage quoted and commented upon by Daniel L. Migliore:

'Sherwood Anderson gives a vivid portrayal of the way distorted images of self and distorted images of God interlock. It is the story of Jesse Bentley, a pious, prosperous, and hardworking farmer. Jesse comes from a long line of strong men.

Jesse believes in an austere and powerful God who controls human destiny even if He remains deeply hidden. In Jesse's mind, he is following God's will by working hard to acquire possessions, by exercising dominion over the earth, by ruling over the members of his family and others dependent on him, and by siring male children who will be rulers in their turn.

Convinced he is God's chosen, Jesse looks upon his neighbors as Philistines, enemies of God. He fears that a Goliath will come from these Philistines to take away his land and possessions. So, Jesse prays for a son whom he will call David. Eventually a grandson by that name comes under his charge. One day the grandfather accompanies the young boy into the forest. The boy wants to go hunting with his slingshot, but Jesse secretly plans to sacrifice a lamb and dedicate his grandson to God. Frightened by his grandfather's strange behaviour, David runs away. When Jesse pursues him, the terrified boy picks up a stone, places it in his slingshot and hurls it at the old man. Jesse is stunned and rendered helpless; the boy is never seen again.

Anderson's story shows how our distorted understandings of God's power are intertwined with our exaggerated understandings of our own power. Jesse's God is a reflection of himself.'[213]

We need to allow our personality to be questioned and shaped by Jesus through scripture, but we are bound to interpret Jesus and scripture to some extent in the light of our own personality. This is

---

213 *The Power of God and the gods of Power*, Daniel L. Migliore, p.17–18
(Westminster John Knox, 2008) referring to *Winesburg, Ohio: A Group of Tales of Ohio Small-Town Life*, Sherwood Anderson p.55–109 (New York: Viking, 1958)

prevented from being a circular trap by the gift of fellowship with those different from us, and by the gift of The Holy Spirit. "'But when he, the Spirit of truth, comes, he will guide you into all the truth... He will glorify me because it is from me that he will receive what he will make known to you.'"[214]

This fresh focus on the earthly life of Jesus is not therefore a means of escapist piety, but rather a call to engage with and understand ourselves and the world around us freshly. Meeting Jesus in this way is to meet someone who leaves everything changed because we can no longer see anything in the same way again. And seeing differently is the largest part of the battle for behaving differently. This prepares us to face the challenge of self-denial that comes to us consistently through Jesus. This is part of the subject of our next chapter.

THE JOURNEY SO FAR

Jesus' deeds, teaching and character should be the lens through which everything is understood, and the example which every individual life and collective culture should attempt to emulate.

Our culture is suspicious of truth claims and power games (often seen as two sides of the same coin). Jesus claims to be 'the way, the truth and the life'. In doing so His approach to power rules out the very power games of which so many are afraid when truth claims are made. He is the answer to the post-modern fear of religious authority.

Jesus is also the answer to the tendency for each of us unwittingly to interpret 'the truth' and to read events in the light of our own temperamental preferences. He is the prism through which the content of all truth claims can be analysed and assessed.

His insistence that we follow his example in breaking down

---

214   John 16:13–14.

barriers and having fellowship with those who are different from ourselves means that we can be rescued from the tendency to interpret truth subjectively or in accordance with vested interests. We are therefore not called to love our enemies solely for their benefit. We need them and their perspectives if we are not to be trapped in an endless self-reinforcing echo chamber of opinions just like ours.

Chapter Four

The Cross as a Way of Life: Dying to Self

'Very truly I tell you, unless a kernel of wheat falls to the ground and dies, it remains only a single seed. But if it dies, it produces many seeds.'

JOHN 12:24

After our excursion to look at how we might, in practice, look through the lens of Jesus, we come now to examine an area where the life of Jesus and our current Western culture are most directly at odds, namely Jesus' call to self-denial, graphically expressed when Jesus said 'whoever wants to save their life will lose it, but whoever loses their life for me will find it.'[215]

The Infantilisation of Culture: From Self-Denial to Self-Indulgence

Philip Yancey reports that 'Daniel Yankelovich, an astute observer of social trends, points to a cultural shift that occurred in the West in the 1970s. Before then, society valued self-denial or "deferred gratification". Spouses sacrificed, even if it meant holding two jobs and accepting transfers to other cities, in pursuit of long-term goals. Parents trapped in an unsatisfying marriage stayed together for the sake of the children. In the 1970s the rules changed: the self-denial ethic morphed into a self-fulfilment ethic. We listen to our emotional

---

215   Matthew 16:25

needs and want them fulfilled now, without sacrifice, without waiting. We buy whatever we want on credit and jettison anything that proves complicated or irksome (like a troublesome marriage, for instance).'[216]

This is a form of infantilisation. Learning to wait, learning not to panic at the first sign of discomfort or even danger, learning to hear the answer "no" is part of growing up. Babies and toddlers scream when they are denied, wail when they hurt themselves even slightly, and yell when afraid. No one condemns them for it; this is what babies and toddlers do. If a grown adult behaves in the same way it raises eyebrows, to say the least.

This 'have it now' culture, with its concomitant infantilisation, does not seem to have produced much joy, partly I suspect because it cuts us off from others. It is a manifestation of an extreme form of individualism. The French Revolution pursued liberty, equality and fraternity, values that speak of how we live *together*. The American Declaration of Independence turned this into 'Life, liberty and the pursuit of happiness', something potentially much more individualistic. Interestingly 'the right to the pursuit of happiness' was taken by Jefferson from a book which referred to 'an equal pursuit of the happiness of all. A very different concept.'[217] As we retreat further into ourselves, and worry more and more about rewarding, pleasing, entertaining and pampering ourselves, the resultant isolation tends to feed into an identity crisis. Where and with whom do we belong? The impact of this upon the politics of the Western world where identity rather than economics seems to be more and more the focus, is becoming obvious, and is often deeply divisive.

Take up Your Cross and Follow Me

Jesus showed another way, with the intention that 'my joy may be in you and that your joy may be complete.'[218] Jesus taught, and

---

216   *Prayer*, Philip Yancey, p.157 (Hodder, 2006)
217   *The Argument Culture*, Deborah Tannen, p.224–5 (Virago Press, 1998)
218   John 15:11

cheerfully lived, self-denial, and restraint. He spoke of dying to self and exemplified it and the life and joy that comes through it, in His cross and resurrection. In their relevance to us, now, the cross and resurrection must not be over-spiritualised. They are an example to follow (in the case of the cross), and a promise of what will follow (in the case of resurrection). In a recent discussion with other clergy, two participants found this idea hard to grasp. The cross is how our sins are paid for, and as such is unique to Jesus. They understood any talk of the cross as an example to follow, as somehow a denial of the uniqueness of what Jesus has done for us. Of course it is 'both – and'. This was an interesting example of the tendency, noted in Chapter 2, to concentrate on the ways in which Jesus is unlike us, at the expense of Him being a plausible example to follow. He is both *fully* human and *fully* God. On the cross He is *both* our unique saviour, *and* an example to follow as we respond to His call to die to self. What else did He mean when He said that we must deny ourselves, take up our cross and follow Him? 'For whoever wants to save their life will lose it, but whoever loses their life for me will find it.'[219] As we turn to follow Jesus, dying to self is a gateway to new life.

This message of self-denial is not fashionable or easily palatable. It never has been. Martin Luther made a distinction between the all too common theology of glory, which appeals to our worldly instincts and appetites, and the true, Christ-centred theology of the cross. The theologian of glory 'does not know God hidden in suffering. Therefore, he prefers works to suffering, glory to the cross, strength to weakness... These are the people whom the apostle calls "enemies of the cross of Christ", for they hate the cross and suffering, and love works and the glory of works... It is not enough for anybody nor does it help him that he recognises God in His glory and majesty unless he recognises Him in the abasement and ignominy of the Cross.'[220]

How we understand God profoundly affects our behaviour. If,

---

219 Matthew 16:24–25
220 Luther, 'Heidelberg Disputation'

Luther argues, we only know God in His glory and triumph, we will be bound to pursue glory and triumph in our own lives. The cross might be something to be taken up as a strategic move on the way to triumph, but little more. Fundamentally, we will be ambitious, power-seeking and self-centred.

A Self-Indulgent Church

These symptoms, as Luther predicted them, are all around us. The prosperity gospel with its concentration on health and wealth and its extreme difficulty in incorporating any idea of suffering into the Christian life is but one example.

Prosperity teaching regards suffering as a sign of spiritual failure. It looks for reward in the same terms as the world looks for reward, namely health, wealth and power. It is as if the Lord's promise to St Paul, 'My power is made perfect in weakness',[221] had never been uttered.

A related symptom is how little preaching and teaching there seems to be, at least in the churches I know, concerning the dangers of wealth. Jesus repeatedly warns against the dangers of riches. He spoke as much about money and its dangers as about any other subject. Sixteen out of the thirty-eight parables are about money. Jesus said, 'You cannot serve both God and Money'.[222] He likened money to a spiritual power, or false god, Mammon.

John Wesley observed that riches are not wrong but are very dangerous. He wrote in his journal, on 31 September 1785 – 'I went on to Macclesfield and found the people still alive to God in spite of swiftly increasing riches. If they continue so, it will be the first instance I have known in about half a century. I warned them in the strongest terms I could.'[223]

---

221   2 Corinthians 12:9
222   Matthew 6:24
223   John Wesley's Journal (Vol. 7, p.256)

Similarly potentially self-focused is the idea of Christianity as a self-improvement programme. In many parts of the Western world the idea of discipleship has been subverted by a therapy-based model of faith. The trouble with Christianity as a self-improvement programme, even a highly commendable moral improvement programme, is that it is focused on self. Our call is to follow and serve Jesus. The kingdom, the power and the glory are His. Self-improvement is involved in all kinds of ways, but as a by-product of focusing on Him.

The cross does not fit easily into most self-improvement programmes. If life gets harder, not easier, then we tend to think that something radical must be wrong. Similarly, if we become more aware of our sinfulness because we are beginning to see clearly in the light of Jesus Christ, we might assume something must be wrong. Dying to self does not seem to be central to most such visions.

SELF-DENIAL, A PATH TO JOY

We seem to need restraint and self-denial in our lives, and to suffer without them. Life with no boundaries, no discipline, no restraint, becomes empty, frantic, meaningless, and distinctly unhealthy.

Referring to a study by an evolutionary psychologist, Donald Campbell, Stephen Pinker says 'The numbers show that it is not the rich, privileged, robust, or good-looking who are happy; it is those who have spouses, friends, religion, and challenging, meaningful work... Campbell echoed millennia of wise men and women when he summed up the research: "The direct pursuit of happiness is a recipe for an unhappy life".[224]

One does not have to be a believer in Jesus to perceive the value of self-denial for well-being. Arguing for the benefits of a closed season for trout fishing, and the renewal and perspective that can come thereby, a journalist in a fishing magazine wrote,

---

224 *How The Mind Works*, Steven Pinker, p.393 (Allen Lane, The Penguin Press, 1998, TSP edition)

'We live in a world not given to pause and where the idea of having to go without seems increasingly mediaeval. The Internet can get you anything short of a foot massage on demand these days, while credit cards bridge ever more implausible gaps between what we want and what we can afford.

While I know this would carry more weight if it came from a man in his twenties rather than one "of a certain age", anything that bucks the trend by bidding us hold fire feels more like a breath of fresh air than the clanking shackles of tradition.'[225]

Note that phrase, 'a breath of fresh air'. It seems that wise self-denial can be a road to refreshment, liberty, even joy. Jesus is not a killjoy, but quite the opposite. The purpose of giving up is to choose something better by far.[226] His goal is that we might enjoy life to the full.[227] Self-denial can be unhealthy and self-absorbed too. What we are talking about here is the kind of self-denial that clears space to allow the life of Jesus to flourish. Over the ages there have developed a series of disciplines, among them fasting, prayer, solitude, generosity and simplicity that lead to joy and life.

Joyful simplicity has long characterised some of the most authentic attempts to imitate Jesus. Without an ongoing attempt to simplify our lifestyle, the sheer busyness and complexity of living takes us over, and our faith revolves around, and is shaped by, our lifestyle, when it needs to be the other way around. Christianity becomes a leisure activity, fitted in among the many idolatrous demands of an over-complicated life. No wonder it is so hard to be a Christian in the affluent West. We are subject to so many pressures to complicate life. The 'hidden persuaders'[228] are telling us that there is so much we need to do, see, and have, in order to enjoy a fulfilled, secure, 'cool' and attractive life, that it takes a determined effort to realise where these messages are

225   Jeff Prest, *Trout Fisherman Magazine*, Issue 388, Jan-Feb 09, p.98
226   Matthew 13:44–46
227   John 10:10
228   *The Hidden Persuaders*, from the title of Vance Packard's 1957 book about the advertising industry and its effects.

coming from, and that there is an alternative. It may take effort to resist, but the failure to resist exhausts us by scattering our energies, dissipating our resources, and fragmenting our attention.

John Taylor describes an example of cheerful simplicity,

'A small community, modelled loosely on the old monastic pattern, with which I shared Easter 1974, celebrated the festival by sharing two boxes of fudge after lunch, and such was the skill of their simplicity, it generated more honest excitement and fun than any expensive self-indulgence could have done. That is the nature of eucharistic living.'[229]

It is those with the least resources who are usually the most resourceful.

He describes the kind of people needed to demonstrate Kingdom living in an age of excess:

'We must try to live by the divine contrariness of Jesus. We need a rapidly increasing minority that is entirely counter-suggestible, a minority that calls the bluff of the trendsetters, is a dead loss to the advertising agencies and poor material for the careers advisers. We must not wait for all Christians to be persuaded of the need for this, neither should we waste our time designing a single rule of life for those who are so persuaded. If we are trying to create a climate of social non-conformity we must avoid moralising like the plague. Our need is for men and women who are free with the freedom of Christ, free to ask the awkward questions that have occurred to no one else, and free to come up with startling answers that no one else has dared to give.

The difficulty of what I want to say now is that it could so totally fall into a nagging series of "oughts" and "ought nots", and that is the very opposite of the spirit I want to engender.'[230]

He suggests a number of slogans, or rather responses to the demands of modern living that such people might find useful; among

---

229   *Enough is Enough*, John V. Taylor, p.76 (SCM, 1975)
230   *Enough is Enough*, John V. Taylor, p.69 (SCM, 1975)

them, 'the price is too high', 'who are you kidding', 'you can't take it with you',[231] and 'you must be joking'. Just try them the next time you are confronted with advertising. These phrases have a power to change your perspective at a stroke.

I have known individuals who have lived like this, and they have been great fun. The simplicity inspired by the spirit of Jesus has nothing grim about it.

Simplicity does not mean a 'hair shirt' existence. It can mean substituting quality for quantity for example. A very good bottle of wine with a meal once a week, instead of something lesser each day, can be really special and an occasion to look forward to. It will probably work out cheaper overall, be less fattening, and reduce the amount to be lugged home from the supermarket, while the 'enjoyment factor' will probably rise. If we have special things every day, nothing is special any more.

But how can we live in the world in a way that is different and simple? How can we be subversives for Jesus when the culture of consumption is so all pervading that it becomes as hard to see as the air we breathe?

I suggest that we can only live like this when we develop a childlike trust in God's daily provision. This can only happen when we allow ourselves to be (or perhaps are forced by circumstances to be) vulnerable, to be in a situation where it is, basically, God or nothing, where we have to be dependent on Him.

I regularly notice the joyful trust in God that seems to characterise those from much poorer cultures than our own. I first noticed this in Benaiah, a Sudanese pastor whom I was privileged to get to know at theological college. Most of his ministry had been during times of civil war, travelling with a minimum of possessions from village to village over a vast area, dodging government troops. He lived with a conspicuous lack of anxiety, and with trust in God's love and provision.

---

231   *Enough is Enough*, John V. Taylor, p70–74 (SCM, 1975)

Since then, in three decades of living in multicultural parishes, I have encountered the same inner freedom and joyful trust a fair few times, nearly always in those who have come from insecure, poor, persecuted, or unstable backgrounds, often overseas. They have to trust God for there is nothing else to rely on.

When I meet clergy from the poorer parts of the world, if their church pays them (many do not) this is something of a miracle and a provision of God to be thankful for. In such circumstances, giving thanks before a meal is not a formality.

We all experience provision from God all the time, wherever we are, but do not always realise it. My monthly Church of England salary payment is the provision of God, but it is easy to lose sight of God behind the smoothly operating institutional machinery. It is when we step out or are driven out of the comfortable and secure routine, that we tend to experience faith-building glimpses of God at work.

When I was a student, my church took a collection for me one Sunday to pay my expenses for going to Iran for a couple of years as a short-term missionary. In the event the collection came to much more than I was aware of needing, and I went to see the rector the next day to offer back the surplus. Wise man that he was, he said that if God had given it, I would doubtless need it, and I should hang on to it. Two days later a letter came from the Church Missionary Society[232] saying that it would be advisable if I could take a course in teaching English as a foreign language over the summer before departing, but unfortunately I would have to pay for it myself. How much did it cost? Exactly the amount I thought was surplus to requirements in the offering I received. I experienced a surge of joy and gratitude and I learned something about God's care for me that day that I never could have if I'd had the money in the bank all along. This is part of the truth behind what the prosperity gospel so profoundly distorts. Jesus said, "'Give, and it will be given to you. A good measure, pressed down,

---

232   Now 'The Church Mission Society'.

shaken together and running over, will be poured into your lap. For with the measure you use, it will be measured to you.'"[233] Sometimes that is wonderful material provision, sometimes it might be a 'No' that helps us realise he has something better in store for us than the Mercedes Benz we were praying for.

The 'Walk' evangelistic missions, founded by the evangelist Daniel Cozens and run by 'Through Faith Missions',[234] work on principles that allow such faith to build. Teams of ten or a dozen walk from place to place, spending a few days in each, working with local churches to share faith in Jesus Christ. Often hospitality is arranged locally, usually sleeping on church hall floors. Just occasionally it is not arranged, and God seems to provide somehow. Team members are asked not to bring a mobile phone, and only to bring two pounds per day, not for themselves, but to buy a drink for others when out gossiping the Gospel in local pubs.

It is all based upon Jesus' commission when He sent out disciples to share the Good News.

'After this the Lord appointed seventy-two others and sent them two by two ahead of him to every town and place where he was about to go. He told them, "The harvest is plentiful, but the workers are few. Ask the Lord of the harvest, therefore, to send out workers into his harvest field. Go! I am sending you out like lambs among wolves. Do not take a purse or bag or sandals; and do not greet anyone on the road.

"When you enter a house, first say, 'Peace to this house'. If someone who promotes peace is there, your peace will rest on them; if not, it will return to you. Stay there eating and drinking whatever they give you, for the worker deserves his wages. Do not move around from house to house.

"When you enter a town and are welcomed, eat what is offered to you. Heal those there who are ill and tell them, 'The kingdom of God has come near to you.'"'[235]

---

233   Luke 6:38
234   www.t-f-m.org.uk
235   Luke 10:1–11

At first it is quite nerve-wracking, then exhilarating and faith building. Life is simplified drastically. God is trusted for daily provision. Distractions (mobile phones, televisions, newspapers) are left behind, and we see God at work quite wonderfully.

The second time I went, I think the Lord knew that my faith needed renewing. I had a dreadful head and throat cold and was late leaving for the train. In order to catch up with the rest of those I was travelling with, I decided to catch the bus to the station, using part of my two pounds for the day. When I boarded the bus, the driver would not accept my fare, despite my vigorous attempts to argue and to pay. He just told me with a smile to sit down. That has never happened to me before or since. In fact, I was a bit embarrassed by it. Maybe I was being taught a lesson in receiving graciously. My throat was hurting and I was coughing, so I was concerned about keeping others awake at the church hall we were to sleep in. I pondered whether to 'cheat' again, and use part of the two pounds to buy some cough sweets, but arriving at Waterloo Station I was greeted by people giving out free sample tubes of cough sweets; one was thrust into my hand and then she said, "Here, have another", and I embarked on the rest of my journey with *two* packets of cough sweets to remind me of God's extravagant provision; 'good measure, pressed down, shaken together and running over, will be poured into your lap.'[236]

The last church I served tried to live without unallocated reserves. We kept enough to pay our running costs, set aside money when we were saving for a specific costed building project, and tried to hold the recommended minimum for salaries in the bank (when we had staff), and the rest was given to the Diocesan Common Fund, to pay for ministry. We experienced both some worrying times, and much wonderful provision that rejoiced our hearts, built faith and encouraged generosity in a poor congregation in a deprived part of London. Reserves kept for a rainy day, we believed, would rob our

---

236   Luke 6:38

faith of much joy and exhilaration, would remove from us a golden opportunity for our faith to grow, and would displease God, because that money could have been put to work for his Kingdom. To squirrel it away would be a way of saying that, in effect, we do not expect Him to be able to provide in the future. Can it actually mean anything to say that our hope is in God, if in practice our real security is in a bank account?

The simplicity and self-denial Jesus calls us to is a gift and a blessing. No wonder Jesus *invites* us into it. Gifts and blessings are not usually imposed or policed. Modern Western society makes it hard to appreciate this, however. This surely is why Jesus said that it is hard for someone who is rich to enter the kingdom of God.[237] We are often left with a pervasive perception among believers and non-believers alike, that faith is mainly a matter of rules, is a bit grim, and needs to be policed somehow.

FEAR AND HOPE IN THE FACE OF DEATH

Death has been described as "'the worm at the core" of our pretensions to happiness'.[238]

We appear as a culture to have become less and less adept at talking about it, which suggests that this is a subject we have particular difficulty coming to terms with.

I suspect that our desperate consumption and frantic activity in the West partly stems from the anxiety that comes with not coming to terms with death, which robs us of Christian hope, and results in the investing of all hope in this life.

The absence of the frame of reference offered by the Christian hope of resurrection has at least three important consequences here. Firstly,

---

237 Matthew 19:23
238 *The Varieties of Religious Experience*, William James (1902 Mentor Edition, 1958) cited in *Beyond the Good Samaritan*, Ann Morisy, p.142 (Mowbray, 1997)

the loss of awareness of eternity leads to a sense of rush, a quite realistic sense, given the prevailing belief, that there is not enough time and we'd better cram in all we can. Life is increasingly lived as though we were sightseers on holiday for our precious two weeks with a list of sights and activities to cram in before the flight arrives to take us away again. The time span of our hope has become shorter and shorter; eternity, the next generation, this life, today. This is unrealistic. From not thinking of heaven we have moved rapidly to a situation where we can fairly complacently make the planet uninhabitable for those who come after us, to finding it difficult even to plan realistically for our own pensions or care in old age. Many are truly marooned in an island of today.

'There's an old *Playboy* cartoon that showed a boy mayfly saying to a girl mayfly, "What do you mean, not tonight?!"'[239] that catches just the right tone of impatient desperation that results.

The lack of a longer perspective lies behind many of our more intractable social problems (perhaps especially global warming).

Secondly, the loss of a Christian frame of reference has robbed us of criteria for assessing what is worth doing, or even what we really *want* to do. We are likely to feel as much under pressure from competing 'wants' as from 'oughts'. When there is nothing to order or assess our lives by, no central organising principle or yardstick, our lifestyles become inordinate and therefore frantic, subject to many competing demands. Whatever does not have eternal value, by definition, has only passing value, but if everything has passing value how do I arbitrate between competing claims for my attention and energy?

Thirdly, bereft of Christian hope, death becomes unthinkable to many, and to avoid thinking we immerse ourselves in an endless round of distractions, as we amuse ourselves or work ourselves to death, in an attempt to stave off having to face our own mortality.

It all points to a world with a diminishing grasp of meaning, combined with an ever accelerating round of activity.

---

239 *Sex, Death & Flyfishing*, John Gierach, p.17 (Simon and Schuster/Fireside, 1990)

In the light of His own cross, perhaps Jesus' call to lose our life in order to gain it might not be entirely metaphorical. How well we have come to terms with death probably has a more than passing relevance to how well we live life.

Canon Andrew White, Anglican Chaplain in Iraq, nicknamed the 'Vicar of Baghdad', has had a considerable impact on non-Christians and Christians in Britain and America, as well as, of course, in Iraq. His clear love for the Iraqi people, his courage in the face of the daily threat of death, his willingness to speak, without hating, to all sides, including the perpetrators of some of the most heinous crimes, catches people's imagination. He has to have twenty armed guards to get to his church, which is the only Anglican church left standing in the country.[240] He has been abducted, attacked and repeatedly threatened. Many of his staff and congregation have been killed, including eleven co-workers in one year.

In a recent television programme[241] he said, "I know it's really dangerous, but the fact of the matter is, I don't really care about my life very much. There is a sense that, certainly as a Christian, I think, well, when my time is up, it's up, and nothing will get me 'till then, but when it comes it comes."

It seems that one key to Andrew White's faith lies in his fairly advanced multiple sclerosis. He has had to adjust his expectation of life, and to put his strength to do the daily tasks, and indeed his very survival, into the hands of God. He seems to be living for God with enormous hope, an eternal hope, and that hope is infectious. Rageh Omar, the journalist who interviewed him and made the programme, commented, "In a city full of cynicism, Canon White is one of the few, if not the only person I have met there, who sustains an innocent, untainted optimism for the future. He restores faith in those he meets

---

240 Since I wrote this it has been badly damaged (in November 2009) in a massive bomb attack on a nearby government building.

241 *The Vicar of Baghdad* (a documentary by Rageh Omaar). (Producers Mentorn & Al Jazeera.) First screened 25 May 2008 on ITV1.

and amidst the heartache and tragedy Iraqis have come to expect, that is a noble cause."

It is no coincidence that Andrew was judged too ill to work within the Church of England. Yet, without his physical weakness I suspect he could not have achieved what he is achieving. He exemplifies what the Lord said to St Paul, "'My grace is sufficient for you, for my power is made perfect in weakness'."[242]

Everything that matters is in the hands of God, who can even bring life out of death, therefore if we but knew it, we are free to live with hope, and without fear. It is that quality in Andrew White that is so infectious, so appealing, so Christlike. It was, surely, how Jesus lived in the face of the realisation that His mission would take Him to the cross. I nearly wrote, 'would end in the cross'... but of course it didn't end.

Those who have discovered this are able to be grateful for Jesus' invitation. Most of them are not to be found in the affluent West.

Those colleagues of Andrew's who were murdered are mentioned honourably in dispatches, in Rev 12:11.

'They triumphed over him
by the blood of the Lamb
and by the word of their testimony;
they did not love their lives so much
as to shrink from death.'

RESTRAINT, OUR PLANET, AND THE BEAUTY OF SIMPLICITY

Restraint and self-denial are central to many key issues today. I do not intend to go into details, as this would take us way beyond the scope of the present book. The importance of self-denial and restraint if we are to deal with justice and inequality, how to live in cities (neighbourliness

---

242   2 Corinthians 12:9

and putting up with each other), the long shadow of the credit crunch, obesity, an epidemic of busyness and stress, and many pressing issues besides, are obvious.

Perhaps pre-eminent among these issues is global warming, and related ecological crises, including the depletion of natural resources. Again, the call to restraint is obvious. Jesus calls us to self-denial because He loves us.

A simpler lifestyle may be experienced as much richer than what we have now. For example, a simpler lifestyle seems to be needed before relationships can flourish. Roy Clements presciently commented, 'The Gospel is making no progress today in any society where relationships are not given priority. There will be no renewal until people realise that what they are seeking can only come from relationships. The only kind of religion that will prosper in the kind of climate we currently have are cults that foster materialism or individualism, e.g. prosperity gospel or new age.'[243]

The values Jesus lived by were, in different ways, just as deeply at odds with the values of His own society. What has changed is the power of society to bribe us with (hitherto) untold riches, and to back up the bribe with relentless multimedia propaganda. The Faustian bargain, however, is turning sour. To whom now will we turn?

FREEDOM, BUT FOR WHAT?

In the absence of anything more objective, human desire itself seems to have become sacred. 'The American dream is that "people can do or be what they want if they just go ahead and do it." Desire becomes sacred and whatever thwarts desire is evil or sin.'[244]

There is therefore fierce resistance today to any suggestion that our desires be curtailed. However, Jesus is not saying they will *be* curtailed.

243　'Planes to Catch and Bills to Pay', a recorded talk by Roy Clements from the 1980s (exact date unknown).

244　Quoted in *The Divine Conspiracy*, Dallas Willard, p.63 (Fount, 1998)

I hope by now that it is clear that He is saying to us "you curtail them, you'll be more free". We have already seen how Jesus' call is to self-denial. The only person He is calling us to police is ourselves, but even here, 'police' is the wrong word. It turns out that He is inviting us to invest in the pearl of great price, not so much to give up as to gain. If we will only let go our grip on what we have, He can fill our empty hands with riches beyond price. Jesus described those riches as being like a fabulous treasure that a man stumbled upon in a field. Realising the value of what he had found he fell over himself in his haste to sell all he owned to raise the funds to buy the field. Did he think he had been hard done by? Did he go home to moan about the sacrifices he had to make? No way! He was overwhelmed by his good fortune and by the wonderfully good deal he had made.[245]

SELF-RESTRAINT, NOT IMPOSED RESTRAINT: DYING TO SELF

Remember, Jesus is radically non-coercive. He calls for *self*-restraint, not imposed restraint, self-denial, not tyranny. At present the most obvious sign to the world of denial on the part of many Christians is the denial they try to impose upon gay people, while often being blind to their own call to self-denial. What is going on?

I'm not arguing here about whether or not gay people are called to celibacy, or about what denominational policies about gay clergy should be. We will return to those issues in Chapter 10.

For now, I just want to note the glaring inconsistency between many churches' strictness about homosexuality, and laxness about Sabbath observance, or greed, or bitterness, or gossip, or even divorce. If our culture is wedded to self-indulgence, and if one of the few things held sacred by it is desire, we are not going to be comfortable with Jesus' guidance that we need to die to self. What a wheeze if, rather than flatly contradicting Jesus, we could find one issue where temptation only

---

245 Matthew 13:44–46

affects a small minority, trumpet that loudly as a call to die to self, and then proceed to live a life of self-indulgence in other areas, safe in the knowledge that we are OK because at least we are not gay. Homosexual acts have become the new defining orthodoxy about who is or is not a real follower of Jesus Christ.

We are all called to self-denial. All of 'us sinners', not just 'those sinners'. We are so called because God loves us and has demonstrated in His Son that taking up our cross, paradoxically, leads to life. The reason for the church's warnings, whether about sexual ethics, unbridled consumption, or anything else, ought to be love. People are wrecking their lives at worst and missing much blessing at best. If our utterances don't sound as though they spring from love and compassion for those in such circumstances, no one will listen. Why should they? 'No one co-operates with someone who seems to be against them.'[246] We are *invited* to self-denial as part of God's loving desire to bless.

Whoever Loses Their Life for Me Will Find It

'Then Jesus said to his disciples, "Whoever wants to be my disciple must deny themselves and take up their cross and follow me. For whoever wants to save their life will lose it, but whoever loses their life for me will find it. What good will it be for someone to gain the whole world, yet forfeit their soul? Or what can anyone give in exchange for their soul?"'[247]

I have spent a while on this chapter not because I have mastered self-denial (far from it), but because the key is to understand that we are lovingly invited to die to self. Then we can make progress even if we can never master it. This message from Jesus is about as countercultural as it is possible to get in the modern West. I keep finding that even my service for Jesus can be self-serving and hide a desire to 'save' my own

---

246 *Dealing with People You Can't Stand*, Brinkman & Kirschner, p.39 (McGraw-Hill, 1994)
247 Matthew 16:24–26

life. The snares of success or of having a 'big church' are as real for the clergy as the snares of 'success' in any secular profession.[248]

I remember, at the age of twenty-one, having just left university, and being about to attend a selection conference for ordained ministry, meeting a fellow Christian at a youth hostel at Rhossili on the Gower Peninsula. I only remember him hazily. He was perhaps fifteen or twenty years older than me, was a teacher, and looked slightly hippyish. However, I remember very well what he said. He referred to my dreams of what I might achieve for God through ordination, and, perhaps sensing that I thought the Church of England, and even God himself, would be lucky to have me, he said,

"What if God wants nothing more of you than He wanted of that thief to whom He said 'Today you will be with me in Paradise'?[249] What if He wants nothing more of you than to suffer with Him a while? Would you still go ahead?"

Well, I went ahead, but only now do I think I am beginning to understand the question.

THE JOURNEY SO FAR

Jesus said "whoever wants to save their life will lose it, but whoever loses their life for me will find it". The invitation to self-denial is central to Jesus' message and example.

This message of 'dying to self' is currently deeply countercultural and unfashionable, but it is also the road to joy. Without it we cannot faithfully represent Jesus.

He invites us to 'take up your cross and follow me'.

It is easy to bypass the cross and to follow so-called theologies of glory, such as the 'prosperity gospel', or self-improvement or therapeutic models of discipleship that leave 'self' in the centre.

---

248 Perhaps more so as the apparent holiness of the cause can obscure the selfish motive.

249 Luke 23:43

Self-denial that practises restraint and simplicity can be a pathway to joy, but it is particularly hard to appreciate this in the affluent West. Self-denial is to be a pathway of blessing not a burden, and as such Jesus invites us into it. Blessings are not usually imposed or policed.

The comforts and securities of Western living, though good in themselves, have tempted us to live for this life only. We consequently find death hard to think about, and dying to self, unreasonable, when there is such a limited time to cram everything in. It is hard not to be frantic, and hard to trust in God's love and provision in such a culture.

It is distinctly odd that the most obvious area of self-denial and restraint in the modern Western church is that which the majority seek to impose on gay people. What is going on? How can this be right if 'self-denial' cannot be imposed, only freely chosen?

CHAPTER FIVE

ANGER, CONTEMPT AND FEAR

> "I tell you that anyone who is angry with a brother or sister will be
> subject to judgment. Again, anyone who says to a brother or sister,
> 'Raca,'[250] is answerable to the court. And anyone who says, 'You
> fool!' will be in danger of the fire of hell."
>
> (JESUS CHRIST, MATTHEW 5:22)

ANGER, CONTEMPT AND FEAR, AND THE FEAR OF DEATH

It's the way of the world that evil begets evil. If we are made to feel
threatened, if experience convinces us that the world is hostile, if the
spores of grievance are allowed to germinate in our soul, these things
have a natural tendency to emerge in bitter and destructive fruit. How
often in history have the persecuted, once they have attained liberty,
and power, become the persecutors?

If we have not come to terms with fear, above all the fear of death,
but also the many 'small deaths' (those lesser losses that tend to loom
less large once we can face death), then it is very difficult indeed not to
become prey also to anger and contempt.

---

250 A contemptuous term roughly translated as 'fool', but far more abusive than the
word 'fool' in modern English.

JESUS AND ANGER, CONTEMPT AND FEAR

We are called to take Jesus as our role model, and one of the trickiest areas for knowing how to imitate Jesus is in dealing with anger. Because Jesus was sometimes angry, we can easily justify our anger to ourselves. We can even convince ourselves that our anger is an expression of Christian virtue. After all, shouldn't we be angry at injustice, hypocrisy or cruelty? Surely the more 'righteous' we are in a sinful world, the more angry we should be? Jesus was angry, so it must be all right?

When worshippers at the synagogue tried to prevent Him healing a man with a shrivelled hand, because it was the Sabbath, we read that 'Jesus asked them, "Which is lawful on the Sabbath: to do good or to do evil, to save life or to kill?" But they remained silent.

He looked around at them *in anger* and, deeply distressed at their stubborn hearts, said to the man, "Stretch out your hand." He stretched it out, and his hand was completely restored.'[251]

We learn from this that in and of itself, anger is not wrong since Jesus experienced it and was Himself 'without sin.'[252]

However, Jesus seems to have regarded anger as incredibly dangerous once it is in *our* sinful hands. Thus he says,

'"You have heard that it was said to the people long ago, 'You shall not murder, and anyone who murders will be subject to judgment.' But I tell you that anyone who is angry with a brother or sister will be subject to judgment."'[253]

It is instructive to look at how Jesus responded in the synagogue when He was angry with those who would have prevented Him healing on the Sabbath. He did not respond with fury, but with 'deep distress', nor did He turn on those who made Him angry, He just reached out with healing to the man with a shrivelled hand, simply ignoring those

---

251   Mark 3:4–5
252   Hebrews 4:15
253   Matthew 5:21–22

who were attempting to stop Him. Jesus' anger seems to have been a function of His compassion.

How often can we honestly say that our anger is purely on behalf of others, arising from compassion? How often is our response to that anger one of constructive love rather than of lashing out or some other form of destructiveness?

The Bible seems to suggest that our fallen state is such that our anger cannot be trusted. 'Human anger does not produce the righteousness that God desires.'[254] That is a pretty categorical statement.

Why is our anger so dangerous, especially if anger was all right for Jesus?

Well, for similar reasons to why it is all right for an expert to handle explosives, but you wouldn't let a child play with them. We need to know what we are doing, and even when we know we tend to make mistakes. It is too volatile ordinarily to be safely handled.

An old preacher's story expresses it well. A man went to a friend's ranch to hunt. 'The friend gave permission to hunt, but asked him to do a favour, to go into the barn and shoot his elderly mule who was sick, as he didn't have the heart to do it himself. When Mick came back to the car, he pretended to be angry. He scowled and slammed the door. Billy asked him what was wrong, and Mick said his friend wouldn't let them hunt. "I'm so mad at that guy," Mick said, "I'm going out to his barn to shoot one of his mules!" Mick drove like a maniac to the barn. Billy protested, "We can't do that." Mick shouted, "Just watch me." When he got to the barn, Mick jumped out of the car with his rifle, ran inside, and shot the mule. As he was leaving, though, he heard two shots and ran back to the car. "What are you doing, Billy?" he yelled. Billy yelled back, face red with anger, "We'll show that son of a gun! I just killed two of his cows!"'[255]

Anger is infectious. Once let loose it spreads like wildfire. In this some of our contemporary populist politicians have discovered a

254 James 1:20
255 *Leadership*, Winter '95, p.38

powerful and pernicious tool. It matters little whether anger is stirred up by truth or lies, once it has caught fire it is not likely to be subject to logical critique. This approach to politics is deeply un-Christlike. It is grievous to see some populist politicians claiming to be standing up for Christian Europe or Christian Britain, or a Christian USA,[256] in a manner that effectively denies Jesus Christ.

Anger rapidly becomes irrational and disproportionate. Once clung to, nurtured, or even enjoyed, it has all kinds of pernicious effects. It makes us want to punish or get revenge. It becomes a barrier to forgiveness. Anger contains a self-justifying dynamic that blinds us to our own faults. It leads to contempt and then to the exclusion or even persecution of our enemies, whom God happens to love very much. It provokes defensiveness and counter anger thus deepening the problem and driving the other person also further from God. It makes the problem much harder to solve. 'No one co-operates with someone who seems to be against them.'[257] It makes consensus and coalition, and therefore a constructive way forward, almost impossible.

Jesus was able to resist the temptations inherent in anger, and so could handle anger safely. This is just one of the ways in which He made a masterpiece of His own life. Even so we only see Him express anger a few times. One is when He strongly criticises the teachers of the law and Pharisees.[258] Jesus is clearly deeply angry. I note, however, that He does not seem, for an instant, to be in danger of losing control, and I note that He takes no revenge, simply warning, at the end, of God's judgment to come.

When He turned the traders and money changers out of the temple, as we have already seen (p.60), He was acting to protect those suffering abuse at the hands of religious power. One would be hard put to see the action as vindictive or selfish or out of control.

---

256   Respectively Viktor Orbán, Tommy Robinson and Donald Trump.
257   *Dealing with People You Can't Stand*, Brinkman & Kirschner, p.39 (McGraw-Hill, 1994)
258   Matthew 23:13–36

Anger, Contempt, Fear, and Us

All of this would seem to show the *possibility* of our anger being righteous. After all, St Paul says, 'In your anger do not sin'.[259] I used to use this line of argument more confidently. Surely it is appropriate to be angry when we see evil? I still believe that but want to say "Yes, but…" Surely there is something morally wrong with us if child abuse, or genocide, or mugging and murder do not make us angry? I want to say "Yes, but…"

I now believe that too often I have used such arguments to avoid having to face the ungodly elements of much of my own anger. Anger has such an inbuilt tendency to create a sense of blind self-righteousness that, unless this is faced rapidly, will tend to evil. This is surely why St Paul, after saying, 'In your anger do not sin', continues, 'Do not let the sun go down while you are still angry, and do not give the Devil a foothold'.[260] It is difficult to keep our anger out of the Devil's hands. Anger creates self-righteousness in the person who is angry, and in the person on the receiving end, who then tends to react in kind.

The boundary between righteous anger, and hatred, bitterness and even revenge, is hard to see even on cool reflection. In the midst of it all, in the heat of anger, it is virtually impossible. Anger should spur the Christian to acts of love, including the righting of wrongs, caring for victims, and forgiving those who have wronged us. If brought speedily to God, in prayer for help and guidance, anger can be a powerful motivator for good, but, as we have seen, if entertained as a long-term guest, it turns sour, transforming via contempt to hatred, rejection or even violence. Then nothing but a miracle of grace can prevent a worsening spiral of angry reaction and deepening distrust, conflict and bitterness.

'If you ask a bomb-throwing teenager in Northern Ireland or a machete-wielding soldier in Rwanda or a sniper in the former

---

259   Ephesians 4:26
260   Ephesians 4:26–7

Yugoslavia why they are killing, they may not even know. Ireland is still seeking revenge for atrocities Oliver Cromwell committed in the seventeenth century; Rwanda and Burundi are carrying on tribal feuds that extend long past anyone's memory; Yugoslavia is avenging memories from World War II and trying to prevent a replay of what happened six centuries ago.'[261]

Our anger seems to produce a self-justifying reaction in our opponent. It starts a chain reaction that can only be stopped by grace.[262] Perhaps anger is only truly to be trusted in the hands of God, who chooses to transmute His anger into astounding grace on the cross. Certainly, the Bible stresses that *judgment and punishment are to be left to Him*. They are His prerogative. He will have the last word and His wrath against sin will be expressed at the last judgment.

It seems that, for those who have not responded to His grace, that grace will be experienced as final judgment. But this really is the 'last-chance saloon'. There will be no more opportunity for a further vicious chain reaction of anger and recrimination. This is the final word, literally the *last* judgment, when all hope of further persuasion or repentance has gone, every opportunity for repentance and forgiveness having already been given.

The trouble often starts when we arrogate to ourselves the right to pronounce this judgment in the here and now, ahead of time, taking God's wrath as justification for our own anger. Over and over the Bible makes it clear that this is not to be. Jesus put it most starkly when he said, '"Do not judge, or you too will be judged"'.[263]

St Paul says, 'Do not take revenge, my dear friends, but leave room

---

261 *What's So Amazing About Grace?*, Philip Yancey, p.83 (Zondervan, 1997)
262 Sometimes this needs to involve deliverance ministry. One area where Jesus seems to me to be very different from our culture is in his diagnosis of evil. He locates it in the human heart, and does not deny our responsibility, but he also takes seriously the involvement of 'unclean spirits' in people's lives. Whenever behaviour is compulsive (and anger often is) I believe we would be wise to use deliverance prayer alongside other methods to help people allow the 'peace of God' to rule in their lives. This subject is, however, way beyond the scope of the present book.
263 Matthew 7:1

for God's wrath, for it is written: "It is mine to avenge; I will repay," says the Lord.'[264]

Or, in the case of judging our fellow believers, 'Who are you to judge someone else's servant? To their own master, servants stand or fall. And they will stand, for the Lord is able to make them stand.'[265]

When we become judges, responding in anger with self-righteousness and contempt, we are guilty of blasphemy, putting ourselves on the throne of God just as thoroughly as Nero or Herod did. We betray a deep lack of faith, that cannot or will not leave final justice for wrongdoers in the hands of God. We are also arrogant, forgetting our own sinfulness, and thinking instead of 'those sinners', no longer of 'us sinners'. No wonder such attitudes cut *us* off from the mercy of God.

The Bible speaks a great deal about the 'wrath' or 'anger' of God. It also promises a final judgment. Old Testament and New Testament, the Law, the Prophets and the Son of God speak with a united voice on these. Embarrassment at, or neglect of, them can make the problems of human anger worse.

Wrath and anger have been given a bad name by our human abuse of them, but, as we have seen, even at a human level, anger is an appropriate initial reaction to all kinds of abuse. If we are not angry at certain cruelties and dishonesties, then many would think that there was something wrong with us. This indignation *should* drive us to God, to trust in His justice and mercy, and if it does not, then I believe it is likely to fester within us. A culture that no longer believes in the cross or the last judgment, to my perception, manifestly finds it harder to forgive. It may excuse, and it may tolerate, to a point, but those are *very* different things from forgiveness.

If the judgment of God cannot be relied upon, then people will tend to take matters into their own hands. Hence the paradox of an age

---

264 Romans 12:19
265 Romans 14:4

that prides itself on being non-judgmental (and which has therefore rejected the idea of the judgment of God) being one of the most unfairly, self-righteously, carpingly moralistic we have ever seen. Just read any newspaper and assess as you read how much of the coverage is blaming and accusing. Bankers, politicians, ethnic minorities, regulators, local councillors, Europe, families on sink estates, single mums, benefit claimants, anyone who is successful, and just about any other group you care to mention, regularly come in for a barrage of angry blame. On almost any blog, including Christian sites, invective and abuse quite regularly take the place of argument and debate. Road rage, shopping rage, queue rage, rage between neighbours is the stuff of everyday life. We are an angry, judgmental society, with angry, judgmental media. The first moments of my waking day every day except Sundays are subjected to a bombardment of dyspepsia and aggression from interviews on the *Today* programme. Yet we live in a society that often claims to believe that no one has a right to judge anyone else as there are no absolute standards. Our behaviour is wildly at odds with our professed belief. It sometimes seems to me that we have simply replaced much principled discrimination and moral debate with irritation, bad temper, cynicism and suspicion.

Yet an angry, judgmental society like this is the almost inevitable result of removing from God the right to be angry, and to judge. We are to leave the outworking of anger and judgment to Him. If we cannot do that, either because we do not trust Him with it, or do not believe in Him, it will come out in other ways (as in the wickedly funny picture of David in Nick Hornby's novel, *How To Be Good*, quoted at the start of Chapter 1[266]).

Judgment is simply not our prerogative. When Jesus was rejected by a Samaritan village, James and John 'asked, "Lord, do you want us to call fire down from heaven to destroy them?" But Jesus turned and rebuked them *(and he said, "You do not know what kind of spirit you*

---

266   p.10

are of, for the Son of Man did not come to destroy men's lives, but to save them") and they went to another village.'[267]

There is plenty of this furious religion about. In Wood Green Shopping Centre some years ago I encountered a street preacher calling on passers-by to repent and escape the judgment to come. There is nothing wrong with that, and I have done some street preaching myself. The trouble was that he sounded furious with the crowd. He called them sinners with a snarl that made it sound as though he hated them. Most telling was his face, which was contorted with rage, as he ranted and sprayed spittle at his audience. I waited, and when he had finished, and was taking a break, I approached him, and as gently as I could, said that though I agreed with his message that we stand under judgment, did he realise that his demeanour indicated fury and rejection, and perhaps this didn't help passers-by to understand that Jesus had died for their sins, whereupon he turned on me and began to rant again. I can't remember his exact words, but the gist of it was that I was lost in sin and couldn't understand the ways of God, destined for hell as I was. I just walked away. In different circumstances he might have been planting bombs for his faith.

God's response to His anger at sin and abuse is His own cross. Our anger tends to obscure that act of mercy, and to make it sound as though the cross of Jesus Christ had never happened.

Talking of the cross as God's response to His anger at sin has been controversial. Some say that it makes God sound like a tyrant or a child abuser (inflicting wrath on His own Son for other people's sins) or an emotional incontinent, like someone who is so impotently furious that they bang their own head against a wall, or have to take it out on the dog. However, the first point is soon dealt with when we realise that 'God was in Christ reconciling the world to himself'.[268] The problem only rears its head when we fail to realise that Jesus is God's son in a way analogous to, not identical with human sonship. It is not and

---

267 Luke 9:54–56. The section in italics is in some manuscripts only.
268 2 Corinthians 5:19 (RSV)

cannot be *exactly* the same. God Himself was on the cross in a way no human father is present in his son.

As for likening God to a headbanger, this is to import into God's anger all the human elements of anger that make it so dangerous for us to entertain. God's wrath is not primarily an emotional response, but rather a moral one. It is not a spasm of irritation, an instantaneous and overwhelming desire to lash out, a loss of control, or an abandonment of love. It is precisely the controlled response of love to abuse. It marks the profound incompatibility between God and sin, such that He cannot entertain, collude with or commit sin, and cannot allow it to remain undealt with in His creation any more than a responsible house owner can ignore dry rot. God's wrath is the response of love and justice to cruelty, bad faith, and abuse. It is all too easy to caricature this as akin to the jealous father who murders his own children for his wife's unfaithfulness, but that is nowhere near the truth of the matter.

Of course, if we are to speak of the cross of Jesus Christ without misleading people and without encouraging the caricature, it is important that, unlike that preacher in Wood Green, we have our own anger under control. Perhaps this helps us to see why 'man's anger does not bring about the righteous life that God desires.'

Dallas Willard goes so far as to say, 'there is nothing that can be done with anger that cannot be done better without it.'[269] My first reaction on reading that was to think 'Hang on a minute. That can't be true.' On reflection I now believe he is right when talking of human anger. Anger may be the spur, the initial stab that provokes movement, but beyond that it is no good. If it becomes the horse we ride we are in trouble. So many actions done in anger would have been better left until calm judgment returned, as I know to my own cost, being temperamentally quick on the draw. 'Speak when you are angry, and you will make the best speech you will ever regret.'[270]

---

269   *The Divine Conspiracy*, Dallas Willard, p.169 (Fount, 1998)
270   Ambrose Bierce. I cannot trace the original source for this widely quoted remark.

Human anger, however perverted, can at least have its roots in something good. Contempt, however, has no redeeming features. Contempt is a greater evil than anger and so is deserving of greater condemnation. Unlike innocent anger, at least, it is a kind of studied degradation of another, and it also is more pervasive in life than anger. It is never justifiable or good. Therefore, Jesus tells us,[271] anyone who says to a brother or sister, "Raca",[272] is answerable to the court.

You can love someone and still be angry with them, but you cannot love someone and hold them in contempt at the same time. Contempt is a way of denying someone's worth, of dehumanising and rejecting them. Contempt nearly always leads to exclusion, and often to mistreatment or violence. Contempt is *always* sinful. It is *never* appropriate for a Christian. However, among religious people it is all too prevalent, as contempt is the common currency of the self-righteous.

Contempt is a way of excluding, or marginalising. We've already seen in Chapter 2 that Jesus has a special place for the marginalised and rejected, so as soon as we start marginalising and rejecting, we automatically make ourselves into Jesus' enemies.

ANGER, CONTEMPT AND FEAR IN THE LIFE OF THE CHURCH

How much of our institutional church life is driven by anger, contempt and fear?

Robert Warren, in a talk to 'The Fellowship for Parish Evangelism' in 1997, said that one of the first motives for Christian action might be anger. 'Anger is one of the first fruits in those who begin to see life clearly.'

I wonder how many of us clergy were propelled into ministry at least partly by anger. We see the injustices of the world and want to change things for the better. But if we don't quickly move beyond

---

271 Matthew 5:22
272 See note 250

anger to love we will not be able to be Christlike. Or having begun with love, thrilled perhaps at the message of God's mercy and love, and passionate to share it with others, we become embittered at people's lack of response, and start to be angry with the world or with other bits of God's church whom we hold responsible for our perceived lack of progress. (That has to raise the question of whose interests we were pursuing in the first place, our own needs, or Jesus' agenda.)

Anger is rather like the body's initial response to an infection. Antibodies produce fever and most of the unpleasant symptoms that we experience when we have an infection. This is fine for a few days or so as an infection is identified and fought by the body. If we could find a way of artificially keeping our immune system operating at the same level, just in case of germs, it would make us very unhealthy, and would eventually kill us. This is what a state of chronic ongoing anger seems to be doing to various parts of the Body of Christ, not least to the Anglican Communion.

In the Church of England in recent years debates about homosexuality, and about women bishops, and increasingly now about gender identity, have been powerfully fuelled by anger, fear, and resentment, spilling over into a fair amount of contempt on each side. In these cases fresh approaches inspired by Jesus' ways of dealing with difference, dispute and anger have been attempted, with some remarkable results.[273] Anger does not have to rule.

Christians tend to care, and if we care very much and are thwarted, anger can result. There are few surer ways to provoke anger than to insult or threaten someone's spouse or family, and the church is like family to many. There are all kinds of good reasons why the church of God can become a bad-tempered place if we see what is dear to us threatened (as we saw at the start of Chapter 1), and the tempter will no doubt do his best to drive us into each and every one of these traps. However, a bad-tempered and disdainful church is not a Christlike church.

---

273 See p.167–168 and 215–217

The evangelist J. John wrote 'I had the privilege of working with the Sisters of Charity and Mother Teresa. And one of the questions I asked Mother Teresa one day was: "Don't you ever become angry at the causes of social injustice that you see in India and around the world?" Her response was amazing. She said, "Why should I expend energy in anger when I can expend it in love?" '[274]

FEARING GOD: THE ROAD TO FREEDOM

Paul Tillich said that our 'ultimate concern is what we recognise as having the power to threaten and to save our very being.'[275] I believe this is the heart of the understanding of the biblical command to fear God. There are so many threats to be feared, but ultimately the only one that it makes sense to fear is the one with ultimate power over our lives. We will then discover that there is nothing to fear except the fear that stops us trusting Him. For those who will trust Him His great power is found to be benign. He has power to throw us into hell, a fate besides which death alone is insignificant. Fear Him says Jesus – and then learn that He loves and cares for you intimately, 'the very hairs of your head are all numbered.'[276] God is love, and He loves us. Once we fear God, we discover the perfect love that casts out fear. As Mr Beaver said of Aslan, "Is he – quite safe?"… "Safe?… Who said anything about safe? Course he isn't safe. But he's good."[277]

FINDING OUR VALIDATION

If we are secure in God's love and acceptance of us, it cuts the roots of anger, fear, contempt, resentment, and jealousy. Nothing and no one can be quite such a threat to us again. Henri Nouwen puts it well.

---

274   J. John in *UK Focus* August 1999
275   *Systematic Theology vol. 1*, Paul Tillich, quoted in *The Power of God and The gods of Power*, Daniel L. Migliore, p.9 (Westminster John Knox, 2008)
276   Luke 12:4–7
277   *The Lion, The Witch & The Wardrobe*, C. S. Lewis, p.75 (Puffin, 1973)

'Almost from the moment I had ears to hear, I heard those voices, and they have stayed with me ever since. They have come to me through my parents, my friends, my teachers, and my colleagues, but, most of all, they have come and still come through the mass media that surround me. And they say: "Show me that you are a good boy. You had better be better than your friend! How are your grades? Be sure you can make it through school! I sure hope you are going to make it on your own! What are your connections? Are you sure you want to be friends with those people? These trophies certainly show how good a player you were! Don't show your weakness, you'll be used! Have you made all the arrangements for your old age? When you stop being productive, people lose interest in you! When you are dead, you are dead!"

As long as I remain in touch with the voice that calls me the Beloved, these questions and counsels are quite harmless.

But when I forget that voice of the first unconditional love, then these innocent suggestions can easily start dominating my life and pull me into the "distant country". It is not very hard for me to know when this is happening. Anger, resentment, jealousy, desire for revenge, lust, greed, antagonisms, and rivalries are the obvious signs that I have left home. And that happens quite easily.'[278]

We clergy are perhaps the worst offenders whenever we lose touch with the one in whom our security really lies. We can become anxious about success (which is hard to measure in parochial ministry) and we wonder 'why does revival tarry?' as our lives and careers move on without transforming the church and the world as we had hoped. It's so easy to believe that we are fully justified in being angry with those who stand in our way because 'our way is God's way, isn't it?' However, if in our resulting petulance, anger and impatience we are not walking as Jesus walked, we are manifestly *not* in God's way.

Unless we have our anger and fear submitted to God, we will

---

278   *The Return of The Prodigal Son*, Henri Nouwen, p.47 (DLT, 1994)

probably find ourselves doing the Devil's work in any stand we take on any issue, however biblical we may be in our conclusions.

'There is no fear in love. But perfect love drives out fear, because fear has to do with punishment. The one who fears is not made perfect in love. We love because he first loved us.'[279]

THE JOURNEY SO FAR

Fear, anger and contempt can be powerful fertilisers for evil.

The dangers of anger are often seriously underestimated. Jesus was angry after all, so it must be all right to be angry? However, though not automatically evil, anger is just too dangerous and volatile for us to safely handle, and we are warned against it in the strongest terms.

Anger tends to lead us to judge others, and this we are categorically forbidden to do.

Downplaying of the anger and final judgement of God has led many, unwittingly, to take the responsibility for judgement and anger upon themselves.

Contempt is always sinful. It is never appropriate for a Christian. However, among religious people it is all too prevalent because contempt is the common currency of the self-righteous.

Anger can be an occupational problem for those who care very much. In a divided and anxious church with existential issues at stake it can become a habit. It is vital to the future health and faithfulness of the church that we build upon some of the more constructive approaches, developed in the midst of anger and fear, during the debates over homosexuality and over the consecration of women bishops.

Learning to fear God more than we fear any other threat, then discovering that we do not need to fear Him because He

---

279   1 John 4:18–19

loves us, can greatly liberate us from fear and anger. 'Perfect love casts out fear'.

Chapter Six

Factionalism and the (Ab)Use of the Bible

'Defend the Bible! I'd as soon defend a lion.'

C. H. Spurgeon

Luke 18:9 'To some who were confident of their own righteousness and looked down on everyone else, Jesus told this parable:'

'The Main Hindrance to the Use of Scripture Lies in the Notion That You Are Already Acquainted With Its Contents.' (Samuel Taylor Coleridge, *A Statesman's Manual*)

We have already quoted Daniel Migliore, 'Karl Barth warns of "the irremediable danger of consulting Holy Scripture apart from the centre", that is apart from Jesus Christ. If scripture is read apart from Him, Barth contends, "the Scripture principle will not stand very long".[280]

If Jesus is the centre of our faith, our criterion for all judgment, including how we interpret scripture, the Bible itself is our source for knowing who Jesus is. I mean the whole of the Bible, not just the

---

280   *The Power of God and the gods of Power*, Daniel L. Migliore, p.121 (Westminster John Knox, 2008) referring to Church Dogmatics IV/1, Karl Barth.

Gospels but the Old Testament, to whose story Jesus is the climax, and all of the New Testament which tells how the ripples from God's arrival among us spread throughout the world. The Old Testament was Jesus' scripture, and He quoted from it, amplified it, and assumed its authority throughout His life.

"'Do not think that I have come to abolish the Law or the Prophets; I have not come to abolish them but to fulfill them. For truly I tell you, until heaven and earth disappear, not the smallest letter, not the least stroke of a pen, will by any means disappear from the Law until everything is accomplished.'"[281]

Jesus underlined the authority of the Old Testament, but He also assumed an authority alongside it, perhaps most evidently in a series of "You have heard that it was said… but I say to you" sayings, that radically intensify the demands of the Old Testament law by going beyond its letter to the heart of God's intention.[282] For example, "'You have heard that it was said, 'Love your neighbour and hate your enemy.'[283] But I tell you: Love your enemies and pray for those who persecute you.'"[284]

Jesus is the interpretative key to the scriptures, and the scriptures are how we know of Jesus. This is not a circular process. The scriptures are reliable evidence, and we would read them differently according to whether we think, say, Moses, Jesus, or Paul is the centre and heart of them. However, the fact that we take Jesus, the Word incarnate, as the supreme authority, and the word written as authoritative in a secondary sense because it points to Him (see pp.76–77), should in no way diminish our respect for scripture. The scriptures are our means of knowing who Jesus is. If we read them trusting in the Holy Spirit's guidance, and in fellowship with others, different from ourselves (and therefore with different perspectives with the potential to correct us),

---

281   Matthew 5:17–18
282   Matthew 5:21–48
283   Leviticus 19:18
284   Matthew 5:43–44

we will hear God speak. God has called us to read the Bible in the widest possible fellowship to save us from succumbing to an avalanche of subjectivity, from interpreting Jesus in the light of our own culture, temperament and interests, as we have already seen, and will explore further in Chapter 7. God speaks, but our own attempts to interpret scripture are not necessarily God speaking.

What does it mean to be biblical? Is 'liberalism'[285] the main danger, as so many of my fellow evangelicals seem to assume? I'm going to concentrate on some of the pitfalls that are easily stumbled into by those of us who may be most convinced we are 'biblical'.

Can we be too certain of, as well as too inattentive to the meaning of scripture? (Too certain and *therefore* too inattentive, perhaps?)

Samuel Taylor Coleridge said that, 'The main hindrance to the use of scripture lies in the notion that you are already acquainted with its contents'.[286]

Sometimes, if we think we know what a passage of scripture says, this will prevent us paying proper attention to what it *really* says. This is a particular danger for conservative evangelicals, because of the easy assumption, frequently made, that 'conservative' equals 'biblical'. It might mean just 'conservative', in the sense of temperamentally not liking change. Andrew Atherstone argues that 'whether we are instinctively radical or conservative, both these tendencies must be brought under the Word of God'.[287] As each age brings up fresh issues the living Gospel must be re-interpreted for each age. 'Reformation is not re-assertion.'[288] There never was a 'golden age' for the church, but even if there had been, it would be madness to simply try to recreate

---

285 A slippery term, and like most 'boo' words it seems to mean more or less what the accuser wants it to mean. I take it here in the fairly imprecise negative sense in which it is often used by 'conservatives', to refer to one who sits lightly to the authority of scripture.

286 *A Statesman's Manual*, Samuel Taylor Coleridge, p.30 (1816 edition http://openlibrary.org/b/OL7193406M/statesman's_manual)

287 *Anvil*, vol. 26, No. 1, 2009. *The Implications of Semper Reformanda*, Andrew Atherstone, p.32

288 Atherstone (op. cit.)

that church in the present. There could be no surer way of making the church irrelevant in our own day. I would add that there could be no surer way of losing touch with Jesus Christ, and of becoming mere conformists to a frozen human ideology. We serve a living Lord.

If we think we know what a passage of scripture says before we even read it, we will not pay attention to its details and particularities. We need to pay close attention to these, and particularly so to those bits we find uncongenial or puzzling.

For example, let us examine Acts 12:1–11:

'It was about this time that King Herod arrested some who belonged to the church, intending to persecute them. He had James, the brother of John, put to death with the sword. When he saw that this pleased the Jews, he proceeded to seize Peter also. This happened during the Feast of Unleavened Bread. After arresting him, he put him in prison, handing him over to be guarded by four squads of four soldiers each. Herod intended to bring him out for public trial after the Passover.

So Peter was kept in prison, but the church was earnestly praying to God for him.

The night before Herod was to bring him to trial, Peter was sleeping between two soldiers, bound with two chains, and sentries stood guard at the entrance. Suddenly an angel of the Lord appeared and a light shone in the cell. He struck Peter on the side and woke him up. "Quick, get up!" he said, and the chains fell off Peter's wrists.

Then the angel said to him, "Put on your clothes and sandals." And Peter did so. "Wrap your cloak around you and follow me," the angel told him. Peter followed him out of the prison, but he had no idea that what the angel was doing was really happening; he thought he was seeing a vision. They passed the first and second guards and came to the iron gate leading to the city. It opened for them by itself, and they went through it. When they had walked the length of one street, suddenly the angel left him.

Then Peter came to himself and said, "Now I know without a doubt that the Lord sent his angel and rescued me from Herod's clutches and from everything the Jewish people were anticipating.'"

I have several times heard this preached on with an exclusive, or almost exclusive, focus on the miraculous deliverance of Peter. I can see why this might appeal to us, especially if our theology is keen on miracles and on 'health and prosperity'. However, if we preach about the miraculous deliverance of Peter, but fail to deal with the death of James in verse two, are we being biblical in any meaningful sense? How often do we wrestle with what scripture *really* says, and especially with those bits we may not want to focus on, those bits we find uncomfortable, or that even challenge our firm beliefs?

David Day, in a superb book on preaching, writes, 'In his influential book *Preaching*,[289] Fred Craddock writes about "looking for trouble"; looking for the surprise in a(n) idea. If you read a passage carefully, imaginatively and prayerfully, the text will often "pop" – that is, some aspect of the passage will surprise you or scandalize you or puzzle you. This is the feature which it is most tempting to overlook, and this is the bump in the terrain which will tell you where to dig for buried treasure… Surprises are precisely those elements which jolt us out of our complacency, which are beyond expectation and which thrust God's way of seeing things up against our taken-for-granted world. You just have to believe that the passage will "pop" if you give it time.'[290]

He then refers to 'the necessary struggle' to enable this to happen, and adds, 'It is necessary work, since the way in which we read the passage directly affects the word which we have to bring to the congregation, and without this discipline we are likely to make do with a few choice thoughts of our own. It is also hard work.'[291]

I am reminded of John Stott's dictum quoted above (p.6), 'the real hallmark of the evangelical is not only a present submission to what he or she believes the scripture teaches, it is a prior commitment to be

---

289   *Preaching*, Fred Craddock, p.196 (Abingdon Press, 1985)
290   *A Preaching Workbook*, David Day, p.32 (Lynx – SPCK, 1998)
291   Day op. cit. p.32

submissive to what we may subsequently learn to be the teaching of scripture – whatever scripture may be found to teach.'[292]

USING ONE TRUTH TO DROWN OUT ANOTHER

We may have a high theology of the Bible, which prevents us from simply disagreeing with it (I do), but that in practice does not stop us doing the same thing by simply choosing to concentrate on what appeals to us. We can often use one truth to drown out another. Most error seems to arise not so much from explicit denial of parts of the Bible, but from focusing so heavily on one aspect as to completely ignore or marginalise other important teachings. The zealot is therefore just as likely to misrepresent the Bible as is the indifferent. This can be apparently innocuous and done with the best of intentions.

We were in a cell group meeting discussing Amos, Chapter 1. Amos paints a picture of the Lord roaring warnings and judgment against the gentile nations that surround Israel. "For three sins of Damascus, even for four, I will not relent."[293] "This is what the Lord says: For three sins of Gaza, even for four, I will not relent."[294] You can imagine the people of Israel and Judah cheering in the stands, the roar getting louder and louder with each pronouncement. So it goes on; Tyre, Edom, Ammon, and Moab, all receive their verdict. The watching crowd must by now be delirious. These are nations that have repeatedly attacked and slaughtered the people of God, worshippers of pagan gods who worshipped with disgusting practices, such as the child sacrifices made to Molech, the 'god' of the Ammonites. A hollow statue of Molech was heated from below, and a child burned to death inside, to appease the 'god'.[295] Imagine their stunned silence, their shock, when the Lord continues, "For three sins of Judah, even

---

292   John Stott, *Church of England Newspaper*, September 1990

293   Amos 1:3

294   Amos 1:6

295   *Commentary on the Old Testament, vol 1, The Pentateuch*, C.F. Keil and Franz Delitzsch, p.416–417 (Grand Rapids, Eerdmans, 1980)

for four, I will not relent."[296] "For three sins of Israel, even for four, I will not relent."[297] Suddenly there is open-mouthed amazement. They have been relying on their status as the chosen people, and looking down on the gentile nations around them, and this has blinded them to the Lord's requirements. In particular they have themselves gone after 'false gods', have adopted similar ethical standards to gentiles, and have abused and exploited the poor. These requirements were always part of the Lord's revealed will for His people, but so focused have they been on His promises and their status as chosen people that, in their pride, they have forgotten them. The chosen people themselves have let one part of the message obscure another.

In our cell group discussion, the irony then was that, as conversation developed about how we might be similarly complacent, and presuming upon the Lord's mercy, just as we were getting to some real honesty and humility, one member of the group said "Thank God that we are forgiven by Jesus." True, important, relevant, but in that moment, it completely blunted the point of that dramatic passage from Amos. The 'bump' in the ground which might have indicated the presence of buried treasure was smoothed over, and Amos was not allowed to speak for himself. One part of the scriptural message had drowned out another in a way that prevented the passage before us from bearing its full weight.

I pick that example because it was not particularly heinous, because what that group member said was not only true, but was important, and ultimately necessary to know. It simply, at that moment, prevented Amos speaking for himself, and therefore effectively prevented us from hearing other things that maybe we also needed to know. But, on reflection, maybe it did more than that. Maybe, and here is the double irony, it prevented us from fully appreciating what it means to be forgiven by God. By jumping too quickly to the assurance of forgiveness, and bypassing any facing up to how we might have

---

296 Amos 2:4
297 Amos 2:6

displeased the Lord, it probably clouded for us how amazing, how necessary and what a relief His mercy is. People who have never realised they were in danger are unlikely to sing songs celebrating rescue with any gusto.

Using one part of scripture to drown out another is something that is difficult to avoid doing, and I am aware that some will accuse me of doing just that in this book, no doubt at times with justification. However, at least we can be aware of the danger and take steps to make sure that we are considering 'the whole counsel of God'.[298]

We might stress personal salvation and ethics, yet ignore the poor, we might stress the Holy Spirit and His gifts and neglect the cross, we might stress the balance needed in understanding the Bible, and ignore the distinctives of particular truths. The useful way to achieve equilibrium on an old-fashioned set of beam scales, as with a see-saw, is to make sure that each end is given its full weight, not to sit in the middle. So it is with scripture. Then you can get an accurate reading.

Each passage of scripture, and especially the 'knots' and 'bumps', must be given its full meaning, and not smoothed out with a premature harmonisation that is likely, if we are not careful, to do nothing more than assimilate the Bible to our own prejudices and interests. No wonder such homogenised preaching is often accused of dullness. We should expect the Bible to contain paradox. To expect anything else would entail assuming that God was somehow less than us, and therefore fully comprehensible to the human mind.

There is a unity and coherence in the midst of the amazing diversity of the Bible that is quite astonishing. Here is a collection of books written over more than a millennium, set in about a dozen modern countries across three continents, in three languages and by at least forty different authors. It has spoken consistently to all conditions and ranks of men and women, across all continents for nearly two further millennia. Despite sceptical claims to the contrary, it speaks with consistency, but

---

298   Acts 20:27 (RSV). More about ways of doing this in the next chapter.

not uniformity. Millions upon millions find it speaks freshly every day in a way that makes sense of their lives and reveals God to them.

It makes the kind of music that does not fight shy of dissonance and irregular meter to create an organic whole. We should beware of levelling out the differences to make an artificial unity, a sort of smooth and bland mood music that encourages sleep rather than attentive engagement. The 'Gospel of John' is different from 'The Gospel of Matthew', and 'The Letter of James' different from 'The Letter to the Romans'. Of course they are, otherwise why did God bother to inspire them. Yet they speak together of God. They are different, not, as many so easily complain, inconsistent. We will not be in too much danger of smoothing out the bumps, as long as we welcome into our fellowships those with different insights from ours. As long as those who wish that St Paul's letters had been lost are in fellowship with those who wish (with Luther) that James had never been written, and are willing to listen to each other and to the 'whole counsel of God', then we will probably not go too far wrong.

The sort of church that insists too readily on excluding those whom it perceives as unorthodox, paradoxically, will probably end up not taking the Bible sufficiently seriously.

Shifting the Centre of Gravity: Making Sexual Ethics the Touchstone

A particularly serious case of 'drowning out one truth with another' seems to be happening over the issue of homosexuality. Being against homosexual practice appears, for some, to have become part of the definition of an 'orthodox Christian'. Thus 'Courage', a so called 'ex-gay ministry', was pressured to resign from the Evangelical Alliance in 2002, after changing its position on whether homosexual relationships were sinful.[299]

---

299   See below p.245, 6

This seems to be a trend we are picking up from the 'religious right' in the USA where 'true faith' seems to be more defined by one's attitudes to certain litmus-test ethical issues (homosexuality and abortion in particular) than by one's allegiance to Jesus Christ.[300] Many Christians who supported Donald Trump did so because of his professed stance on homosexuality and abortion. I find this staggering, but *potentially* understandable from a tactical point of view. However, the astonishing thing is that the issue of character and Christlikeness did not seem to arise for many of these Christians. Trump is a man with no track record of proven Christian commitment at all, and with a character about as far from Jesus as could be imagined, yet many US Christians seem to have reduced the whole Christian message to a stance on two hot-button issues. This is what happens when Jesus Christ (and therefore Christlike discipleship) has become marginalised into invisibility. Ideology takes over.

One's attitude to homosexuality seems, for some, to define whether one is a Christian or not, hence the inability of some Anglican bishops to receive Communion with one another at the 2008 Lambeth Conference.[301]

Since when was our faith *defined* by our attitude to homosexuality? We are in danger of denying the faith here, in our zeal for a misplaced orthodoxy, in a similar way to the Galatian church.

'You foolish Galatians! Who has bewitched you? Before your very eyes Jesus Christ was clearly portrayed as crucified. I would like to learn just one thing from you: Did you receive the Spirit by works of the law, or by believing what you heard? Are you so foolish? After beginning by means of the Spirit, are you now trying to finish by means of the flesh? Have you experienced so much in vain… if it really was in vain? So

---

300 I am not arguing here that abortion and homosexuality do not matter, far from it. I believe that the silence of many Christians about abortion is one of the great scandals of our age. I just do not believe that therefore they cease to be Christian.

301 Some stayed away, and some attended, but abstained from receiving at the eucharist. *The Times*, 21/7/08.

again I ask, does God give you his Spirit and work miracles among you by works of the law, or by your believing what you heard?'[302]

The Galatian Heresy Rides Again

The Galatian mistake was to make circumcision a *sine qua non* of being a Christian. Paul immediately perceives what is at stake, the place of Jesus Christ in salvation, no less. Are we saved by faith in what God has done for us on the cross, or by faith in what God has done, plus something else that we can bring to the table (circumcision at that time, an attitude to homosexuality, or perhaps a particular political approach of the right or the left today)?[303]

Gal. 5:4 'You who are trying to be justified by law have been alienated from Christ; you have fallen away from grace.'

It is important to be clear here. Paul was not saying that if you are circumcised you have forfeited your salvation. This would simply be an equal and opposite form of the same mistake, like a mirror image. He *appears* to be saying this earlier in the same passage, when he says, 'Mark my words! I, Paul, tell you that if you let yourselves be circumcised, Christ will be of no value to you at all.'[304] However, in context, he clearly means if you are circumcised *as a way to salvation,* then you have not put all your hope in Jesus Christ and are missing the point of what He has done for you. This Paul makes clearer a few verses further on when he says, 'For in Christ Jesus neither circumcision nor un-circumcision has any value. The only thing that counts is faith expressing itself through love.'[305] Perhaps we see this most clearly when Paul has Timothy, his new missionary companion, circumcised. This

---

302 Galatians 3:1–5
303 For example, the association of Jesus' concern for the poor with a particular kind of left-wing programme, to the extent that those who will not vote that way cannot be Christians, or the claim by some nationalists, such as Viktor Orbán in Hungary, to be defending 'Christian Europe'. To both claims Jesus sometimes seems to be marginal.
304 Galatians 5:2
305 Galatians 5:6

is not because circumcision is necessary for salvation. It is a tactical move to make Timothy's ministry acceptable to a Jewish audience.[306] Paul is not, therefore, being inconsistent. Context is everything. Just as a carving knife in a kitchen drawer is an item of cutlery, taken out into the street to be used in self-defence it becomes an offensive weapon that can attract a long prison sentence. Circumcision is harmless in itself, but used as a means of salvation it becomes the enemy of the cross of Christ.

Therefore it is not all, or even most, who object to homosexual behaviour who are falling into the 'Galatian heresy'. Otherwise we could not argue for righteousness as we best understand it, within God's church. Clearly some standards of behaviour are appropriate for Christians and some are not, and this is a subject worthy of debate. It's a question of whether we are insisting that certain kinds of behaviour are required *in order* to be saved. Those who insist that homosexuality is a 'salvation issue'[307] are making a fundamental mistake. The only 'salvation issue' is Jesus Christ. They are making essentially the same mistake as the circumcision party who are in the background of the letter to the Galatians. We may well feel compelled by our loyalty to Jesus to hold that homosexual sexual acts are sinful. But to contend that of themselves these acts exclude a person from the Kingdom of God, or even that someone who argues a contrary position to ours is no longer a true Christian, is to fall into one of the most basic heresies of all, and to deny the grace that bought us.

Paul is pretty robust about those who would pervert the Good News into a different Gospel by requiring circumcision:

'I am astonished that you are so quickly deserting the one who called

---

306 Acts 16:1–3

307 There are many polemical claims that homosexuality is a 'salvation issue'. For an example, see 'Ways Forward in the Present Crisis for the Church of England' (2004), a paper written in preparation for Reform's 2004 National Conference, www.reform.org.uk/pages/bb/issueshsex.php or Robert Gagnon in *Homosexuality and The Bible: Two Views* by Robert A. J. Gagnon and Dan O. Via, Location 502 (Fortress Press, Minneapolis digital edition, 2003).

you to live in the grace of Christ and are turning to a different gospel – which is really no gospel at all. Evidently some people are throwing you into confusion and are trying to pervert the gospel of Christ. But even if we or an angel from heaven should preach a gospel other than the one we preached to you, let them be under God's curse! As we have already said, so now I say again: if anybody is preaching to you a gospel other than what you accepted, let them be under God's curse!'[308]

Who is preaching a different Gospel? Is it liberals who are letting 'anything go', or sticklers for the law whose misplaced zeal has led them to make something other than 'Jesus Christ and Him crucified'[309] into a 'salvation issue'?

THE USE AND ABUSE OF SCRIPTURE

The verses usually relied upon by those who define homosexuality as a 'salvation issue'[310] are from 1 Corinthians 6:9–11. 'Do you not know that the wicked will not inherit the kingdom of God? Do not be deceived: Neither the sexually immoral nor idolaters nor adulterers nor male prostitutes nor homosexual offenders nor thieves nor the greedy nor drunkards nor slanderers nor swindlers will inherit the kingdom of God. And that is what some of you were. But you were washed, you were sanctified, you were justified in the name of the Lord Jesus Christ and by the Spirit of our God.'

However, this passage is surely pointing out that *all* sinful behaviour and the Kingdom of God are incompatible. It is not setting up a special class of heinous sin. It is a similar list to 1 Timothy 1:9-11, that refers to 'lawbreakers and rebels, the ungodly and sinful, the

---

308   Galatians 1:6–9
309   1 Corinthians 2:2
310   Another typical example of many that could be chosen is taken from a talk by Revd Paul Carter, Executive Director of 'The Anglican Communion in New Westminster' – at The Church Society AGM in 2003. '1Corinthians 6:10, this is not just a moral issue, but a salvation issue... This is a salvation issue and we are doing the most loving thing for homosexuals to warn them of this.'

unholy and irreligious; for those who kill their fathers or mothers, for murderers, for adulterers and perverts, for slave traders and liars and perjurers...' and concludes 'and for whatever else is contrary to the sound doctrine that conforms to the glorious gospel of the blessed God.'

The Bible is being misread to make homosexuality out to be uniquely sinful, and to elevate the issue of homosexuality to a central position in our faith and salvation that it does not have. Note that I am not here arguing that homosexual practice is biblically acceptable, simply that the issue cannot legitimately occupy the prominent place in our faith that some would have it occupy.

Some might wish to reply that homosexuality is not uniquely sinful, *all* sin is a salvation issue. To which I would reply, "Fine, but why then do you not make a similar stand about other sins that are both prevalent in the church, and contentious? Perhaps, taking 1 Corinthians 6 as our guide, idolatry, greed or slander might make a good start." To which my imaginary interlocutor might then say, "Yes, but idolatry, greed or slander are not clear cut. They have blurred edges as issues." My response would be that homosexuality is nowhere near as scripturally clear cut as many have assumed (though more of this in Chapter 9).

Clearly scripture can be disrespected as much by the dogmatic certainty that is no longer open to revelation as by a 'liberal' indifference to what the Bible actually says. I fear that much 'biblical' assertiveness is not so much rooted in the Bible itself, as in a conservative subculture that prides itself on being biblical, which might be a very different thing.

The late Marlene Cohen, who came from a church tradition that equated being a real Christian with abstaining from alcohol (and who valued much from that background) said that the hidden assumptions operating in some traditions (all traditions if we are not careful?) run as follows: 'a) 'I agree with it (so it must be biblical).' b) 'It's in a famous hymn (so it must be biblical).' c) 'It's in the prayer book (so it must be biblical).' d) 'My minister says it (so it must be biblical).' e) 'It's in a Christian book (so it must be biblical).' f) 'A famous Christian said it (so it must be biblical).' g) 'It's common Christian practice (so it must be biblical).' [311]

THE JOURNEY SO FAR

Jesus is the interpretative key to the scriptures, and the scriptures are how we know of Jesus.

We can as easily miss what the Bible has to say to us by over confidence that we already know what it says, as by a cavalier attitude to its authority.

Without care it is easy to think we are being biblical when in fact we are simply giving a biblical gloss to the prejudices of our own temperaments or cultures.

It is commonplace to marginalise significant parts of the Bible at the same time as claiming to have a very high view of scripture's authority. It is easy to ignore passages and messages we do not find congenial by concentrating instead on those parts that we do.

A particularly serious case of 'drowning out one truth with another' seems to be happening over the issue of homosexuality. Being against homosexual practice appears, for some, to have become part of the definition of an 'orthodox Christian'. We are in danger here of a rerun of the so-called 'Galatian heresy', namely that Jesus is insufficient for salvation. On this view it has to be Jesus plus.

---

311   *The Divided Self*, Marlene Cohen, p.143 (Marshall Pickering, 1996)

CHAPTER SEVEN

DO WE READ THE BIBLE,
OR DOES THE BIBLE READ US?

'The vision of Christ that thou dost see is my vision's greatest
enemy: Thine has a great hook nose like thine, Mine has a snub
nose like to mine. Both read the Bible day and night, But thou
read'st black where I read white.'

(*THE EVERLASTING GOSPEL*, WILLIAM BLAKE)

LETTING THE BIBLE READ US

When Hillary Clinton went to a Washington bi-partisan Bible study
full of suspicion because of the vicious personal attacks she had
experienced from many Christians, why was she amazed and moved
to receive an apology for such behaviour? Why is this not what the
world expects from Christians? Why did she want a way of introducing
her daughter, Chelsea, to similar Christians of her own age, because
'Chelsea had not met many "grace-full" Christians'?[312]

Perhaps the answer to these questions lies in the fact that not
many Christians seem to be reading the Bible. Of regular churchgoers
reading the Bible in the UK, sixteen per cent read something every
day, ten per cent several times a week, forty-two per cent less
frequently but at least once per year, fourteen per cent have not read

---

312 *What's So Amazing About Grace?*, Philip Yancey, p.243 (Zondervan, 1997)

anything in the last year, and eighteen per cent never personally read it except during church services.[313] In other words nearly three quarters of regular churchgoers had only a passing acquaintance with the Bible. Research in 2017 by ComRes for the Church of England shows similar results.

If we immerse ourselves in the pages of the Bible with disciplined regularity and invite the Holy Spirit to convict and change us as we read, we should come to see ourselves as in a mirror,[314] and we should see Jesus more clearly despite the mists and fogs of our preconceptions. If we do not so immerse ourselves, then vision becomes clouded and un-Christlike behaviour can flourish. In particular, 'ungrace' (as Philip Yancey calls it) can rule when the Bible is not read searchingly and submissively. An unexamined faith is likely to degenerate into little more than a collection of bigotry and prejudices.

To read submissively is important. A well-known preachers' trap is to slide into reading the Bible for others, looking for a message for the congregation, but blind to personal application. Or we read looking for confirmation of what we already believe, and so miss the things that need to disturb us (a particular peril if we over rely on favourite verses). Or we might read out of mere curiosity, like W. C. Fields, who embarrassed to be caught reading the Bible, said, "I'm looking for loopholes".[315]

In submissive Bible reading, it is as true to say that the Bible reads us as that we read the Bible.

'For the word of God is alive and active. Sharper than any double-edged sword, it penetrates even to dividing soul and spirit, joints and marrow; it judges the thoughts and attitudes of the heart. Nothing in all creation is hidden from God's sight. Everything is uncovered and laid bare before the eyes of him to whom we must give account.'[316]

---

313   *Quadrant* (Christian Research Association Newsletter), March 1998
314   James 1:23–24
315   *What's So Amazing About Grace?*, Philip Yancey, p.35 (Zondervan, 1997)
316   Hebrews 4:12–13

It's much harder to persist in ungracious behaviour under that kind of scrutiny. And this is not a scrutiny to be feared. God's scrutiny is gracious and aims to restore. He works co-operatively, *with* us, and aims for our salvation, not our condemnation. It is this that makes a submissive approach on our part safe. Submissiveness could not be more contrary to the spirit of our age, but as we saw in Chapter 3, 'crucified truth threatens no one'.[317]

To enable this life-changing dialogue with the Bible we need to invite the Holy Spirit to assist our reading, and to get into the habit of reviewing our life, including, as we become aware of them, those inner reactions that tend to drive us, and then we can bring what we perceive to God. As Rowan Williams has said, "To be willing to put one's belief, action and thinking under judgement, under scrutiny, is a mark of a Christian".[318] Here again, the input of those who do not always agree with us can be invaluable.

When reading the Bible it helps to dwell on those passages we might feel inclined to skip over, such as those that surprise us, those that are hard to understand, those that we wish were not in the Bible, those that seem to be at odds with a cherished position we hold (remember what David Day had to say about 'the bump in the terrain which will tell you where to dig for buried treasure', p.121)., If we hold on to such passages, possibly writing them down in a journal, or on a postcard put where we will see them regularly, if we chew on those passages to see whether they yield anything fresh, we may be surprised. If we just rush past the awkward bits, we are unlikely to hear much from the Bible beyond the echo of our own voice.

I was greatly blessed when years ago I took up Robert Murray M'Cheyne's Bible reading programme.[319] This consists of four passages per day, usually one chapter in each. Over the course of a year this goes through the Old Testament once, and the Psalms and New Testament

---

317   p.67
318   Rowan Williams at The Stepney Episcopal Area Advent Lectures, 1999.
319   www.edginet.org/mcheyne/calendar.php

twice. Some prefer to read just two passages a day. There are numerous other Bible reading plans with a similar idea. The strength of such a system is that not too long can go by without the reader entering into 'the whole counsel of God'.[320] There is no alternative for those who are serious about their faith, and certainly for those who aspire to be teachers, to embracing the whole Bible on a regular basis so that the overall sweep and narrative, as well as the details, become a fixed part of our mental furniture. Life is always throwing up new issues for us, and as we re-think and re-interpret, if we follow such a scheme, we cannot go for more than a year or so without our thinking and our actions being tested against *the whole* of scripture. If we slide off at a tangent from God's revealed will, either through novelty or through stubbornly clinging to inherited understanding with little root in scripture, we will, if we pay attention, hear the summons back, which says, 'This is the way; walk in it'.[321] And as Jesus *is* the way, a scheme that goes through the New Testament twice, and keeps us immersed in His life and teaching while we read the Old Testament, has much to commend it.

More selective schemes are likely to be deliberately or unconsciously biased. Reading passages according to some pre-selected plan that picks and chooses, whether it is key verses learned by rote, or the local preacher's plan, or the favourite verses of our favourite authors, can tend to reinforce an ideological position and leave us choosing an interpretation that suits our temperament or circumstances, and so tend to stifle the whole counsel of God.

As we read and reflect we need to pray for an open and receptive mind. As Karl Popper wrote, 'If we are uncritical we shall always find what we want: we shall look for, and find, confirmations, and we shall look away from, and not see, whatever might be dangerous to our pet theories.'[322]

---

320   Acts 20:27 (RSV)
321   Isaiah 30:21
322   *The Poverty of Historicism*, Ch. 29, 'The Unity of Method', Karl Popper (1957)

It is surprisingly easy to impose our own filters and frames of reference upon scripture,[323] either consciously or more likely, unconsciously, and by so doing we will be limiting our ability to hear from God. Without knowing it we are exercising our own lordship over the Lord's Word – and censoring what we will hear. This is why I quoted John Stott in the preface to the effect that our commitment to the authority of scripture has to mean more than commitment simply to what I *now* believe it to say. It has to mean commitment to whatever scripture might in future be shown to teach, even if such revelation might be deeply uncongenial to me.[324]

Reading the whole Bible in a year might seem too heavy a commitment to some, and there are similar schemes that go through the whole Bible over a longer period. However, I rarely meet anybody who thinks they have time for Bible reading *before* they develop a regular pattern. Once we start reading the Bible in this way, however, we begin to reassess our priorities and our use of time and it is remarkable what then seems possible.

Gradually we find that we see ourselves, the world, our friends, our enemies, everything, in a new light through the words of the Bible, and in particular, in the light of Jesus Christ. This is a cumulative process over years, and it takes time and thought day by day, as we pause to make connections. We need not only to read, but to think, ponder and pray. This is one reason why the Bible does not seem to get boring the more we read it, but rather quite the reverse.

'Until our thoughts of God have found every visible thing and event glorious with His presence, the word of Jesus Christ has not yet fully seized us.'[325] This will take us a lifetime. Until then the Bible will not usually be boring to an attentive, submitted person (though

---

323 Or perhaps more likely, we allow someone else to impose their filters and frames of reference when we follow some Christian 'guru' or submit to the group think of the Christians we particularly identify with without testing these conclusions against scripture for ourselves.

324 p.6

325 *The Divine Conspiracy*, Dallas Willard, p.71 (Fount, 1998)

it might seem stale to us for a season from time to time, particularly when we are out of sorts).

It should be obvious by now that reading the Bible simply to obtain ammunition for a polemical case one wishes to make, or defensively to buttress an opinion one already holds, is not 'letting the Bible read us'. It is a question of who is in control. In this sense our reading needs to be submissive, but there is a danger that this could be misunderstood. It is not a passive process. There is struggle involved. A person of integrity will often say "Do you really mean that Lord?", or "Surely that's not right?" at the very least. 'Submissive' does not mean 'unquestioning'. Quite often we will find ourselves shouting at God. Philip Yancey points out how all the great figures of faith in the Bible argued with God. Abraham, Moses, Jeremiah, Isaiah, and supremely Job, all did. Job's friends refused to get into the argument with God and were roundly condemned by God for it.[326] God seems to positively welcome argument as part of our struggle for truth. The Old Testament characters who argued were concerned to do God's will, but they were not pushovers. The person who doesn't struggle to understand will probably never get beneath the surface, and will be either servile towards God, or like a teenager who says "Whatever" without wanting to really engage. Healthy submissiveness is sometimes like joining in a vigorous debate, arguing fiercely, but all the time with the intention of giving way to whatever this process eventually reveals of the truth. Moses, Job, Abraham and the others were often (not always) proved wrong, but the process developed a relationship with God and revealed Him to the protagonist more fully. God does not seem to mind using people who get it wrong and who argue, as part of His plans. Actually, He seems to prefer them to 'yes men and women'.

Could it be that the dissident groups, the awkward squad, are part of His mind for the church, part of His blessing to lead us further into truth, *even* on those occasions when they might be wrong? If so, we

---

326   Job 42:7–8

must engage in the conversation, or argument even, with God and with others. We need to engage vigorously, but without resentment, self-righteousness, hate or exclusion and then to bring the fruits of those conversations honestly into our own reading of the Bible.

All these things, reading the whole Bible, with feisty submission, with honesty and attentiveness to the awkward bits, in fellowship with those who disagree with us, and, as we saw earlier, through the lens of Jesus Christ, will help avoid the all too frequent spectacle of Christians using the Bible simply to buttress the conclusions their temperament would have come to anyway, or to support their own vested interest. Christians who claim to respect the Bible rarely just reject the bits that don't suit them. They just marginalise them.

In *Uncle Tom's Cabin*, Eva says, "'Don't the Bible say we must love everybody?" "O, the Bible! To be sure, it says a great many things; but then, nobody ever thinks of doing them," ' replies her cousin.[327]

This surely is partly why St Paul said, 'Examine yourselves to see whether you are in the faith; test yourselves.'[328]

THE GIFT OF DIVERSITY:
CULTURAL PERSPECTIVE AND THE BIBLE

We have already remarked on the diversity of the Bible's origins. The inspirer of a Bible of sixty-six books written by about forty authors, in three languages, set in about a dozen modern countries, across three continents, over 1,500 years must know a thing or two about difference and diversity, and is clearly not afraid of it.

One sure (and biblical) way of avoiding the trap of only seeing the Bible through the tinted spectacles of our own culture, temperament or vested interest, is to interpret the Bible in fellowship with those whose cultures, temperaments, and vested interests, are different from ours, as we noted on p.77. Jesus came to break down barriers,

---

327 *Uncle Tom's Cabin*, Harriet Beecher Stowe, Ch. 23
328 2 Cor 13:5

reaching out to Samaritans, and Gentiles, Jews, lepers, Pharisees, and prostitutes, revolutionary zealots, and members of the establishment. These were people divided by a potent brew of politics, history, mutual incomprehension, race, religious rules, fear and large measures of contempt. Jesus spent His life widening our circles of sympathy, not only from 'Jerusalem', and to 'all Judea and Samaria, and to the ends of the earth',[329] but from family to strangers, from friends to enemies, from those who assist us to those who persecute us, from those with whom it is safe to be, to those who might infect us with a dreadful disease, from those who are respectable, to those who will leave us religiously tainted, and on and on, breaking down every barrier of race, religion, class, gender, taste and choice.

The church therefore cannot be the Body of Christ unless it embraces and reconciles human diversity. It was no accident that the church was born as God gave the gift of tongues through the Holy Spirit, thus enabling 'Parthians, Medes and Elamites; residents of Mesopotamia, Judea and Cappadocia, Pontus and Asia, Phrygia and Pamphylia, Egypt and the parts of Libya near Cyrene; visitors from Rome (both Jews and converts to Judaism); Cretans and Arabs'[330] to hear and respond to God's word.

In particular the voice of the poor and the relatively powerless surely has a privileged place because they have so few vested interests to skew their reading of the Bible, and because their concerns are close to Jesus' heart; 'Blessed are you who are poor, for yours is the kingdom of God.'[331] As Robin Gamble has graphically put it, 'At the incarnation Jesus "signed up" to play for the under privileged. This is not surprising, for they had always been his Father's favourite team.'[332] Without their voice we will seriously misunderstand the Bible. A simple survey illustrates this.

---

329 Acts 1:8
330 Acts 2:9–11
331 Luke 6:20
332 *The Irrelevant Church*, Robin Gamble, p.109 (Monarch, 1991)

The 'percentage of Americans earning less than $30,000 per year who believe that "the meek shall inherit the earth": 61. (The) percentage of Americans earning more than $60,000 who believe this: 36.'[333] I have had many discussions about this and find that many middle-class Christians have genuine and persistent difficulty in really believing that they need their often less articulate and less educated brothers and sisters from the council estate to help them to understand the Bible. I know what it feels like. I remember struggling with the very idea. It is counter-intuitive for the educated. After a while I reluctantly gave mental assent, but not really doing much about it because *in practice* I still doubted it was true. I've now been in too many Bible discussions where people who may (or may not) need some of the more abstract or complicated words explaining to them, have come out with the questions and comments that have got to the truth more directly than anything else said all evening. These are people who, when they read of the woman caught in adultery, read the passage from the woman's point of view, and so see things that those who automatically identify with Jesus may miss. These are people who don't have money in reserve and have not been trained to look upon it as security. They *know* what Jesus means when he says, "'Do not store up for yourselves treasures on earth, where moths and vermin destroy, and where thieves break in and steal. But store up for yourselves treasures in heaven.'"[334] They may not be easily able to put it into words, but if they are allowed the space (a big 'if', as many will have come to a discussion before and been patronised or bamboozled with long words, and made, quite unintentionally, to feel inadequate, and thus never came again)... if they are allowed the space, they will ask the right questions, and push the whole group nearer to the mind of Christ. I find they are also more generous, of themselves, of their time and definitely with their money.

If the voice of the poor, marginalised and relatively powerless, is not heard in the fellowship of discernment, we are almost bound to go

---

333   Harper's (3/96) quoted in *Leadership Magazine*, Fall '96, p.73
334   Matthew 6:19–20

wrong. Every part of the church needs the poor and the powerless even more than the poor and powerless need the rest of the church.

Christ died for all, therefore 'You are all children of God through faith in Christ Jesus, for all of you who were baptized into Christ have clothed yourselves with Christ. There is neither Jew nor Gentile, slave nor free, nor is there male and female, for you are all one in Christ Jesus. If you belong to Christ, then you are Abraham's seed, and heirs according to the promise'.[335] The body of Christ was created and called to be diverse. In human communities, however, like tends to attract like, and so there is a tendency to become monochrome. A good question for any church or individual to ask is "whose perspective is missing whenever we work out our faith together?"

The church of God is at its best when it is culturally diverse. Our staff team in the Upper Holloway Team Ministry had members from England, Nigeria, Eritrea, India, Tanzania and Guyana and from English middle-class and working-class backgrounds. The congregations were even more diverse. In many ways we had so little in common, but because of Jesus we had so much in common. The staff team would annually go away for forty-eight hours together, often with a team consultant to help us to reflect. Often it was a wonderful, enriching time. Sometimes it was hard work. Very different styles of arguing, discussing and leading meant that we needed to work at understanding each other, but that was a blessing, turning us into better listeners and showing each of us that ours was not the only way. Above all, because Jesus was the reason we were together, and the main factor we had in common, it became that much harder not to see Him as He is, the centre of our fellowship and the reason we were called together. I don't want to romanticise. We had some fierce arguments and some fallings out, though they never lasted for very long.

Being together often changed how we thought. When we were talking about the clergy pension crisis, and one of our number was

---

335   Galatians 3:26–29

concerned over whether her family in Tanzania would starve in the drought, it changed perspective and challenged assumptions. When we had fallen into grumbling about our lot, and one of our number came to the discussion with news of five members of his former church who had died that month in the same prison in Eritrea that he himself was held in for a year, it rather changed how we thought and prayed, not to mention the light it shed on what Jesus might have meant by 'dying to self'. Not least, I came to a fresh appreciation of how individualistic most of my assumptions and preferences were compared both with my colleagues, and with the values of the Bible. This is hard, but immensely liberating.

Unless diversity is present in the life of the church, I suggest that we are almost bound to misread scripture and to misrepresent Jesus Christ. The very differences of perspective, culture and temperament that make fellowship such hard work are God's gifts that enable the Bible to speak and to release us from the captivity of our own little ghettoes, into the wideness of God's Kingdom. It's rather like surveying. It is not possible to fix a point's position unless it is 'triangulated', that is looked at and measured from two other points. It is why we have two eyes and not one. You cannot adequately gauge distance or size from only one point of view. There is no perspective. We should therefore be suspicious of strident but largely monocultural voices in the church.[336] This is one of the reasons why it is not wise for one part of the worldwide church to move ahead with innovation

---

336 The 'homogenous unit principle' in church growth theory suggests that evangelism works best when single cultures are reached in a way suited to them, thus black churches, student churches, and middle-class churches will best reach black people, students and middle-class people respectively. I believe that there may be something in this, up to a point, but only if it is recognised that this is only a starting point. People can only be reached where they are, but the gospel demands that these barriers are broken down as people mature in their faith. This is one of the reasons why churches that reap on the homogenous unit principle must, having prepared them, try to build their converts into more culturally diverse fellowships to complete their maturing. Usually they will not, fearing 'relativism' and dilution of faith. If only they could see that a Christ-centred and biblical faith requires such breaking down of cultural barriers.

until the voice of others has been weighed and considered extremely carefully, especially, as recently in the Anglican Communion, if that province is rich and powerful (the Episcopal Church of the USA) and the alternative voices are predominantly from among the poor (the so-called churches of the 'Global South').

A strange picture of what can happen when a Christian community becomes closed and self-referential was given in a description by Tom Whipple of a community of monks at Esphigmenou on Mount Athos.[337] It is a community with a defensive mindset, not surprisingly having endured centuries of humiliation from Ottoman Turks, and now having been excommunicated by their own patriarch, physically attacked by fellow monks and the Greek state in order to evict them, and blockaded in order to starve them out. Its lands have been seized and its bank accounts frozen. They have even had a warship despatched against them.

The monks object to Patriarch Bartholomew's friendly relations with the Pope, believing that ecumenism, 'is not just heresy, it is the final heresy that precedes the end of the world'... "'You are Catholic," states Dimitrius, after I arrive at the monastery, having lied about my destination to the Greek officials controlling entry to Mount Athos and walked ten kms through the forest. "The father wants you to know you cannot go in the church, and you cannot eat with the monks in the trapeza [dining hall]." Between us, a thick booklet shows pictures of the Patriarch, Bartholomew, embracing the Pope and other Catholic leaders. Its caption Dimitrius translates with a slightly embarrassed smile. It reads: "The Kiss of Judas"... There are a few biblical pictures on the wall, but most are of stern men with excellent moustaches: "Greek heroes," Dimitrius explains. Another pilgrim is more descriptive. "They kill Turks," he says, grinning as he makes a throat-cutting gesture.

'The monks here belong to a small minority of Orthodox called Old Calendarists, who reject the Gregorian Calendar, by which most

---

337 *Boys in the Hood: The Fight for Religion's Soul,* by Tom Whipple, *The Times,* 4 March, 2009

of the world counts its years. It may seem absurd, but the monks regard themselves as the guardians of their faith. For them, it is deadly serious.'[338]

We can perceive a process of exclusion at work here over centuries. First of all Greeks not Turks, then only Orthodox Christians, then only Greek Orthodox old calendarists, then only 'our own' monastery. Such separatism leads to some strange views and behaviours. '"The Patriarch tells us that we have no love for Catholics – no love in our hearts," explains Father Savvas who, after twenty years in the monastery, is one of the more senior monks. "Well, is it an expression of love to let people live in deceit? In Europe, with your Protestantism and your Catholicism you are in…" He stops, to find the *mot juste* in his English-Greek dictionary. "Oh yes, perversion." The word pleases him. "Popism is a perversion of Christianity."[339] He seems quite unaware that the journalist in front of him, and most of the so-called Catholic and Protestant West are probably non-observant or non-believing and desperately in need of Jesus Christ.

'The monks believe that ecumenism, hand in hand with globalisation, will prepare the world for a single world government "run by the Antichrist, the Messiah of the Jews"… "The coincidences are so many that you cannot turn a blind eye. For example, globalisation requires the barcode system." He finds a magazine and points to two lines on its barcode that are longer than others, repeated three times. "Do you know which number each double bar is?" This is conspiracy theory bingo, and I am about to get a full house. 6? "Yes ! It is 6!" 666: the mark of the beast. Technically, I later learn, those lines do not represent 6 but I doubt that the monks, who proudly call themselves zealots, would have taken my word for it.'[340]

The Monks were not 'evil'. They were, despite their rules about Catholics, very hospitable. They are not wrong about everything.

---

338 *The Times* (op. cit.)
339 *The Times* (op. cit.)
340 *The Times* (op. cit.)

Globalisation doubtless is full of dangers and ecumenism can be unprincipled. They are willing to stand for their understanding of truth at great personal cost. They have recognised the great dangers of worldliness. Nevertheless, they have shut themselves off from as many manifestations of diversity as they can, they only listen to their own interpretation of the faith, and most of us would conclude that they have drifted a long way from a true understanding of Jesus.

There is great danger in worldliness but there is also great danger in a closed world. Separating off into a subculture does not guarantee separation from worldliness. Only Jesus, who calls us to be in the world but not shaped by it, can help us with that. Separating into a closed subculture merely guarantees an eccentric and particular form of worldliness. We do not have to live in a closed monastery behind high walls to be so cut off. Those silent, unspoken exclusivities that ensure that our congregations are full of people just like us will do just as well.

The Bible and Dissonant Experience

What do we do when the facts of our experience seem to be in contradiction to our understanding of the Bible? This of course has happened repeatedly, perhaps the most famous example being the assumption that the Earth was the centre of the universe, and the adjustments required to Christian thinking when Galileo (following Copernicus) established that the Earth in fact revolves around the sun. If the scriptures and the universe reflect the mind of God who brought them about, then surely we should expect some congruity between the two. If our experience of the world does not sit easily with our understanding of scripture, then a person of integrity will re-examine their interpretation of the data from both sources.

This challenge to our existing understanding might come from scientific discovery, from a fresh way of looking at things, from someone from another culture, or from our own experience. Plenty of people who believe that God never heals have had to reassess that belief in the light of repeatedly answered prayer, and plenty of people who believe God heals to order have had to reassess that belief in the light of disappointing experience. Do we see such challenges as a threat or as an opportunity? If God is the creator of all we see, and the inspiration behind scripture, then surely we can afford to welcome every challenge to our way of thinking and believing as containing the potential to increase our understanding of the Bible, of God and of life? Christians with a defensive attitude against science, for example, probably betray not a high view of scripture, but a lack of confidence in both God and scripture.

This is emphatically not to say that our judgment trumps scripture, as if we and not God define truth. Nor is it to say that science trumps revelation. In the words of the Lausanne Covenant, scripture is 'without error in all that it affirms'. However, as John Stott writes: 'Not everything included in scripture is true, because not everything recorded in scripture is affirmed by scripture.'[341] He gives the example of the Book of Job, which contains long speeches by Job's friends about God. God then says, '"You have not spoken the truth about me".'[342] So, Stott argues, in our commitment to scripture as true, we are also committed to 'the responsible work of biblical interpretation, so that we may discern the intention of each author and grasp what is being affirmed'.[343]

This is obvious now, when we look back on Copernicus and Galileo. This revolution in understanding overturned many assumptions and resulting misinterpretations of scripture. It in no way challenges the teaching and authority of scripture itself.

It is in fact a form of idolatry to objectify *our interpretation* of scripture as if that were the 'Word of God'. The trouble is that we often

---

341 Chapter by John Stott in *The Authority and Power of the Bible*, in Rene Padilla (ed.), *The New Face of Evangelicalism* (Hodder and Stoughton, 1976)

342 Job 42:7

343 John Stott (op. cit.)

do not realise that this is what we are doing. If we cannot conceive of another way of interpreting the data, we easily assume that there cannot be any other legitimate way of looking at it. If we are paying attention to our experience, to the world around us, and to people who are different from us, however, this might give us some clues.

I have already described (p.105) how my experience of anger and its tendency to do no good led me to look more closely at scripture, and forced me to the realisation that reading the verse 'in your anger do not sin' as a justification for 'righteous anger' might not be a fair representation of what God was saying. More contentiously I would suggest that our experience of the 'credit crunch' in 2007-9 might drive us back to the Old Testament teaching on usury to see whether we do not have lessons to learn that we might only now be in a position to see in the light of our experience. I recall a paper from 1993 by Paul Mills, then a Cambridge economist,[344] questioning a debt-based economy as inherently unstable, and in particular, as likely to exaggerate the economic swings of boom and bust. By taking the biblical model of finance, and using it to critique modern practice, he accurately identified many of the problems that have since come to light in the post-2008 financial crisis and recession. The details are not important for our purposes now, and no doubt they are contentious. What is important is that experience brought us to the point (certainly it has brought me to the point) where the relevance of Old Testament teaching about usury that, frankly had seemed rather quaint, now seems rather obvious. If we pray with our Bibles in one hand and our newspapers in the other, we will hear the Bible more clearly. Our experience and the Bible should be in dialogue if the Bible is to be given its full weight and authority.

We have seen that the central message of scripture must control its interpretation, which means interpretation must be Christ-centred. Thus, when the facts of experience produce major dissonance with

---

344   *The Ban on Interest: Dead Letter or Radical Solution?* by Paul Mills,
      Cambridge Papers, Vol. 2, no. 1 (Jubilee Centre, 1993)

what we think we know of Jesus or scripture, or between Jesus and scripture, it may be that God is inviting us to think again.

This will become important again in Chapter 10, when the experience of gay people is admitted to the debate about scriptural interpretation. Suffice it to say here that if the way the church handles any issue tends to lead to behaviour that is strikingly un-Christlike, then we must be getting something (though not necessarily the obvious thing) wrong. For example, in some communities in the 1950s, if unmarried teenage girls got pregnant, their 'Christian' families would throw them out on the streets. It is difficult to read about Jesus, and His treatment of 'sinners', without a few alarm bells going off in the light of this kind of parental behaviour. Such incongruity is an invitation to a rethink and to a fresh look at the Bible.

Integrity demands that when the Bible and experience of life are at variance, we look at both afresh with care and with prayerfulness, for as long as it takes. As we have observed, a commitment to the authority of scripture, 'is not only a present submission to what he or she believes the scripture teaches, it is a prior commitment to be submissive to what we may subsequently learn to be the teaching of scripture – whatever scripture may be found to teach.'[345] This is not to undermine the authority of scripture, it is to uphold it and take it very seriously indeed.

ALL THEOLOGY IS CONTEXTUAL

John Stott once succinctly commented that 'all theology is contextual.'[346] This is implicit in God's preferred *modus operandi*, namely incarnation at a particular time and place.

Quite what this contextuality means is well illustrated by Raymond Fung in the preface to Ann Morisy's book, *Beyond the Good Samaritan*.[347]

---

345   John Stott, *Church of England Newspaper*, September 1990
346   *Get A Grip On Mission*, Martin Goldsmith, p.191 (IVP, 2006)
347   Raymond Fung in *Beyond the Good Samaritan*, Ann Morisy (Mowbray, 1997)

'The title of this book reminds me of a bible study I once participated in with a house church in rural China. Some twenty peasant believers, sitting on low wooden benches on a dirt floor, were reflecting on the parable of the Good Samaritan in Luke 10. As conversation drew on, I became acutely aware of an unfamiliar slant towards this all too familiar text. It almost seemed to me they were dealing with a different scripture. Then it struck me: the peasants were not identifying with the priest or the Levite as I was wont to do – nice people – faced with the challenge of whom and whether to help – rather they were seeing themselves in the wounded person, the one who had been robbed and beaten up. The question is precisely that offered by Jesus: who is neighbour to the ones who are hurt? The Christian is not to see things from the perspective of the comfortable and the strong, but from the perspective of the vulnerable and the weak.'

Sometimes our insularity and the skewed interpretations it gives us can seem startling to others, while we remain unconscious of it. It wasn't exactly wrong, but neither did it give quite the correct picture when a London local newspaper's post-Christmas front page led with the headline 'Queen Broadcasts to People of St Pancras'.[348] Despite our perceptions, we are not the centre of the world. Like the famous headline, 'Fog in the Channel, continent cut off', it reveals a wrong apprehension of our place in the scheme of things.

Perhaps these two examples are quaintly amusing, but context matters because it affects our understanding of everything else.

This can be of the utmost significance. If this is God's world and we refuse to give the world any credence as we try to listen to God, then we might find ourselves immersed in scripture but a million miles from Jesus. Martin Goldsmith recalls, 'It was back in the early 1970s, in the dark days of rampant apartheid in South Africa. I was invited to give some lectures at a white evangelical Bible school. The students were enthusiastically open to all I taught them, and the staff

---

348   *A History of London*, Stephen Inwood, p.7 (Macmillan, 1998)

were warmly friendly, too. After my lecture, the principal kindly spared me some time to show me round the college and tell me more of their work. After a while, I asked in what ways the multinational context of South Africa influenced the content of the syllabus. The atmosphere changed and electricity ran around the room. Defensive hostility replaced the warm friendliness. "It makes no difference to our teaching," he growled. "After all, Calvin is the truth."[349]

As Jesus said,

"'You study the Scriptures diligently because you think that in them you have eternal life. These are the very Scriptures that testify about me, yet you refuse to come to me to have life'."[350]

REJECTION OF SCRIPTURE OR INTERPRETATION OF SCRIPTURE?

Am I then saying that virtually anything goes when it comes to interpreting scripture? God forbid! I'm arguing that the interpretation of scripture is so important that we need all the help we can find to get it right, and for that we need each other, especially those different from ourselves. We need to relate the Bible to the world we see around us, we need the Holy Spirit, and we must interpret everything we read in a Christ-centred way. We need great humility in doing this: firstly the humility to listen to those who we might think are quite wrong, as their perspective might bring fresh light to us, and, secondly, if we still conclude that we disagree, we need the humility to argue our case without hostility or contempt, and within the bonds of fellowship. This will usually involve us in the conclusion that even if we disagree, even if we have listened carefully and still are convinced that the other person is wrong, we have no warrant to conclude they are not Christians if they are trying to wrestle with the Bible, however mistakenly in our opinion, and if they are still

---

349   *Get A Grip On Mission*, Martin Goldsmith, p.217 (IVP, 2006)
350   John 5:39–40

seeking to follow Jesus Christ, however falteringly or imperfectly in our opinion.

WHAT CAN JUSTIFY THE CONCLUSION THAT SOMEONE IS NO LONGER 'IN CHRIST'?

But does no amount of wrong thinking put a person outside the Christian faith? Explicit and complete abandonment of any willingness to recognise the authority of the Bible surely does. Scripture is the word of God in a secondary and derivative sense, Jesus being the living Word. However, this effectively enhances, and does not weaken, the authority of the Bible, which is the only objective authority for how we know Jesus and who He is. Rejection of the Bible cuts off our understanding of Jesus from objective roots. Similarly, turning against Jesus and rejecting Him as our Lord surely puts a person outside the boundaries of the Christian faith. We should, however, be slow to reach such conclusions about those who claim to be followers of Jesus. We know so little of each other's inner minds and are so prone to errors of judgment ourselves. We so easily assume that because someone does not think as we do about scripture they must have rejected the Bible. We need to heed Jesus' words, 'Who are you to judge someone else's servant? To their own master servants stand or fall.'[351]

But surely there comes a time when we must judge? What about those times when we feel, in conscience, that we must take a stand against what someone else is saying or doing? What about when institutional decisions have to be made, such as when people are being selected for ordained ministry, or decisions have to be made whose books shall form part of a training curriculum? Some form of judgment is unavoidable. The next chapter is about how we might disagree in a way that imitates Jesus, and Chapter 9 is about whether,

---

351   Romans 14:4

when institutional decisions are involved, the imitation of Christ is even possible.

THE JOURNEY SO FAR

The majority of churchgoers do not seem to read the Bible regularly. This probably explains a great deal.

However, it is not enough just to read the Bible. We need to read it actively, searchingly, and questioningly, but submissively. This could as well be called 'letting the Bible read us'. Submissive Bible reading can be feisty, even argumentative. Indeed it is probably better if it is.

We need to read all of it. Selective Bible reading inevitably has an agenda, whoever does the selecting.

God called the church to be diverse and to cross boundaries. When, in the church, we find ourselves mainly with others just like us, this should be a danger signal. We need to read and interpret the Bible in fellowship with those whose cultures, temperaments, and vested interests are different from ours, if we are to avoid the trap of importing our own prejudices into the process.

If our experience of the world does not sit easily with our understanding of scripture, then a person of integrity will re-examine their interpretation of the data from both sources.

Sometimes, often through long familiarity, we just cannot imagine another way of understanding scripture. It is here in particular that the insights of people different from ourselves can be helpful, as can close attention to our context.

We should similarly be alerted when there seems to be a divergence between the character and values of Jesus, and the fruits of any of our interpretations of scripture. After all, He is the interpretative key to the scriptures that all bear witness to Him.

It is in fact a form of idolatry to objectify our interpretation of scripture as if that interpretation were the 'Word of God'.

Given all of this, we must be very cautious in concluding that someone else is not a Christian if they claim to follow Jesus as Lord and are seeking to be faithful to scripture.

CHAPTER EIGHT

DISAGREEING WITHOUT BEING DISAGREEABLE?

'The primary task of the leadership of the church
is to help in the receiving of grace.'

ROBERT WARREN[352]

PANDERING TO THE SPIRIT OF THE AGE?

In Chapter 3 I raised the question of whether what I'm saying isn't just an accommodation to the spirit of the age.[353] Just be nice to everyone, be tolerant and all will be OK. 'Faith, hope and niceness remain, and the greatest of these is niceness.' Of course, in theory it is much easier to take this approach if you believe that there is no such thing as 'truth', if at best there is only truth 'for you'. Once we believe that Jesus is 'the way, the truth and the life',[354] we are in a different ball game.

Christians have a bad reputation for arguing, condemning and falling out for at least two reasons. Firstly because whenever we forget the example of Jesus, we are (like most people) simply not very good at handling diversity, disagreement and power. The second reason is that, unlike many today, we believe in 'truth' that is real and discoverable.

---

352   *Being Human, Being Church*, Robert Warren, p.117 (Marshall Pickering, 1995)
353   Or possibly the age that is just ending and ushering in a new age of intolerance and aggression?
354   John 14:6

To those who believe in no such thing many of our debates will sound pointless, however politely or respectfully conducted.

As Antonia Senior put it, 'To the atheist, most theological schisms look, well, barmy. Bonkers. From the moment Paul and Peter first started squabbling about the great man's legacy, Christianity has been riven with splits that seem comically absurd to those of little faith.'[355]

Firstly, when we have failed to disagree well, we need to respond with repentance and humility. Secondly, we need to respond by living in a way that shows to those who do not believe in revealed truth that truth matters. We also need to show that by 'truth' we do not just mean 'my view of the truth', and that, like Jesus, we do not intend to use 'truth' as a power hold over others. Truth is nailed down in Jesus in a way that defuses these threats. To these tasks we now turn.

Integrity May Demand Contention

It is not necessarily wrong to be contentious. Jude writes 'I felt compelled to write and urge you to contend for the faith that was once for all entrusted to God's holy people.'[356]

Perhaps one of the clearest examples of the necessity for contention in modern times was Dietrich Bonhoeffer's resistance to the Protestant Reich Church.[357]

Bonhoeffer had moved into outright opposition to the Nazis after 1933, when the government forced Protestant churches to merge into the state-controlled Protestant Reich Church, and to support Nazi ideology. The central question for Bonhoeffer was 'Whose church is it?' The answer, of course, was Jesus Christ's, not the state's, therefore the state had no authority to ordain anything contrary to the word of God

---

355   *The Times*, 31/10/09. Of course she misunderstands the dispute between Paul and Peter, but that is partly the point. People often don't understand and so do not see the point of what we are arguing about.

356   Jude 3

357   I am indebted in what follows to *Dietrich Bonhoeffer*, Eberhard Bethge (Fount, 1977).

in scripture. The sharpest issue was the so-called Nuremberg Laws, which restricted Jews, and the application of these laws to exclude Jews from the church. Bonhoeffer was clear that compromise with the state by the so-called German Christians, or Reich Church, was nothing less than heresy and idolatry, and that one could not therefore remain within the Reich Church without betraying Jesus Christ. It was time to separate.

He was up against his non-negotiables, the place where compromise becomes a sin, not a virtue. He expressed it graphically by saying 'If you board the wrong train, it is no use running along the corridor in the other direction.'

Most, if not all, today would readily agree that Bonhoeffer was right, but, at the time, the overwhelming majority who claimed to be Christian did not go with him. So what grounds do we have for the rather naïve assumption that we would necessarily have been any different? What was it that helped Bonhoeffer to discern where to take a stand, and could this help us to discern similarly?

Firstly, he feared God more than he feared Hitler. He trusted in heaven and overcame his fear of death.[358]

Secondly, he was a careful and biblical theologian. He had a very high regard for the ultimate authority of the Word of God in Scripture, and he took care and prayer to work out its meaning and implications. He was no quoter of proof texts, taking passages out of context and waving them like battle standards. He knew that the truth is not always obvious. It takes care to discern, particularly the care to know the Bible inside out and back to front.

Thirdly, he was centred upon Jesus Christ. When defining God, Bonhoeffer liked to quote Luther, who would point to Jesus and declare: "This man is God for me." This had huge implications. Jesus was a Jew, thus he could not go along with anti-Semitism. Jesus is Lord, therefore neither the state, nor the Reich Church, nor Adolf Hitler could claim

---

358   See p.19

that authority. He recognised that false gods and false religion could easily masquerade under the banner of the church.

Fourthly, he had learned to look from the perspective of the poor and outcast. He had been exposed to the plight of the poorest and weakest while in the United States, where he had witnessed racial discrimination in the 1930s. As a pastor he had come alongside the poor. He knew and had befriended Jews. These experiences provided him with what he called 'the view from below', that is, the perspective of those who suffer from maltreatment, powerlessness and oppression. This for him was a key to the right understanding of the Gospel.

Thus Bonhoeffer saw when others failed to see. It cost him dearly.

Dietrich Bonhoeffer was executed by the Nazis on 9 April 1945 at Flossenbürg concentration camp.

I am not arguing for 'niceness' in the way that we disagree or live together with difference. We do not have a calling to be 'nice', but rather to be Christlike. This means that we are liable to be those who will be oppressed, or even like Bonhoeffer, liable to lose our life, but we will not ourselves become the persecutors.[359] I wonder how people would perceive us if we conducted a survey using the question, 'What do you think Christians are more likely to be: persecutors of others or the persecuted?'

On the 'Yahoo! Answers' website there are a few clues. One thread starts,

'In your opinion why are Christians so mean?

I asked a question – when we're standing in line for judgement – will refreshments be served?

I had one tell me "Yes. The cup of wrath", another, "Yep, your head on a platter. Mmmmmm. Dead atheist on rye", and another that said

---

359   Of course Bonhoeffer's part in the Stauffenberg plot to assassinate Hitler raises questions at this point. This is far too big an issue to explore at length here, but an outline of a response would be that Bonhoeffer was following Jesus in acting coercively against those who were using their power to coerce others (see pp.60–61). In fact his involvement was tangential and limited, but he knew about it, and was in regular contact with the plotters.

"You won't have to worry 'bout that, just remember you need lots of fire-retardant clothes".

I am not an atheist, and hope I'm not going to hell. But the assumptions and rude remarks show me why some people say Christians are evil people.

I was just asking because I would imagine the line would be long and we would be there for a while. Yet my light-heartedness was met with viciousness.

Why were they so rude?'

Among the replies on the website were: 'Every Christian is different, most are jerks without realising it, "cup of wrath" is just a part of their vocabulary although it seems harsh to the rest of us. Just steer clear of "Christians".

and

'Christians are the only religion opposing human rights and persecuting gays, pro-choice and so much more – but far worse, whilst they demand freedom of religion they deny it to all non-Christians and persecute them!!!

Simple answer is that they have abandoned the loving god and now worship terrible human emotions!!'

Now, I could take issue with a number of these statements, which clearly contain some inaccuracies and prejudice, but for now that is not the main point. The point is that this is how Christians are seen by many. Our public image is not Christlike. If we're going to be vilified or even persecuted, let us at least be sure it is for Jesus' sake.

Just examine one of the replies, from a Christian; 'What are we supposed to say when you ask such an insulting question? We born again Christians take our Salvation and our Lord seriously. You ask a stupid question you deserve the same back. Christians aren't mean, just fed up with ignorance.'[360] Is that full of grace *and* truth?

There were some gracious responses from Christians, and quite a

---

360   Yahoo! Answers: Religion and Spirituality: Resolved Questions, http://answers.
        yahoo.com/question/index?qid=20081014222248AAGEqcI

number of rather complacent ones, along the lines of 'Well, I'm a nice guy, and so are all the Christians I know'. However, the point is for us to humbly recognise that we are not usually seen as Christlike. If we were, the opposition would probably be far worse.

Now, I may well be preaching to the converted here, in which case I rejoice. But when I look at the reply of the Christian guy who posted the ungracious response, I can recognise, if I am honest, a large element of my own irritated inner response to much of the intemperate and vituperative comment that Christians are increasingly receiving from atheists. My first instinct is often to want to respond in kind. But, 'Human anger does not produce the righteousness that God desires'.[361]

Jesus promised us that we would offend people, in fact, that they would hate and persecute us.[362] There is a huge danger that we might use Jesus' promise of opposition and hate to cover up the offence that we (rather than Jesus) cause. It is so easy to remain impervious to how rude or judgmental we have been by saying, if only to ourselves, 'Well, the Gospel is bound to cause offence'. Yes, but are we quite sure that it was *the Gospel* that caused the offence?

However, some are probably by now squirming with frustration, wanting to make the point that, when Jesus is maligned, we must speak up. The danger again arises that it is so easy to interpret what I am saying as a call to be 'nice'. If we try to be 'nice' we will almost certainly fail to be true to Jesus lest we offend. This is the danger that many German Christians fell into in the 1930s during the church crisis.

'Between 1933 to 1935 in Germany there was further, quite naturally, a certain distaste for anything to do with the distant "church disputes", a term which those in authority, both in party and in state, employed in preference to the term "church struggle". Astutely, they reckoned on widespread aversion among the population to

---

361 James 1:20
362 Matthew 10:22–23

involvement in ecclesiastical or theological disputes. It could even be assumed that a good and pious Christian would rather keep away from "church disputes".[363]

If, guided by the Holy Spirit, we try to concentrate on imitating Jesus, we are going to have to say some fairly unpalatable things. If we speak of the judgment to come, or maintain that 'all have sinned and fall short of the glory of God',[364] or speak of self-control and self-denial, or speak up for the poor and the oppressed, or repeat Jesus' call for repentance, then we will cause offence and stir up opposition. We must make sure, however, that we do not divert attention from Jesus by our own unacceptable behaviour. We are not here to promote a 'cause', but to reflect Jesus.

If we do not speak up, even at risk of causing offence, we play along with the prevailing assumption that all truth is relative, that truth 'for you' is all that matters.

An article by Antonia Senior explains why our philosophical position about 'truth' matters and has important practical consequences. Speaking just after a highly contentious appearance on the BBC programme *Question Time* by Nick Griffin, the then leader of the far right and racist British National Party, she wrote:

'The dominant philosophical framework of the post-war era has been moral relativism; the notion that there are no universal truths. I think bacon is divine; you are a vegetarian; he thinks pig meat is an affront to God. Each of these positions is true, because truth is in the eye of the believer. I think Nick Griffin is a buffoon; you think he is a dangerous fascist; he thinks he is a fearless hero of the Right.

'It (relativism) took off in the twentieth century, prospering in a haze of post-colonial guilt, feeding off a desire to atone for our forefathers' racism and assumptions of superiority. It is a moral code for those who do not want to be impolite or rude. It's the ideology of holding hands in a circle or drinking tea together. Small wonder

---

363   *Dietrich Bonhoeffer*, Eberhard Bethge, p.262 (Fount, 1977)
364   Romans 3:23

it has been so seductive within these shores. Moral relativism, as philosophies go, is just so nice.

'It's a shame, then, that it is also incoherent, logically flawed and utterly tired. Few philosophers take it seriously any more. Yet having escaped the ivory towers, it has taken on a life independent of the theorists. It sits at the heart of our society like a jolly, beaming tumour, eating away at our ability to take on the BNP and their ilk... even though we know we must. We are squeamish about dealing in moral absolutes. It feels counter-intuitive and unbearably arrogant to stand up and say: "I am right and you are wrong."

'There seems to be no middle ground between an absurd relativism and a shouty, strident nastiness.[365]

'The only way to decide if a proposition is true or not, or if an action is right or wrong, is to test it and debate it. This takes more rigour than a lazy assumption that all views are truth and rightness is relative.'[366]

Not only does Christianity (in common with other religions) provide a helpful starting point for the necessary debate by offering philosophical ground to stand on, but Jesus also offers another way between 'an absurd relativism and a shouty, strident nastiness'. Jesus *is* the truth and He is no bully.

Integrity, then, demands a willingness when necessary to dispute and to disagree, and Christians are called to integrity. Jude knew the importance of this and pulls no punches: 'I felt compelled to write and urge you to contend for the faith that was once for all entrusted to God's holy people. For certain individuals whose condemnation was written about long ago have secretly slipped in among you. They are ungodly people, who pervert the grace of our God into a licence for immorality and deny Jesus Christ our only Sovereign and Lord.'[367]

---

365 Senior it seems did not foresee a situation in which the absurd relativism and the strident shouting nastiness could coexist in the same person. The disdain for truth of the propagandist and a certain bullying nastiness seem to have characterised a great deal of the Brexit debate in recent years.

366 Antonia Senior, *The Times,* 23/10/09

367 Jude 3–4

Culture, Temperament and Contention

In Chapter 3 we noted how our culture and temperament both need to be subject to the rule of Christ. We need to become aware of how they affect us, and aware of how they are likely to lead us to see things, or to respond in ways that are not Christlike.

How we handle discussions, arguments and disputes is likely to be strongly influenced by our culture and temperament. I believe that this is an area that receives precious little attention, mainly because our culture and our temperament are like tinted sunglasses that we have forgotten we ever put on. Several times, when fishing, I've said to my companion "Those clouds look a little dark and ominous" only to receive the reply "Not if you take your sunglasses off they don't." Our whole frame of reference is influenced by our culture and character and the world view that results from them, making it very hard indeed to realise that our view has been at all coloured. Other people's cultures and temperaments, however, tend to be obvious to us, especially if they clash with our own.

When I first moved into one particular house, I was amazed at the aggression our Greek neighbours showed to each other. Time and again there were raised voices, and I began to wonder whether their marriage could last much longer. As I got to know them I discovered that they had a good relationship, as far as I could tell, and as I got to know other Greek people I realised that speaking loudly, emphatically and demonstratively was a common Greek characteristic. I had completely misread them, and no doubt they would be amazed to know how, at first, they appeared to me.

I suspect that part of what some see as Nigerian aggression and intransigence in the dispute over homosexual bishops in the Anglican Communion, may be distorted by cultural issues relating to how we debate. What appears to an English person as verbal bullying can be seen by a Nigerian as necessary plain speaking. What appears to a Nigerian as duplicity and dishonesty can appear to an English person as a necessary reticence and sensitivity in not pushing our view down someone's throat. Consider one possible Nigerian perception, that the English person has no need to push his views, because for centuries the English (the former colonial power) have had the power to do what they want anyway, without consultation or discussion. The English person may be quite oblivious to this and reply if asked, "What power?" The ground is then set for major misunderstanding.

Such uncovering of assumptions and cultural luggage is a necessary step if we are to understand and really hear each other. However, it is only a start. Jesus requires us to go further.

Firstly, culture does not explain all of the perceived aggression and bitterness that is going on within the Anglican Communion as I write. Secondly, all cultures are under the judgment of Jesus Christ; they are not sacrosanct. In this instance, at the risk of oversimplifying or stereotyping, it could be that English unwillingness to speak plainly, Nigerian assertiveness, and possibly American unilateral wilfulness, are all challenged by the example of Jesus.

It took me a long time to begin to be aware of these issues. My father-in-law, a very wise and humane man, often used to warn me that, in a debate, I would "win the argument and lose the person". I grew up in a disputatious family with levels of aggression in argument that, I now realise, seemed extraordinary to some outsiders. Many mealtimes developed into a political debate (most would say argument), of some ferocity. In particular, manifestations of contempt for opposing opinions were quite normal. It was how one made one's point if one felt strongly, and we seemed to feel strongly about most things. No doubt that is partly why I am now writing this book. It took a long time to understand that in most disputes there were at least two distinct issues, firstly, the substance of the issue, and secondly, how I spoke to (and about) my opponents. Eventually it dawned on me that Jesus (normally)[368] modelled a very different way of dealing with disagreement.

---

368   See p.57f. for the exceptions and their significance.

I used to attend the conferences of a Christian movement that made frequent use of Jude 3, 'I felt I had to write and urge you to contend for the faith that was once for all entrusted to the saints'. I have already argued that truth matters, and we need to give this verse its full weight.

However, this was all at around the time that I was becoming aware that I had, perhaps, a slightly (some would contest the 'perhaps' and the 'slightly') contentious personality. I began to wonder how much of this contention was from me, and how much from a Jesus-centred biblical mandate. As I wondered, I could not help noticing that, of the participants in the conferences I attended, very many (but not all) had a personality like mine. This would not have been such an issue if there had been *some* sign of an awareness that verses like Jude 3 played into and fed off elements of a contentious personality that other verses might challenge, for example Romans 12:18, 'If it is possible, as far as it depends on you, live at peace with everyone'.

Our personalities are part of God's gift to us of ourselves. I do not believe that, when we are converted, God gives us a personality transplant, turning extroverts into introverts, and the spontaneous and impulsive into careful planners, or vice versa. Why should He want to? The world needs these various types and many more, and so does God. However, I believe that the Holy Spirit, as a secondary part of leading us into all truth,[369] will help us to understand our own personality better so that we can hear Jesus better, and be aware of when our own instinctive preferences are causing a distorting echo. A good soul friend, pastor or spiritual director is valuable beyond price in this process.

In itself it need not be a problem that some of us are by nature contentious. If truth and love sometimes demand contention, we could

---

369 The primary part, of course, is helping us to know and understand Jesus. The secondary part, however, is crucially important because, as I hope I have already demonstrated, we cannot adequately know or imitate Jesus unless we adequately know ourselves.

be a gift to the Kingdom of God. However, lack of self-knowledge has the potential to deafen us to much that Jesus says to us. I looked at this in a little more detail in Chapter 3.[370] This applies to every personality type. After all, every self-selecting group has dangerous tendencies towards homogeneity if we are not careful. I'm sure that I could equally have found more eirenic groups of Christians with similar personality traits to each other, giving inadequate attention to those parts of Jesus' life that provoked opposition (much of the centre ground of the Church of England?). We need, as I noted in Chapter 3, to allow Jesus' personality to be a lens, or perhaps in this case a prism, to allow us to better understand the elements that make up our own.

The Argument Culture

Linguistics professor Deborah Tannen has analysed the discourse of dispute and discussion, and persuasively demonstrated a number of ways in which our increasingly media-driven practice falls short of what is decent, fair or constructive.[371]

She argues that deeply embedded in Anglo Saxon culture is the assumption that an adversarial approach is the best way to sort out problems. However, the habitual oppositional stance that often results can prevent listening and learning and even, in the end, subvert democracy.

'Democracy begins in conversation and gets derailed in polarised debate. Of course, it is the responsibility of intellectuals to explore potential weaknesses in others' arguments, and of journalists to represent serious opposition when it exists. But when opposition becomes the overwhelming avenue of inquiry – a formula that requires another side to be found or a criticism to be voiced; when the lust for

---

370   p.74–79
371   *The Argument Culture*, Deborah Tannen (Virago Press, 1998). What is true of the conventional media that Tannen analyses is now even more true of social media.

opposition privileges extreme views and obscures complexity, when our eagerness to find weaknesses blinds us to strengths; when the atmosphere of animosity precludes respect and poisons our relations with one another; then the argument culture is doing more damage than good... smashing heads does not open minds.'[372] She argues that this produces cynicism, especially about leaders and public figures, and leads to an atmosphere of hopelessness.

Tannen has here fairly accurately described the course of and outcomes from the Brexit campaign in the UK with its simplistic polarisation of complex issues, and resulting vitriol, threats and political paralysis.

Particularly in journalism, but increasingly in everyday conversation, metaphors of war and battle are used for any debate, however friendly. Positions are attacked, enemies are routed. Synod does not discuss, it has a 'fight'. People do not 'disagree', or 'express an alternative point of view', they are 'angry with', they 'dismiss' or 'rubbish'. Arguments are 'shot down'. An exchange of views becomes a spat.

This need to approach all issues adversarially leads to the assumption that every argument has two equal sides (it may not, or the other side might be so trivial or so extreme as not to deserve equal attention, or there may be many sides). She cites a campaign to place holocaust denying adverts in student newspapers across the US. 'In justifying his decision to run the ad, for example, an editor at the State University College at Buffalo student newspaper explained, "There are two sides to every issue and both have a place on the pages of any open-minded paper's editorial page."'[373]

Listen to the *Today Programme* on any weekday morning in the UK and you will regularly hear the two most extreme proponents of opposing cases slugging it out. This is supposed to get us nearer to 'the truth'. But much 'truth' is nuanced, and often the truth is not to

---

372   Tannen (op. cit.), p.27–8
373   Tannen (op. cit.), p.41

be found at the extremes. This approach commonly leads to cynicism and apathy. 'Persistent putting of "the other side" leads to a culture that believes there is always another side, so it is not worth committing to anything at all.'[374] The system we have developed privileges extreme views and obfuscates the truth.

The very word 'debate', which I have used a good deal in this book, is problematic. Debates can be useful, but the word implies a contest with a winner and a loser. Often a *conversation* would be more appropriate. A conversation is a *mutual* attempt to discover truth and to enlarge shared understanding. A conversation tends to build relationship rather than producing winners and losers.

The 2008 Lambeth Conference, with its background of polarising disagreements over homosexuality, was set up to avoid the debate format with its winners and losers, and rather to encourage conversation, in small groups, based around Bible study and mutual listening (the so-called 'Indaba'[375] process). There was much criticism of this approach as an avoidance of the issues, as a pandering to one side or the other, or as unprincipled. I wonder. The *issue* was not suppressed, but power games were. This, to me, appears a rather Christian thing to have done.

This model was again adopted for a series of 'Shared Conversations' across the Church of England between 2014 and 2016. In 2013 the House of Bishops Working Group on Human Sexuality recommended that 'The subject of sexuality, with its history of deeply entrenched views, would be best addressed by facilitated conversations or a similar process to which the Church of England needs to commit itself at national and diocesan level.'[376]

'The facilitated conversations have taken place to create safe spaces in which questions of difference and disagreement can be explored in relation to questions of scripture, mission and human sexuality.

---

374 Tannen (op. cit.), p.13
375 A Zulu word for a process by which a community takes time to chew over divisive issues in an attempt to discover common ground and to facilitate living together.
376 'Shared Conversations' website: http://www.sharedconversations.org/

They started with the premise that sound judgements about others must start with adequate knowledge about who the "other" is, and what they actually believe and practise. When members of the church draw different conclusions from their reading of scripture and hold that God's call to his people has implications for conduct and ethics which others within the church dispute strongly, knowing the "other" becomes crucial.'[377]

These conversations were not designed to change minds or to reach decisions, but to better understand one another as well as the issues, and to model a better process through which decisions might eventually be made. I took part in the regional shared conversations in 2016 and my experience was that in terms of these aims they were a resounding success. Painful and difficult decisions still have to be made within the Church of England and the Anglican Communion, but I believe there is a realistic hope that the way we make the decisions is likely to be greatly improved, probably leading to better decisions in the end (whatever they may be).

Deborah Tannen pertinently asks, 'In an argument, do we listen? Is our aim to win, or to reach the truth?'[378] If Jesus is the truth, and we prefer winning, then we have chosen an idol in place of the truth.

Just before the passage in which we are assured that man's anger does not achieve the righteousness of God, James writes, 'Everyone should be quick to listen, slow to speak and slow to become angry.'[379] It is hard to believe that he was not thinking of the character of his brother, Jesus, as he wrote this.

Listening is not assisted by the impersonal (often anonymous) nature of much modern communication. I'm still troubled by an online discussion that I read an hour before writing this, while looking up something on *The Times* website. It was all in response to an article critical of the Post Office. Words like 'rubbish' and 'clown!'

---

377 'Shared Conversations' website ibid.
378 Tannen (op. cit.), p.7
379 James 1:19

appear, and sneering references to 'uneducated and unwashed union masses'. The stench of contempt was pervasive. It was not an exercise in enlightenment, but an exercise in point-scoring at best, and in hatred at worst. This example is fairly typical and, in fact, rather mild compared to many I could have chosen from even the more civilised internet discussions. I simply choose this example because I happened to stumble upon it in the last hour. I fear for our future. Such mutual disdain, regularly stoked as it is, can fuel a roaring furnace of anger and is likely to end in an inability to trust or co-operate with anybody. If anger is stoked for long enough it is likely to issue in repression and violence. We are sowing the wind, and who knows what whirlwind we will reap?[380]

We would not normally dream of speaking to anyone face to face in these terms, but the rise of abrupt and sometimes anonymous electronic communication, blogs, social media, emails, texts, is facilitating the ratcheting up of conflict at an alarming rate.[381]

Sometimes clear decisions need to be made. Then a debate and a clear vote might be necessary. Sometimes an Indaba-type consensus building approach can be open to manipulation. However, often, face-to-face listening is what is required even more than a clear decision. A clear decision that leads to nearly half the participants taking their ball away and leaving the game is probably not going to be very productive, nor is a majority decision to oppress a minority. Quality listening and conversation tends to lead to better decisions in the end, to more people owning those decisions, and to mutual respect between protagonists.

We have seen that Jesus broke down barrier after barrier, widening access to the Kingdom of God to all sorts of unlikely comers, and then insisting that, as brothers and sisters, the members of that Kingdom break down the barriers between themselves.

Many problems in the Christian community can be solved by

---

380   I wrote this before the Brexit and Trump campaigns, which I think have ratcheted up these problems considerably.

381   Tannen (op. cit.), p.245–248

a willingness to listen and a refusal to rush to judgment. Marlene Cohen describes how a new vicar moved into a parish to find the vicarage unprepared. The sub-committee responsible had felt that they were leaving choices open for him, such as choosing the colours. He just perceived lack of care. This simmered for a while until, with Marlene's facilitation, discussion of the issue quickly removed misunderstanding and defused perceived hurts and slights that could easily have festered in the background for years after the initial cause was forgotten.[382]

This kind of approach is not a way of avoiding conflict, which would be unhealthy and a way of storing up unexploded bombs for the future. Rather it is a way of facing conflict. Peace at any price is unprincipled and counterproductive. 'Co-operation is not the absence of conflict but a means of managing conflict.'[383]

If Deborah Tannen's analysis of the trends of our culture is at all right, then the last thing our society needs is a church that avoids conflict. It desperately needs a church that models a better way of handling conflict.

In the face of a worldwide crisis of democracy, with rising populism, resulting in Trump, Brexit, the rise of the extreme right in Europe and increasing disenchantment with mainstream politicians, we find polarisation and anger all around us. Christians could and should have a key role to play in demonstrating a better way forward. Jesus offers and demonstrates better ways to disagree, better ways to treat our enemies, and a model for respecting, listening to and empowering the excluded and marginalised in our communities. A faithful and Christ-centred church has it within its grasp to be profoundly transformative in such circumstances.

However, we are not always good news at present. The tendency to disfellowship one another, and to use communion as a weapon, reinforces all that is worst in the world around us. The use of tools

---

382 *The Divided Self*, Marlene Cohen, p.74–75 (Marshall Pickering, 1996)
383 Tannen (op. cit.) p.28

such as 'Shared Conversations' points in a much more positive direction. I am just beginning to hope that Christlike responses might just be beginning to outweigh the un-Christlike. In particular the vastly more gracious way in which the issue of the ordination of women bishops was resolved, after the use of a similar 'indaba' process to Shared Conversations, is a powerful pointer to a better way forward.[384] I recently reviewed the contents and in particular the letter pages of the *Church of England Newspaper* from recent months, in order to monitor the tone and standard of debate. Some years ago I found this contained so much that was contemptuous, disdainful, abusive, hateful and fundamentally un-Christlike (especially from those on the same side of the argument as me), that I ceased to subscribe. This time I found a much more gracious approach to disagreement. It was no less clear (in fact probably clearer), and no less firm, but markedly less hateful. I found hope for the church's witness beginning to creep back into me.

It is too early to tell whether these signs of hope are just a lull in the storm, or a harbinger of something better. There is always a danger in times of contention and controversy that we tend to hear from the 'stroppy' and contemptuous, while the majority keep their heads down and assume that it is somehow un-Christian to take part in an argument at all.

Robert Warren has written that,

'The danger here is that the church handles conflict by sweeping it under the carpet, often because the feeling is abroad that "Christians should not disagree". A church where there was no conflict has little relevance to our society. A church that has found a way to handle conflict creatively will be good news to all around and in it.'[385]

Joshua 22:10–end is a good example of the kind of listening I am talking about, in a dispute about a hard or a soft border. Immediately after the initial conquest of the Promised Land 'the Reubenites, the

---

384   See p.215–217
385   *Being Human, Being Church*, Robert Warren, p.17 (Marshall Pickering, 1995)

Gadites and the half-tribe of Manasseh built an imposing altar there by the Jordan'.[386] The rest of Israel was furious and alarmed, believing that the three tribes were founding a new religion and deserting the God who had saved them. War was in the air. There was already a history of suspicion between the two sides, which had once before been resolved by straight talking and mutually submissive listening (despite some intemperate words from Moses).[387] On this second occasion Israel expressed its concern to the three tribes, saying "If you rebel against the Lord today, tomorrow he will be angry with the whole community of Israel. If the land you possess is defiled, come over to the Lord's land, where the Lord's tabernacle stands, and share the land with us. But do not rebel against the Lord or against us by building an altar for yourselves, other than the altar of the Lord our God. When Achan, son of Zerah, was unfaithful in regard to the devoted things, did not wrath come on the whole community of Israel? He was not the only one who died for his sin."[388]

I notice that though they were alarmed, angry and talking of war, they addressed the supposedly 'rebel' tribes face to face. They did not soft-pedal their anxieties and concerns but explained them fully. They made a potentially costly gesture, offering to share their own land to keep the unity of the tribes intact. They did not wait for a climb down, but first made a real offer that showed good faith and a desire to reach a settlement. They were not primarily looking for 'victory' (which they no doubt could have achieved with their overwhelming numerical superiority) but for a mutually helpful solution.

They then listened while the three tribes responded. Their explanation was that they had no intention of ceasing to worship the Lord, in fact quite the opposite: 'No! We did it for fear that some day your descendants might say to ours, "What have you to do with the

---

386   Joshua 22:10
387   Numbers 32
388   Joshua 22:18–20

Lord, the God of Israel? The Lord has made the Jordan a boundary between us and you... you Reubenites and Gadites! You have no share in the Lord." So your descendants might cause ours to stop fearing the Lord. That is why we said, "Let us get ready and build an altar".'[389]

The three tribes had the humility to respond in a detailed and conciliatory way. They allowed themselves to be called to account and gave a detailed explanation designed to inform rather than obfuscate. Point-scoring and face-saving do not appear to have been part of either side's agenda.

Peace and mutual understanding were achieved.

'When Phinehas the priest and the leaders of the community... heard what Reuben, Gad and Manasseh had to say, they were pleased... (and said)... "Today we know that the Lord is with us, because you have not been unfaithful toward the Lord in this matter. Now you have rescued the Israelites from the Lord's hand".'[390]

Phinehas seemed to feel no need to defend his original misunderstanding. He was in fact able to rejoice that he had been wrong. In an argument culture, or an 'out to win' culture, people will often not admit it when shown to have made the wrong assumptions, even, as here, when the correction gives news that they want to hear. It is somehow a loss of face to admit to having misunderstood the situation. Or perhaps it is just not playing 'the game' (which is to argue). I'm sure we have all heard debates between politicians, in which it quickly becomes apparent that the differences between each side are minimal or non-existent, but as the game is arguing, they have to continue, and so resort to scoring cheap points or misrepresenting the other side. It is tedious almost beyond endurance. On many mornings it is in the middle of such a discussion that my radio gets switched off.

---

389 Joshua 22:24–26
390 Joshua 22:30–31

WINNERS CAN BE SUCH LOSERS

Constructive argument, perhaps better called conversation or discussion, is more demanding than criticism. Tannen says 'One reason the argument culture is so widespread is that arguing is so easy to do. Lynne Hewitt, Judith Duchan, and Erwin Segal came up with a fascinating finding: Speakers with language disabilities who had trouble taking part in other types of verbal interaction were able to participate in arguments. Observing adults with mental retardation who lived in a group home, the researchers found that the residents often engaged in verbal conflicts as a means of prolonging interaction. It was a form of sociability. Most surprising, this was equally true of two residents who had severe language and comprehension disorders yet were able to take part in the verbal disputes, because arguments have a predictable structure.'[391]

'Criticising relieves you of the responsibility of doing integrative thinking, and can make you appear "smarter" than someone who has spent years studying the problem.'[392] Perhaps if it were more widely known that argumentativeness sits so well with mental limitations, this approach might cease to seem so superficially 'smart'.

Criticism has its place. It is an important tool for testing hypotheses, but it is only one tool among many, and if we use it to the exclusion of other methods of engaging, it will prevent us learning. If we cannot bear to discover that the other person has something to teach us, if we have to prove that we are right all the time by proving others wrong, we will be the proud possessors of invincible ignorance. Such an attitude is close cousin to that which Jesus criticised in the parable of the Pharisee and the tax collector. Luke introduces this by saying, 'To some who were confident of their own righteousness and looked down on everyone else, Jesus told this parable:'[393] Those who

---

391   Tannen (op. cit.), p.278
392   Tannen (op. cit.), p.281
393   Luke 18:9

need to prove others wrong to establish their own rightness will have a hard job seeing that they need to be forgiven and justified by Jesus Christ. They will be too proud and defensive. They will be like those of whom Paul writes, 'Since they did not know the righteousness of God and sought to establish their own, they did not submit to God's righteousness.'[394] At the heart of this problem of negative arguing is a profound spiritual problem. It was the problem of the Pharisees. It is an attitude that Jesus said made it impossible to perceive Him or His message.[395] It is a form of pride that too often characterises religious people. If we find ourselves arguing in a mainly negative way within the church, whatever the rightness of our cause, alarm bells should ring for us. We are probably doing ourselves even more harm than we are doing to our opponents.

Scott Peck calls such people, 'People of the Lie', arguing that real evil is the refusal to receive any criticism or acknowledge any personal sin. 'The central defect of the evil is not the sin but the refusal to acknowledge it.'[396] Thus he speaks of finding in prisons what he calls 'honest sinners', people who do not feel they have to pretend any more. After a visit to Pentonville Prison during Christmas 1988, the late Bishop Jim Thompson said, "It's such a relief to be working with people who have already been found out."[397] These are not really evil people. The truly evil normally cloak themselves in respectability and will not acknowledge, even to themselves, that they could be guilty of any serious sin.

'Unpleasant though it may be, the sense of personal sin is precisely that which keeps our sin from getting out of hand. It is quite painful at times, but it is a very great blessing because it is our one and only effective safeguard against our own proclivity for evil. Saint Theresa of Lisieux put it so nicely in her gentle way: 'If you are willing to serenely

---

394   Romans 10:3
395   Matthew 13:13–15
396   *The People of the Lie*, Scott Peck, p.77 (Arrow, 1990)
397   *STAR* (*The Stepney Area Newsletter*, January 1989)

bear the trial of being displeasing to yourself, then you will be for Jesus a pleasant place of shelter.'[398] The truly evil really cannot bear the trial of being displeasing to themselves.'[399]

A predominant feature of 'the people of the lie' as Scott Peck calls them, is scapegoating.

'Scapegoating works through a mechanism that psychiatrists call projection. Since the evil, deep down, feel themselves to be faultless, it is inevitable that when they are in conflict with the world, they will invariably perceive the conflict as the world's fault. Since they must deny their own badness, they must perceive others as bad. They project their own evil onto the world. They never think of themselves as evil; on the other hand, they consequently see much evil in others.'[400] Such people are often destructive because they devote a great deal of energy to destroying the evil they therefore see in the world.[401] People who are only ever against things are bad news. This is a characteristic sin of certain types of Christians. Usually they hanker after some imagined golden age in the past and see every change as a decline from this. Surely Jesus rather calls us to build for a better *future*.

Peck further argues that 'The words "image", "appearance", and "outwardly" are crucial to understanding the morality of the evil.

---

398 Ibid. p.77

399 Peck, in a passage that might shed some light on Donald Trump's notoriously thin-skinned inability to face truth, further comments (op. cit. p.83) that the 'people of the lie' might equate 'the fear of self-criticism with the fear of death. Self-criticism is a call to personality change. As soon as I criticise a part of myself I incur an obligation to change that part. But the process of personality change is a painful one. It is like a death. The old personality pattern must die for a new pattern to take its place. The evil are pathologically attached to the status quo of their personalities, which in their narcissism they consciously regard as perfect. I think it is quite possible that the evil may perceive even a small degree of change in their beloved selves as representing total annihilation. In this sense, the threat of self-criticism may feel to one who is evil synonymous with the threat of extinction.' This of course links with Chapter 4, 'Dying to Self' (and the fear of death).

400 Ibid. p.82

401 Again, as a description of President Donald Trump's way of working, this is eerily accurate. Only a group of Christians who have lost sight of our primary calling to be imitators of Jesus Christ could possibly facilitate the election of such a person.

While they seem to lack any motivation to *be* good, they intensely desire to *appear* good. Their "goodness" is all on a level of pretence. It is, in effect, a lie. This is why they are the "people of the lie".

'Actually the lie is designed not so much to deceive others as to deceive themselves. They cannot or will not tolerate the pain of self-reproach: The decorum with which they lead their lives is maintained as a mirror in which they can see themselves reflected righteously'... 'Since the primary motive of the evil is disguise, one of the places evil people are most likely to be found is within the church. What better way to conceal one's evil from oneself, as well as from others, than to be a deacon or some other highly visible form of Christian within our culture?'[402]

I hesitate to say this, but some who are strident, unwilling to listen, 'sure of their own righteousness', contemptuous or otherwise destructive in their crusade against sin are probably just such people as Scott Peck describes. I hesitate to say it because it can be infuriating and utterly unfair for the many people who are contending for what they believe to be right out of genuinely held conviction to be so labelled. However, if we are apparently more concerned in our zeal to overcome evil in the world than in ourselves, then the cap may fit.

To be obsessed with criticising others is to lead the most joyless of existences, replacing the excitement of discovery with the monotony of certitude and the fear of defensiveness. 'The truth' however, 'will set you free'.[403]

Willingness to be proved wrong is the basis on which scientific discovery operates. Tim Lenton once wrote an article in the *Church of England Newspaper* headlined, 'Being Right Versus the Joy of Discovery'. It described how the 'Voyager' visit to Neptune has shown scientists that many of their previously held theories about the planet were in fact quite wrong. Pointing out that the more we find out about a subject,

---

402   Ibid. p.84–5
403   John 8:32

the more it seems we have to throw out many of our previously held assumptions, he asks why it is that people are often most dogmatic about those areas of knowledge about which they know least. 'The excitement of science lies in discovery rather than in theorising. Unfortunately in science as in so many other areas, including religion, there are many who are more concerned with being conventionally right than with making incredible discoveries. Christianity seems to have shifted away from discovery and into "rightness". Churches today are more concerned with being sound than with finding out more about the richness of God. The paradox is that those who are so concerned with being right turn out to be wrong. Not only that, they lose the opportunity to revel, like those Voyager scientists, in the joy of discovery.'[404]

WEAKER BRETHREN

Winning an argument can be harmful even when we are technically right. One of the best biblical examples of how *winning* the argument might not always be our best aim, occurs in 1 Corinthians Chapter 8, which deals with a dispute between two Christians (or groups of Christians). The difference is over whether meat that has been first offered to a pagan idol (probably a form of ritual slaughter) and then offered for sale in a meat market, should be eaten by a follower of Jesus. The first group knows that idols are not gods and says that no harm is done in consuming such meat as long as you are not personally participating in pagan worship. The other group, probably converts newly escaped out of just such pagan practices, is much more disturbed by the idea of eating such meat. To them it seems like the thin end of the wedge, the first movement in a slide back into their old bondage to idols. Paul says to the first group, "Yes, you are probably right in your argument, but nevertheless if you go ahead and eat this

---

404   Tim Lenton, *Church of England Newspaper*, summer (precise date unknown) 1989

meat, and it becomes a stumbling block for these new converts whose faith is not yet strong enough to handle these subtleties, then you are still guilty of sin, the sin of not loving your brothers and sisters who find this a stumbling block." He deals with the insufferable arrogance of the habitually right, the wilfulness of the expert on everything, with the wonderful observation, 'knowledge puffs up while love builds up. Those who think they know something do not yet know as they ought to know. But whoever loves God is known by God.'[405]

We are rarely so much in danger of getting it badly wrong as when we are utterly convinced we are right.

Leaving Your Weapons Outside the Room

We have already established that Jesus was fundamentally non-coercive. This approach was overwhelmingly reinforced by the fact that He was, in worldly and political terms, weak and vulnerable. He had no powerful connections, no army, not even a mass movement. When God came to earth, He chose to leave His weapons at the door. This, of course, presents an immediate challenge to anyone in hierarchical authority who attempts to speak for Jesus (more about this in Chapter 9). One great advantage of Jesus' weakness was that, where necessary, Jesus could speak out very challengingly without being coercive, and without even the appearance of bullying.

His cousin, John the Baptist, seems to have learned from Him, speaking out publicly and directly about King Herod's sin, and paying for the privilege with his life.[406] Remember, meekness means power under control,[407] not wimpishness. Imitating Jesus in His meekness does not mean lack of plain speaking, or even, when appropriate, unwillingness to confront. However, there is the world of difference between the confrontational person who is willing to die, and the

---

405   1 Corinthians 8:1b-2

406   Mark 6:17–29

407   See p.53

confrontational person who is willing to kill. The latter can be a Hitler, the former can be a Gandhi. Wherever possible we must leave our weapons outside the room, including manipulation, and subterfuge, position and authority, as well as threat and anger.

In the light of this, I wonder how those Anglican churches who threaten so-called 'quota capping'[408] if their requirements are not met, can expect to operate in this way, and still receive the Lord's blessing on their ministry, however justified their original requests.[409]

I do try to look at it from their point of view. Often 'quota capping' is wielded against doctrinal or ethical stances that are perceived as illegitimate. The 'cappers' may see it not as blackmail, but as an unwillingness to pay for ministry that they regard as fundamentally unsound. They do not wish to pay for more than the cost of their own local ministry because they do not wish to subsidise what they regard as 'unsound' or 'immoral' ministries. There is a part of me that understands and sympathises with this. However, the churches that engage in the practice are usually large and comparatively wealthy, and usually situated in commuter suburbs or in city centres, where it is possible to grow large churches of comparatively affluent and stable people. Those who suffer from the effects of quota capping are often poorer people with less stable lives, on council estates and in deprived districts. As we have seen,[410] the poorer members of the Church of England often give more per head than the richer. However, due to a number of sociological factors, their congregations are smaller, and their budgets more limited. Two such factors are the tendency of the more stable, and therefore more prosperous, to move out to the suburbs and commuter towns, thus depleting inner city congregations,

---

408 'Quota capping': A refusal to pay the 'quota' or payment to their diocese towards the cost of ordained ministry, or, more usually, to pay more than a certain proportion of it. This has sometimes been invoked over concerns about policy towards homosexuality.

409 At first I wrote 'demands' instead of 'requests'. The constant journalistic and political use of the word 'demands' is another of those uses of language that escalates conflict and reduces the scope for conversation and compromise.

410 p.140

and the often extreme instability of the lives of those who are left behind. Effectively therefore, those churches that quota cap are saying that they are prepared to limit the chances of the poor finding Jesus, in order to have their own way about church policy. This is so unlike the ways of Jesus that it is hard to know where to start. It is coercive, it devalues 'His Father's favourite team',[411] the poor, it is manipulative, it disrespects the ministry of others, it is certainly not leaving weapons at the door. If Church of England ministry is so compromised that it can no longer be financially supported, then the response of integrity is to leave the Church of England altogether on the one hand, or to stay and argue the case robustly and straightforwardly without manipulation or power games on the other. Quota capping is sub-Christian in its lack of generosity, its ungraciousness, and its un-Christlike use of power.

Honest and robust disagreement is no shame to Jesus. However much we disagree, we are to interact with straightforward honesty and respect, and without playing power games. It should hardly need to be said that deviousness, manipulation or lack of openness are not what Jesus has modelled for us. If we disagree, we need to say so, directly, to each other's faces, and not behind each other's backs, not dissembling because we find disagreement embarrassing, not sweeping things under the carpet that would be better out in the open. When Peter said one thing and did another, Paul did not first write about it in his letters, or threaten his funding, or sweep it under the carpet. Rather he 'opposed him to his face'.[412]

RECOGNISING CHRIST IN OUR OPPONENTS

Recognising Christ in our opponents and enemies, however hard that may sometimes be, is key to responding to them as Jesus would wish.

This applies irrespective of whether or not they are Christians. Each

411   See p.139
412   Galatians 2:11ff.

of us is created in the image of God. However much we have marred and distorted that image through sin, it is still there. Furthermore, Jesus has died for the salvation of every person, even those whom we would rather curse, a salutary thing to call to mind in the middle of a heated dispute.

With other Christians, however irritating we may find them, we are dealing with family members who share the same spiritual DNA, the Holy Spirit. Like us, they are living temples of God, in whom the Spirit dwells. 'Don't you know that you yourselves are God's temple and that God's Spirit lives among you? If anyone destroys God's temple, God will destroy that person; for God's temple is sacred, and you together are that temple.'[413] Are our disagreements like the healthy structural tension, such as that between a buttress and a wall, which helps support the temple, or is it more like the axe of a vandal who would damage a part of the building that is very precious to its owner?

Paul expresses the same truth in a different image when he says, 'Now you are the body of Christ, and each one of you is a part of it.'[414] I hesitate to call this an image, as it is closer to literal truth. Once we have received the Holy Spirit, the hands, the brains, and tongues that Jesus is acting through are ours.[415] This being the case, if we turn on a brother or sister in Christ in a destructive or a rejecting manner, then we are effectively cutting off our nose to spite our face (or perhaps our 'Head' who is Christ). The Body of Christ is indulging in self harm.

Most of us are much more likely to worry about offending our neighbours than complete strangers. It is in our own interest to avoid starting a civil war with those we have to live among. If we detect the note of contempt, anger, coldness, petulance, dismissiveness or disrespect in our voice or heart when speaking to, or about, a Christian brother or sister, it might be salutary to remember that we will one day be neighbours. We will spend all eternity with this person. 'Who

---

413 1 Corinthians 3:16–17
414 1 Corinthians 12:27
415 'Ours' plural, not 'ours' alone.

are you to judge someone else's servant? To their own master, servants stand or fall. And they will stand, for the Lord is able to make them stand.'[416] The Lord will not agree with us if we mentally consign them to hell.

Therefore, I would ask of those bishops who would not receive Communion at the Lambeth Conference in 2008[417] whether they can be very sure indeed that those with whom they would not share Communion are no longer Christ's? Without this conviction their action was indefensible. At present I do not see how they can possibly have such certainty. Being in communion does not imply agreement about policy. It only assumes we are each 'in Christ', and on this issue we must bend over backwards to give each other the benefit of the doubt. If Jesus gave Holy Communion to Judas moments before Judas betrayed Him, who are we to be more strict?

I wonder if the thoroughly biblical concept of 'spiritual warfare' has led some astray here.[418] Once we believe that we are part of a cosmic struggle between good and evil, between God and the Devil, it *can* be but a short step to demonising our opponents. When Jesus said, 'Get behind me Satan', He recognised that at that point Peter was speaking for the Devil. But this did not lead Jesus to treat Peter like the Devil, or to identify him in other ways with the Devil. In fact, He made a particular point of restoring Peter after the resurrection.[419] It can sometimes be just too tempting to demonise our opponents, either silently in our hearts, or more openly. Even if we only silently

---

416 Romans 14:4
417 http://news.bbc.co.uk/1/hi/uk/7516497.stm 'Though he (Archbishop Greg Venables) came to Canterbury and participated in the service, he was one of several bishops who did not take communion, arguing that he is no longer in communion with many of his colleagues.' (20/7/08)
418 I write as a committed believer in such a concept. If we take Jesus' life and example seriously, I believe we must conclude that His understanding of the Devil and his angels is much more likely to be correct than ours. Such an understanding was not universal in His culture, and cannot be dismissed as a culturally limited view. As one who came from heaven to reveal God among us, I would rather trust Jesus' assessment of these things than go with modern scepticism, which I believe is culturally bound and partial.
419 Mark 16:7, John 21:15–19

demonise people in our thoughts, it will leak out in other ways, in contempt and disdain, or suspicion or even fear. Is it even remotely possible to demonise our opponents and at the same time love them?

It can help enormously to pray for our opponents and enemies and as we do, to identify a number of things about them to thank God for. Regularly repeated this can transform our innermost attitudes.

I have tried to establish that there are times when it is our duty to contend for truth. To do so we must understand ourselves well enough to be properly submitted to Jesus Christ, and that we need, as far as possible, to recognise Christ in our opponents. Are there any other biblical guidelines for handling disputes in a Christlike way, and are there any principles that can guide us as to whether or when it is necessary to walk apart?

BELIEVE THE BEST OF EACH OTHER

We should believe the best of each other. Love 'always protects, always trusts, always hopes, always perseveres'.[420] Or in the Authorised Version, 'Beareth all things, believeth all things, hopeth all things, endureth all things'. This is the exact opposite of cynicism, but it is not naïvety. It is an attitude with grit, which can put up with disappointment, and will not say of someone, "Oh, I give up". Take for example teachers who can inspire inner city pupils in struggling comprehensives because they have not given up hope. Such teachers are not naïve. Naïvety would not survive for long in an inner city comprehensive school. They somehow convey to pupils, who have been repeatedly written off, that *they* will not write them off. We all know that low expectations *create* low achievement, and yet it is so easy to fall for cynicism, the science of low expectations. 'Blessed are those who aim at nothing, for they are sure to hit it.'

---

420   1 Corinthians 13:7

Believing the best of each other is not naïve. It is hard-headed – and hopeful. It plans in the light of realities – and it doesn't give up. Believing the best is not burying your head in the sand. If, say, you are supporting an alcoholic, you recognise the strong possibility that they will relapse, but you hope for change and ask God for the faith to believe change possible when that faith begins to flag. Therefore, you encourage them to attend their twelve steps group, and you don't get the bottle of wine out when they come to dinner. The cynic says, "Why bother? They'll probably never change". That is soft: soft-headed, because people do change, and soft on oneself, ducking the cost of offering constructive, up-building support even in the face of disappointment. The only thing that is hard about it is its heart. The person who 'hopes all things, and believes all things' is soft-hearted, but hard-headed, and is 'hard' in the colloquial sense, meaning hardy, able to endure all things. Cynicism is self-defensive and is the refuge of softies who cannot stand the cost of love and truth.

So, when Christians caricature their opponents, choosing to believe the worst, they are doing the Devil's work, not Jesus'. I've already given an example of this (slander of Gene Robinson) on p.11, but it can take many other forms, from the insinuation that all who are concerned for social justice are Communists, to the opposite insinuation that all those who believe in a market economy cannot be true followers of Jesus Christ. It is too easy to assume that anyone who disagrees with us on an issue we regard as 'biblical' is not a true believer.

Dennis Bratcher argues that this is not just a human failing, but a sin that is becoming characteristic of some aspects of 'Christian' culture. 'A growing concern I have about modern holiness groups, and indeed about many evangelical groups, is that we have a tendency to accept almost anything negative we hear about other people, groups, or churches if it fits our own agenda or touches on issues that we have declared to be important. We seem to have developed certain litmus tests of orthodoxy or ethical correctness or righteousness, and then draw conclusions about other people or groups based on how they rate against our test-list of concerns. So, when we hear something negative reported about others, whether through the media or by conversation, we tend to react on the basis of our test. And that is often done blindly, without taking the time to find out if we are being manipulated, whether we have the facts straight, whether there is even any basis to what we have heard, or whether we are indulging in a knee jerk reaction because it is what we want and expect to hear.

How and why have we come to the point that we are driven more by fear and negativity than we are by hope and the possibility of renewal and transformation? I think we have come a long way from the optimism of grace that characterised not only Wesley, but the American Holiness Movement as well!'[421]

The habit of believing the worst happens quite routinely in everyday conversation. 'You *always* forget (insert whatever is your pet frustration)', or 'you betrayed me' when what happened was just an oversight. We all do it at times. We do it to strengthen our case and to express our frustration, though as soon as there is time for a moment's reflection, of course, it weakens our case.

Dennis Bratcher continues, 'It seems to me that too many Christians cruise the media looking for bad news to confirm their worst views of the world. They seem to want to find the worst that goes on, the most outrageous acts of sin or stupidity, and then present them to the rest of us as reflective of what is happening in the world. At best I think that is imbalanced and imprudent; at worst it is a sinful addiction.'[422]

As always the main problem is that it is not Christlike. The Devil is the accuser, not Jesus.[423]

'For God did not send his Son into the world to condemn the world, but to save the world through him.'[424]

---

421   *The Jonah Syndrome*, Dennis Bratcher, now slightly re-written at http://www. crivoice.org/jonahsyndrome.html
422   Ibid.
423   Revelation 12:10
424   John 3:17

The true prophet speaks as a fellow sinner under judgment, not with the accusing voice of the Devil. Amos delivered a message of judgment from God to Israel, but knew that he was part of Israel and pleaded for her out of pity.[425] Jeremiah had a tough message of judgment to deliver, but could also say, "'Discipline me, Lord, but only in due measure – not in your anger, or you will reduce me to nothing'".[426]

If we demonise others, it is hard to feel compassion for them, but Jeremiah could say, "'Oh, that my head were a spring of water and my eyes a fountain of tears! I would weep day and night for the slain of my people'".[427] This is strongly reminiscent of Jesus lamenting over Jerusalem. "'Jerusalem, Jerusalem, you who kill the prophets and stone those sent to you, how often I have longed to gather your children together, as a hen gathers her chicks under her wings, and you were not willing!'"[428] A little later in the same Gospel we read that Jesus wept over Jerusalem.[429] To be Christlike does not necessarily mean refraining from repeating God's words of judgment, but it means that to pronounce such judgment is a bitter grief, not a pleasure, because of mourning for both sinner and victim, and because of an uncomfortable awareness that we are not ourselves above judgment, and must rely upon mercy. Sometimes I have heard sin and sinners condemned from the pulpit with a relish that does not sound remotely like Jesus.[430]

CHRISTLIKE DISAGREEMENT

We have looked at some of the fundamentals for Christlike disagreement. If we attend to these and to the promptings of the Holy Spirit, it will become increasingly obvious what we should do and how

---

425   Amos 7:1–6
426   Jeremiah 10:24
427   Jeremiah 9:1
428   Luke 13:34
429   Luke 19:41
430   I think also of the street preacher in Wood Green Shopping Centre, see p.109.

we should do it. To help get us started I suggest a few specifics. We will avoid generalisations, such as 'you always do x', avoid attacking the person rather than engaging with the issue, avoid unfair assessments of their position, be careful of raised voices, be prepared to apologise, don't let our relationship focus solely on the area of dispute, be careful about hostile body language (a hand on the shoulder and a suggestion of going for a pint to talk about something else can work wonders), be slow to take offence. Before long we may be surprised at what a blessing our opponent turns out to be for us.

AN ESCALATING CONFLICT: THE PRIME MINISTER, AFGHANISTAN AND MRS JANES

An incident that exemplifies many of the themes in this chapter occurred in November 2009.

The prime minister, Gordon Brown, wrote a handwritten letter to the mother of a soldier recently killed in Afghanistan. He misspelled the family's name, addressing Mrs James, rather than Janes, the handwriting was poor, and he was accused of other misspellings in the letter. Appalled at his mistake, the prime minister phoned the lady concerned to apologise, was met with a tirade, and unknown to him, the whole conversation was secretly recorded and then reported in *The Sun* newspaper. The poor bereaved mother was, in my opinion, badly exploited by the newspaper for political reasons. She had potentially legitimate concerns about the conduct of the war in Afghanistan, and these were lost in a welter of comparative trivialities about the letter and the phone call. *The Sun* and the bereaved mother both assumed the worst, claiming that the letter was dashed off carelessly and hastily, and that the prime minister 'couldn't be bothered' to spell the name correctly, and had shown 'disrespect'. In fact, Gordon Brown had no sight in one eye, and very poor sight in the other. It was claimed that there were over twenty spelling mistakes in the letter, but (probably) there was only one, the young man's name (a serious error, admittedly).

The rest were down to illegibility due to the poor handwriting. I would guess, as an article in *The Times* suggested, that there are class differences operating here as well. In middle-class circles a handwritten letter, even with poor handwriting, is a mark of personal warmth and respect. A computer-processed letter in such circumstances would be impersonal and 'infra dig'. To (some) working-class people, the neater presentation of a type-written letter shows more respect. A handwritten note is what you leave out for the milkman.

This was argument as point-scoring, not an attempt at constructive conversation. There was a lack of straightforwardness involved in the secret recording of a personal conversation, and there was a lack of willingness to allow any credit for Gordon Brown's attempt to write personally, and then to try to apologise. The dangers are many, among them, that in future prime ministers at least, possibly all of us, are a little more reluctant to write letters of condolence or apology, in case they cause offence, or are made public in an unhelpful way. It makes it a little more difficult for a disabled person to fill a public role (basically the prime minister was pilloried for his poor eyesight). It obscured a good case that the mother wished to make about lack of equipment for troops in Afghanistan. Everyone, as far as I can see, was the loser, because anger and cynicism got the upper hand. If Mrs Janes' focus had rather been on how remarkable it was that the prime minister had made the time to write a personal, handwritten letter, something that is particularly difficult for him, it may be that the bereaved mother could have found *some* comfort, while not compromising her legitimate grievances.

Mrs Janes' anger was understandable, and, to her great credit, she later accepted Gordon Brown's apology and expressed some sympathy for him over how he had been treated. *The Sun's* part in this is less easy to explain or defend. However, the point of retelling this is not to apportion blame but as an object lesson in what happens when we choose to believe the worst, when we treat our 'enemies' with contempt, and when we conduct our disputes in an unprincipled way. No one is a winner. Followers of Jesus Christ are called to be different.

THE JOURNEY SO FAR

Christians often have a bad reputation for arguing, condemning and falling out. We believe that truth matters and is discoverable, and integrity demands we stand up for that truth. How can we do that in a way that is glorifying to God?

Firstly, when we have failed to disagree well, we need to respond with repentance and humility. Secondly, we need to demonstrate that we are not those who will use truth claims to wield power and control over others. We need to exemplify that truth sets free.

We are not called to 'niceness', but to 'Christlikeness'. The imitation of Christ means that we will be called to stand for truth, but it will also control how we make that stand. Jesus is the truth and He is no bully. When He chose to become incarnate in weakness, without a position of power, or armies, He chose that His mission would not involve bullying, manipulation or power games. If we choose to act in those ways, we betray Him. We are called to be those who will never persecute or bully, though we may risk persecution ourselves.

Jesus Christ offers another way in a culture caught between 'an absurd relativism and a shouty, strident nastiness'.

Personalities and cultures vary greatly in their tendency to dispute and contend, and in how *they might dispute and contend. We need to allow Jesus to help us understand our own instinctive and cultural preferences better, so that we can take account of them in learning to become more Christlike. We need to be sure that any offence we cause is inherent in the Gospel and not from us.*

We need to beware the adversarial approach to solving problems that is so deeply embedded in our culture. This does not necessarily promote understanding or listening and tends to promote the will to win above the will to discover the truth.

We are not primarily called to oppose (though we may have to oppose at times), but to find a better way forward together.

All are made in the image of God (all, not just believers) and Jesus Christ died for all. Therefore, it is necessary that we recognise Jesus Christ in our opponents or enemies. It is hard, or even impossible, to do this if we demonise them or hold them in contempt. Similarly, we need to choose to believe the best of others, not always looking for the worst. Where we do dispute or challenge, we need to speak as a fellow sinner, not as a judge.

Good disagreement will aim to bless our opponent. It will have anger under control. It will listen well and hope to learn. It will seek wherever possible to keep the relationship alive. It will argue for something (people who are only ever against things are bad news), and above all it will enjoy shared fellowship with Jesus Christ wherever that is possible.

In an era of increasing polarisation, intolerance and aggression and lessening trust, the world needs Christians to show a better way of handling difference. We must learn to argue well. The church has the potential to be a gift to a disputatious world. This potential has been glimpsed in the contribution of 'indaba' type conversational processes when dealing with polarising issues in the Church of England.

Chapter Nine

'Jesus Is OK – but the Church?'

'The final act of an institution,' Cicero wrote in AD31, 'is to write
down its rules and regulations.' [431]

'Every organisation seems to start with a prophet and end with a
policeman.'

Cardinal Newman

Can We Have Non-Coercive Institutional Governance?

Here we come to the heart of the problem many people see with
religion, namely institutional culture, decision making and discipline,
and their tendency to be experienced as coercive. As we argued in
Chapter 2, Jesus did not coerce obedience, He invited it. He calls us
to follow that example, and commands us not to judge. Jesus is the
answer to post-modern fears of coercive religion and ideology. [432] So,
if it is difficult, if not impossible, for institutions (religious or non-
religious) to avoid coercion, does what Jesus drives out of the front
door, by his non-coercive example, simply come in again at the back
door as Christians come together as church? Institutional decisions
can affect a large number of people for good or ill, and therefore can
often be experienced as oppressive. The larger the organisation the

---

431   *Priorities, Planning and Paperwork*, Peter Brierley, p.120 (Monarch, 1992)
432   p.66, 67 & 72.

harder it is for institutional governance to be relational, and the more likely it is therefore to feel coercive. The integrity of an organisation necessitates rules, principles and guidelines about all kinds of things. These can be experienced by individuals as coercive.

For all these reasons, institutions have garnered a bad name in our society, particularly now in what is probably one of the most individualistic societies that has ever existed.

One reaction to this is to eschew institutions altogether, so 'organised religion' becomes a term of contempt. This is often expressed in the phrase, 'Jesus is OK. It's the church I can't stand'.

However, this flight from anything institutional is, I suggest, an inadequate and immature response. It is unrealistic and unachievable unless we are to live lives of atomised and fragmented individualism, having as little to do with each other as possible. Such a situation would be a form of anarchy. Jesus has made us members of one body, so the radical individualism that is the only alternative to institutions (in their broadest sense) is not an option for us as Christians.

As soon as people begin to co-operate, they begin the process of forming institutions. Flat mates need some rules and decision-making mechanisms, however informal. The most informal, 'non-denominational' house church needs and will develop, openly or by default, leadership, assigned roles, rules and procedures. It is a truism that by the second Sunday the most radical of new church plants is establishing traditions, all the more difficult to resist for being unconsciously followed. If these things are not dealt with openly and with free discussion, the organisation will be prone to hidden power struggles and manipulation. It is notorious how decision-making groups that forswear voting and rules of procedure in order to decide by 'consensus' can become playgrounds for the manipulation and power politics of dominant personalities. I suggest that we need to forget myths about having non-institutional church (the so-called 'house churches' discovered decades ago that it cannot be done) and instead concentrate on making our institutions as Christlike and as non-coercive as possible.

So, if we cannot simply refuse to have anything to do with institutions, what can we learn from Jesus that will help institutions and those with institutional authority act with Christlike integrity?

Firstly, is it possible to have non-coercive institutional governance?

The honest answer is, 'not totally, no'. We have seen that Jesus was radically non-coercive, but even He, on rare occasions, acted coercively.[433] This is because principles conflict. They are rarely absolute. Thus, principles of non-coerciveness and of the protection of the weak can obviously conflict. Sometimes we face a stark choice between coercing an oppressor or allowing the oppressor to coerce the weak.

A related example might be the need for selection of those who will be a recognised representative of an organisation (and therefore not selecting others), and for removing them when they behave inappropriately (if the organisation is to have any integrity). The ongoing scandals over child abuse by clergy in churches across the world testify to the importance of such discipline, and the harm that results if it is neglected or avoided. Clearly the church has been experienced by many as abusive and coercive because it would *not* act with appropriate coercion and discipline towards rogue clergy.

Many institutional decisions involve winners and losers. Losers will often experience such decisions as coercive. A Christlike approach might be to try to create a 'win-win' situation if possible. It was refreshing to see the eventual decision on consecrating women bishops finally beginning to be handled in this spirit by both sides.[434]

I still want to say that the answer to the question, 'Is it actually possible to have non-coercive institutional governance?' is, substantially, 'yes', even if not always. Institutional decision making and culture can be characterised by the meekness of Jesus, and, indeed, it must be if the church is to adequately reflect its Lord.

This is partly a matter of making sure that the individuals who

---

433   See p.57–61
434   See p.141ff.

govern any institution are as Christlike as possible, and partly a matter of making sure that our systems and culture are as non-coercive as possible, and are enabling Christlike behaviour. I am no expert in systems management, and all I can do is sketch out a few ideas and hope that others can develop these ideas further.

INSTITUTIONAL LEADERS AND THE IMITATION OF CHRIST

Jesus laid out the terms for holding institutional authority when he said:

"'You know that those who are regarded as rulers of the Gentiles lord it over them, and their high officials exercise authority over them. Not so with you. Instead, whoever wants to become great among you must be your servant, and whoever wants to be first must be slave of all. For even the Son of Man did not come to be served, but to serve, and to give his life as a ransom for many.'"[435]

Institutional authority is a very difficult thing for a follower of Jesus to hold. This does not mean that it is wrong to hold it, but that the best people to hold it are those who recognise the pitfalls, are aware of a needy dependence upon God's mercy, who stand trembling and reluctant on the threshold of receiving authority, whether by ordination or consecration, as church warden, or cell group leader or in any other way. In the film *The Godfather: Part III*, Cardinal Lamberto is elected Pope. A look of shock crosses his face as he says, under his breath "Oh, no! – No, no, no." He accepts the election as his calling, but rather in the manner of Jesus accepting His cross. The whole scene conveys an aura of Christlike humility, combined with a willingness to serve, that is a long way from worldly ambition, and contains no shred of a desire to 'lord it' over others.

---

435   Mark 10:42–45

I am struck by a description of a Victorian bishop. 'It was said of Edward Bickersteth, Bishop of Exeter, that whereas the previous bishop, Frederick Temple, pushed along, carrying work and workmen with him in the enthusiasm of labour, Bishop Bickersteth fell upon his people like dew. He came to his parishes and went his way, and those whom he visited found themselves refreshed. Temple's own verdict on him was "That man will do; he is so transparently good." '[436] Here was a leader whose authority was, like that of Jesus, intrinsic, rooted in character and godliness, not extrinsic, rooted in position and hierarchy.

When Christlike leaders have to discipline someone, they will be deeply conscious of what Jesus said about not judging, and their hearts will be grieved at what they have to do. I suspect that institutional authority *should* be a hard thing for a follower of Jesus to bear. Religious leaders are liable to a whole raft of temptations that will pull them away from Jesus if not resisted (Matthew 23 is a good overview of some of them).

Jesus made a point of demonstrating that His way with power is not the world's way, so we find in Him a safeguard against our deep-seated tendency to misuse power, and His example just might make institutional leadership possible for the deeply submitted Christian. Therefore, the most important characteristics of any Christian leader are that they should be submitted to Jesus Christ, be self-aware, and have become recognisably Christlike themselves. However good leaders may be at setting direction and policy, however skilled at people management, however gifted at handling bureaucracy, or ideas, or resources, however orthodox in their beliefs, the prime requirement is holiness (as demonstrated by Jesus Christ).

---

436 *Evangelicals in the Church of England 1734–1984*, Kenneth Hylson-Smith, p.165 (T & T Clark, 1988)

GENTILE AND JEWISH LEADERSHIP MODELS

Martin Goldsmith, a disciple of Jesus from a Jewish background, contrasts the Gentile and Jewish culture of leadership, and questions whether the exercise of raw power can *ever* be justified in Christian leadership.

'So, Jesus points the finger at the Gentiles, criticising the fact that "their high officials exercise authority over them" (Mark 10:42). In saying this, Jesus is attacking authority, not just authoritarianism, in leadership. Jesus strongly rejects this pattern of leadership, and declares, "Not so with you". He then teaches his disciples that primacy means being "slave of all". Jesus himself gives the model of serving rather than being served. He comes, not to save his own life, but to "give his life as a ransom for many" (Mark 10:43–45). While it is true that these last words teach that Jesus offers himself as a sacrificial offering in our place, this is not the main point of his teaching here. He is underlining that Christian leadership should not include the exercise of authority, but rather should be characterised by self-sacrifice. Jesus was following a traditional Jewish approach to leadership here. But as the Gentiles increasingly dominated the church, their patterns of leadership obscured the Jewish background, and one-man leadership with authority became the standard pattern, and now in our time it is almost unthinkable that the Western church could possibly live with leadership which did not have any authority except the authority of God's word.'[437]

This is radical stuff! It raises all kinds of questions. Surely sometimes the exercise of power and authority is necessary (as in the many child abuse cases that went undealt with by the church for so long)? Decisions have to be made by someone, leadership has to be exercised. However, I conclude on reflection that Martin Goldsmith's challenge, which gives full weight to Jesus' teaching on this matter, is a necessary corrective to my cultural assumptions, and I should be slow

---

437 *Get A Grip On Mission*, Martin Goldsmith, p.211-12 (IVP, 2006)

to modify his conclusions with caveats and exceptions. This is a classic example of how our normal Western culture might have blinded us to the full import of what Jesus meant. It takes someone from a different (this time Jewish) culture to help us see what Jesus might have to say to us. Martin Goldsmith has a point. Leadership that rests upon position and juridical authority ('because I say so', or even, 'because the church says so') is hollow. Authority can only come from God's Word (because Jesus says so) and from a character manifestly shaped by Jesus.

Goldsmith continues, 'Christian leaders carry no authority in themselves. But their biblical teaching and preaching convey the authority of God's Word. In the context of not being despised for his youth, Timothy is instructed to "command and teach" (1 Timothy 4:11). The Greek word used for "command" was a military one for soldiers passing an officer's message down the line. It was not used for the officer commanding the men, but merely for passing on words of command. In those days, the army lacked electronic means for conveying an order. We merely pass on his Word through our preaching and teaching. His Word has authority, not us!'[438]

Leaders who understand this will exercise authority differently. Christlike authority will at the very least seek to consult and persuade. It will be collaborative, accountable, probably collective, not authoritarian. Church leaders, following the example of Jesus, will probably only need to be authoritarian when those in authority under them are exercising their power in a way that is abusive and damaging to those whom they are called to lead.

Martin Goldsmith gives an example of the different attitude to leadership that is required. 'We are bound to question the traditional European and American patterns of leadership, in which young people are chosen and trained theologically and are then let loose on our congregation, teaching and pastoring Christians who are often older, more mature and more experienced spiritually than they are. One

---

438   Ibid. p.214

young Anglican curate remarked to me that he was "only number two" in the congregation where he was serving. It was a large well-taught church, with many mature, godly and biblically well-read members. He was somewhat shocked when I suggested that actually he was merely number seventy-seven.'[439]

POWER

Church leaders should be aware that the power they have is the power that God the Father gave to Jesus, real power, power which caused bystanders to repeatedly ask, "By what authority do you do these things?"[440] Therefore it is power that is dangerous as well as potentially helpful. If the Devil can tempt Jesus to misuse it who are we to think that we will escape such temptations? However, it is not a responsible Christian option to *refuse* to exercise power. The only Christian option is to accept the responsibility with enough awareness of the dangers to say, 'God help me' and then to try to exercise that power in a Christlike way. It is very dangerous to attempt to pretend that one has no power. Clergy who have just been defeated on their pet project at their church council, or who find that motivating and organising volunteers is like herding cats, might be tempted to believe that they have *no* power, whereas in fact it merely means they do not hold *all* the power (which should be a cause of relief and thanksgiving). Clergy, for better or for worse, hold very real power, power of preaching week by week, of deciding to whom to delegate, of chairing the church council, of moral authority and of office, of having the whole working week free to devote to the ministry (if they are paid ministers), and the intangible power of influence. If the fact of the possession of this power is denied, if it is not faced up to, accepted, and submitted to Jesus, it will probably result in the misuse of power (and abdication is a misuse of power, just as much as bullying). I have heard it said several times that one of the

---

439   Ibid. p.213–4
440   For example, Matthew 21:23

problems with the Church of England is that everyone believes power is located elsewhere. This can be a safeguard, if power is dispersed, but it can also make bullying more likely as members feel frustrated and do not realise the power that they do hold.

As we have seen in Chapter 2, Jesus chose not to use power for His own convenience or glory, but to liberate others. Often this meant giving power away (a very different thing from abdicating it). Giving power away means using power to empower others, especially those who are otherwise weak or at the margins.

A Christlike leader will always be trying to empower others. He or she will be experienced by others who are trying to serve Jesus as encouraging and blessing their efforts rather than as controlling. As Elizabeth Fry, the early pioneer in prison reform, is reputed to have said, 'There is no end to the good a perfectly ordinary person can accomplish provided they do not mind if someone else gets the credit.'[441]

Jesus had great authority. The crowds often remarked on it.[442] However, as we have seen, it was authority exercised with meekness, which is power under control,[443] submitted power. It was leadership exercised as a servant, with no clinging to an inflated sense of dignity. It was power directed to the setting free of 'captives'; the sort of power that could liberate an Auschwitz, not the power that would conquer and dominate either nations or individuals against their will. It was power bent towards blessing those He was serving. People will soon sense, even if they can't correctly name, power that is intent upon using them. It is all too easy in ministry to say, 'Thine is the Kingdom, the power, and the glory,' whilst actually, perhaps unconsciously, building our own empire and basking in the reflected glory that comes from it. The minister who talks of 'my church', who wants to appear a success

---

441   I have been unable to track down the original source for this widely used quotation.
442   See Luke 4:32 & 36
443   See p.53f.

and sees the people as the means to that end, who regards their present congregation as a staging post on the journey of their ambition, will not have any authority other than the un-Christlike authority that can be asserted, but is never earned. 'Budding preachers have often been admonished by the words, "Your people will not care how much you know until they know how much you care." The preacher's authority over his people will not depend upon how much he can relate of the Bible but how much the people can relate to him. People hate to feel used. People love to feel useful.'[444]

CHRISTLIKE LEADERSHIP

Church leaders have a seemingly impossible job, running an organisation that exists in the world, with all the normal dynamics of a worldly organisation such as budgets, receiving both fair and unfair criticism, being involved with people playing power games, only having twenty-four hours in the day, and yet called to play by the rules or, rather, values of the Kingdom of God. They need to believe that Jesus' ways do work in the world, when it would be so much quicker (it can seem) and simpler to take short cuts. They need the faith to trust in God's vindication, even when countless voices are blaming and criticising. They need to have enough faith to trust in Jesus' verdict and His mercy, and not be so scared of the inevitable criticism that they lose heart. They need to know that such misunderstanding and criticism is part of the vulnerability that God experienced when He became man and is, therefore, part of the calling of Christian leadership. Leaders who are not willing to be vulnerable will never lead like Jesus.

In particular, they need to be sufficiently vulnerable not to hide their own failure and struggle. This is difficult to do appropriately. If a male minister confesses to lust half his congregation may end up feeling threatened. There is such a thing as inappropriate confession.

---

444   *Leadership for New Life*, David Pytches, p.176 (Hodder & Stoughton, 1998)

The secret is not to hide things for our own protection, but only for the protection of others.

William Challis writes, 'my own experience of pastoral ministry in the Church of England has been challenged by the realisation that many people who themselves feel failures find that the average Anglican clergyman, with what a Catholic friend of mine called a typically Anglican effortless superiority, cannot relate to their failure. But we do meet with failure whether we like it or not: we meet it in others, but not only in others, for we also meet it in ourselves and in the Church we serve.' [445] If we are only able to model success, how on earth can we model the ministry of the one who was crucified?[446]

Heeding Jesus' criticisms of the religious leadership of His own day, Christlike leaders will practise what they preach,[447] and they will be careful not to place heavy burdens on people's shoulders.[448] Rather they will copy Jesus who said, '"Come to me, all you who are weary and burdened, and I will give you rest."'[449] If they sound harsh, they are probably not speaking for Jesus. A Christlike church leader will have a sense of proportion. Jesus charged the religious leaders with giving 'a tenth of your spices... mint, dill and cumin. But you have neglected the more important matters of the law – justice, mercy and faithfulness. You should have practised the latter, without neglecting the former. You blind guides! You strain out a gnat but swallow a camel.'[450] David Prior comments that 'The Pharisees had become so enmeshed in subsidiary matters that they had allowed the primary commandments to fall by the wayside.'[451] Could this have some relevance to recent

---

445 *The Word of Life*, William Challis, p102 (Harper Collins, 1997)
446 In what follows in this section I am deeply indebted to Chapter 7, *The Guardians of Tradition – Religious Power* from *Jesus and Power*, David Prior (Hodder and Stoughton, 1987)
447 Matthew 23:3
448 Matthew 23:4
449 Matthew 11:28
450 Matthew 23:23–24
451 *Jesus and Power*, David Prior, p.130 (Hodder and Stoughton, 1987)

debates about women bishops and about homosexuality? I wonder what Jesus would say about what seems to be occupying our attention in the Anglican Communion, if instead of asking Him about narrow and technical issues of biblical interpretation we instead asked Him to comment upon our priorities, our sense of proportion and our practice of grace and graciousness?

From time to time I hear of clergy who feel bullied by their congregations, and of congregations who feel bullied by their clergy (sometimes both in the same church!). If we are indulging in bullying it doesn't matter what we say, no one will be able to perceive Jesus in our words. Bullies do not, however, always know that they are bullying, especially if, as bullies often do, they *feel* powerless. The only way to learn how others experience our behaviour is to be willing to listen humbly, and if others say that we are bullying, to enlist a trusted but independent-minded third party to help us to perceive the truth of the matter. If we are in leadership, we will need to make efforts to ensure that people feel that they can approach us with what could be seen as critical insights. If people are not doing this it may well be a sign that they are afraid of us, and that we need to take heed.

Christlike leadership involves trying to be as open and consultative as possible about decisions, while not ducking issues or letting them be swept under the carpet. We are called to servant leadership, which does not mean weak leadership, but it does need to inspire trust, be open, non-manipulative, and avoid coercion as far as humanly possible given the necessity of making some hard decisions. Hard decisions need to be faced, preferably by helping all involved to face them squarely, otherwise it is too easy to use hard decisions as an excuse and cover-up for bullying. Because it is so easy to deceive ourselves, leaders need to be accountable to someone who will challenge them if they are acting in a way that is un-Christlike. In fact, they need to be accountable in two directions, to someone under whose authority they operate (a line manager or supervisory body in worldly terms) and to a spiritual director or pastor who is outside the immediate 'power structures' of their church. After all, even Jesus was accountable to His Father,

"'Very truly I tell you, the Son can do nothing by himself; he can do only what he sees his Father doing, because whatever the Father does the Son also does.'"[452]

Jesus spelled out the requirements for leaders in His Kingdom in a way that rules out self-assertion, domination, vainglory or selfish ambition when He said, "'But you are not to be called 'Rabbi', for you have only one teacher and you are all brothers. And do not call anyone on earth 'father', for you have one Father, and he is in heaven. Nor are you to be called instructor, for you have one instructor, the Messiah. The greatest among you will be your servant. For those who exalt themselves will be humbled, and those who humble themselves will be exalted.'"[453] How does this sit with cathedral processions, with their fine robes and finer sounding titles, and specially reserved seats graded according to rank, on the one hand, or with the evangelical tendency to venerate gurus of the publishing, broadcasting or conference circuit on the other?

Christlike leaders are surely called upon to bless and encourage more than they are called to control. In the Church of England only ordained ministers are permitted (officially) to pronounce a formal blessing. A new light was shed on this for me when Richard Chartres became Bishop of Stepney. He was keen to bless anything that furthered the cause of the Gospel, and if an episcopal licence did not exist for a particular ministry, he would invent one. We planned a new church plant on a local estate, and his support in licensing the building for use, and licensing members of the congregation for ministry and

452   John 5:19
453   Matthew 23:8–12

leadership roles, was extremely affirming and released a great deal of energy. It struck me at the time that this is what the ministry of 'blessing' is really about, releasing energy and authorising what will build God's kingdom. The reason it needs a certain authority to bless, and why it cannot be effectively done by just anyone, is because the people with the power to stop something release great energy when they recognise an initiative as good and godly, and instead 'bless' and thereby authorise it. It is sad when we reduce such a powerful ministry to restrictive rules about who can pronounce a simple prayer for God's blessing at the end of a service of worship. Clergy and bishops in my experience divide fairly neatly into two camps, those who are primarily concerned with regulation and who try to police and control and thereby unintentionally set us on the road to death, and those who are concerned to pronounce blessing and empowerment on anything that can be seen to build the Kingdom, and who bring life wherever they go. The former go 'armed' into every meeting and encounter, and people are wary of them, whilst the latter leave their weapons outside the door, and leave people feeling that Jesus has just been involved in the encounter. This is especially important in these times of numerical and therefore financial decline in the church. A declining church tends to be anxious, and it is difficult for an anxious person to exercise leadership in the second of these ways.

Above all, the responsibility of a leader in God's church is to help people walk with Jesus. Jesus Christ is God in their lives; if we are a leader we emphatically are not to be. David Prior put it well when he said, 'those who assume – or are entrusted with – official (or unofficial) religious power today must be specially sensitive to any tendency to play God in the lives of others.'[454] Helping another to walk with Jesus is the single most empowering thing we can do for anyone.

---

454   *Jesus and Power*, David Prior, p.138 (Hodder and Stoughton, 1987)

CAN INSTITUTIONAL CULTURE REFLECT THE CHARACTER OF JESUS?

As we have just been seeing, a large part of whether institutions can operate in a way that is recognisably like Jesus depends upon the quality, and the Christlike integrity, of the people who comprise it, and especially those who lead it. Is there anything else about institutional culture that can make an organisation more or less in tune with the character of Jesus? Clearly there are difficulties in trying to read from an individual character (Jesus) and to apply the results to the character of an organisation, but I believe it can be done.

The most basic question is whether the organisation is dedicated wholly to the furtherance of Jesus' interests. Like individuals, institutions can become focused on the preservation of their own power and prestige.

AN EXAMPLE FROM THE MISSIONARY CHURCH: THE EUTHANASIA OF MISSION

An example of good practice over a long period has been the Church Missionary Society[455] (CMS), which from early in its life, under the leadership of Henry Venn,[456] general secretary from 1841 to 1873, worked for the establishment of indigenous leadership and governance in mission churches. Venn believed that mission churches should become self-supporting, self-governing, and self-propagating.

'The main underlying principle which appears to have guided Mr Venn in this and all analogous questions is, that foreign missions to the heathen must always be treated as a transition state, in which novel problems must and will arise'... 'not to be decided by the rules or usages of settled Christian Churches, but requiring much mutual

---

455   Now 'The Church Mission Society'.
456   I was thrilled to discover, sometime after I came to the Upper Holloway Team Ministry, that Henry Venn was vicar of one of our churches, St John's Upper Holloway, 1834–46.

forbearance on the part of all concerned, and always to be approached so as to facilitate and not to hinder the growth of an independent native Church – the true death-birth of a mission. European missionaries have no vested interest, as have clergymen in England, labouring amongst their own countrymen, and as ministers of their own National and Established Church. The foreign mission is to be gradually and silently removed as the nascent community advances towards completion… but when we aim at making Christianity indigenous and not exotic, with many centres instead of one as at Jerusalem and Antioch in the earliest days, the problem becomes delicate and difficult.'[457] That last sentence is a prescient description of where we are now, experiencing great difficulty in holding the Anglican Communion together. It is good to pause and encourage ourselves with the thought that we are experiencing one of the problems of success, because the Anglican Communion has followed Jesus in His attitude to power, and was not formed as a centralised, authoritarian, culturally imperialist church.

Venn came to speak of this institutional dying to self as 'the euthanasia of mission', and the culture of CMS was shaped to achieve it. His first biographer writes, 'his Minutes on Corresponding Committees, etc., involving the whole machinery by which the CMS missions are regulated, are all conceived and constructed so as to tend to this euthanasia'.[458]

More recently CMS, as a logical corollary of these values and policies, has worked for mission to be seen as the duty and need of all, not just Western Christians, with its slogan, 'from everywhere – to everywhere'. Thus a Western mission organisation has, ever since the heyday of colonialism, when such ideas were neither fashionable nor popular, worked to give away power, to risk its own existence, and to shape its institutional policy so as not to preach 'ourselves, but Jesus

---

457　*Memoir of Henry Venn, BD*, William Knight, p.157–8 (Seeley, Jackson and Halliday, 1882) available at www.archive.org

458　Knight (op. cit.) p.159

Christ as Lord, and ourselves as your servants for Jesus' sake.'[459] This vision of CMS was an inspiration to me as my own call to ordained ministry was developing, when I encountered it as a short-term volunteer with the organisation. I could sense there was something remarkable and godly about it long before I understood its roots, either in the history of CMS or in the character of Jesus. I suggest that the example of CMS, and the persistence of that example down the decades and centuries, indicates that it is not a forlorn hope for institutional culture and practice to reflect the character of Jesus in a way that is not overly tied to whether the particular staff or leadership at the time is Christlike. Particularly significant in this regard is the comment (above) that 'the whole machinery by which the CMS missions are regulated, are all conceived and constructed so as to tend to this euthanasia (of mission)'.

This willingness to die is the very opposite of party spirit. As Tom Wright commented once in a lecture to clergy, '… any church party that lasts for more than a generation is likely to be an occasion of sin. Yes, we need people who glimpsed a fresh vision to get together and tell the rest of us about it, but no, we don't need their children and grandchildren to pride themselves on their heritage, on being the people who really know what's what. If we are to become God's people for tomorrow, it is time to repent and believe. "Don't think to say to yourselves, 'we have Abraham for a father'… " '[460]

Churches that follow their Lord incarnate will themselves incarnate in the form of an indigenous culture. Martin Goldsmith comments that in mission 'we need to go with such humility that we desire to learn rather than to teach. Some church leaders fall into the temptation of trying to teach overseas Christians about Christian leadership. How dare we attempt such teaching with little or no understanding of the local leadership structures! Christian leadership must relate to local

---

459   2 Corinthians 4:5
460   Tom Wright – Stepney Advent Lecture – 1994, p.28

cultural and religious patterns. We don't want to export our forms of leadership; that is cultural imperialism.'[461] This means that there is no single Christlike church culture. The church must incarnate itself in the local culture wherever it is. It seems to me that the Church of England has been markedly better at understanding this in its involvement with overseas mission than it has at home in its own cross-cultural mission to its own inner cities and to the poor, and to the working class.[462]

'MY POWER IS MADE PERFECT IN WEAKNESS'

I suggest that institutions that are to be modelled after Jesus should welcome power 'made perfect in weakness'. Our churches' histories often show us resisting the dilution or reduction of our power. However, speaking from the edge of society and from outside the corridors of power is probably necessary if we are to have a truly prophetic voice, if we are to be and be seen to be non-coercive, and if we are to share Jesus' bias to the poor and excluded.

It certainly helps if our institution does not have a monopoly. If we are surrounded by other denominations with which we are in fellowship, it should help to keep us humble. It can function as the institutional equivalent of a church made up of individuals from many cultures.[463] If we know that our church, in its earthly, institutional manifestation, is provisional, contingent and temporary, it should save the church from demanding the allegiance that belongs to God alone. It might also help us to refrain from panic if crisis threatens our part of the church. Should, for example, the Church of England go under, God will not find His hands tied.

---

461 *Get A Grip On Mission*, Martin Goldsmith, p.169 (IVP, 2006)
462 Probably because of a failure to recognise just how middle class we are, and that there are therefore cultural issues to address.
463 See p.138ff.

A Christlike institution will probably practise subsidiarity (a clumsy word for a beautiful concept), namely allowing decision making to take place as low down the chain, and therefore as close to the point of implementation, as possible. This engages participation and empowers. It can also enable governance to be relational to some extent. Declining organisations, in an anxiety-driven response, often begin to multiply central staff, and when we see this in the church it is a serious danger signal. Power that is faceless, an unseen tyrant or 'central committee' pulling the levers and not susceptible to conversation, questioning or even lobbying, a sort of '1984' style 'Big Brother', can be terrifying. Surely that is one reason why God became incarnate in Jesus Christ, to put a face to His power. If we know personally some of the people who make decisions in our institution it will be that much harder for the decision making to be or to appear to be coercive.

A Christlike institution will keep rules and regulations to the absolute minimum needed for the organisation to function, maximising human freedom. Anything else will make it too much like the Pharisees.

A Christlike institution will prioritise the poor. Whilst being non-coercive it will not be afraid to be prophetic, and to speak truth to power with courage. It will facilitate generosity and mutuality. An organisation where cut-throat competition and backstabbing are necessary to 'get on' is not a reflection of Jesus. It will be culturally diverse, modelling reconciliation and unity in Christ across divisions of race, class, culture, age, gender and temperament.

An Example From the Infant Church

Acts 6:1–7, I believe, gives us an early example of the institutional expression of Christlike values.

'In those days when the number of disciples was increasing, the Hellenistic Jews among them complained against the Hebraic Jews because their widows were being overlooked in the daily distribution of food. So the Twelve gathered all the disciples together and said, "It would not be right for us to neglect the ministry of the word of God in order to wait on tables. Brothers and sisters, choose seven men from among you who are known to be full of the Spirit and wisdom. We will turn this responsibility over to them and will give our attention to prayer and the ministry of the word."

This proposal pleased the whole group. They chose Stephen, a man full of faith and of the Holy Spirit; also Philip, Procorus, Nicanor, Timon, Parmenas, and Nicolas from Antioch, a convert to Judaism. They presented these men to the apostles, who prayed and laid their hands on them.

So the word of God spread. The number of disciples in Jerusalem increased rapidly, and a large number of priests became obedient to the faith.'

The 'Twelve' kept their focus on the mission that Jesus had given them (v.2) but, as far as they could, they made sure that trust and unity were maintained in the embryonic church, as this racially charged grievance threatened to tear them apart. The 'Greek' Christians were complaining that their widows were not receiving a fair share of the aid that was being distributed. The 'Twelve' appointed deacons to look after this matter. Did they appoint deacons in equal representation from each community? No, they bent over backwards to reassure those who had felt excluded. Every name in the list of deacons is a Greek name. The group that felt aggrieved was put totally in charge of the distribution of support to both Jews and Greeks. The Jews in the church were willing to surrender power in the pursuit of justice and unity. They did not count equality with Greeks as something to be grasped, to paraphrase Philippians Chapter 2, but made themselves nothing. In other words, the character of Jesus determined their actions, with the result that the church grew rapidly (v.7). Jesus should not need to leave the room when church politics is being practised.

AN EXAMPLE FROM THE MODERN CHURCH

The twenty-five churches of Islington Deanery,[464] in which I used to live and work, met annually to set the rate of 'Common Fund', that is the amount that each church would contribute to the Diocese of London towards clergy and other costs. I had been accustomed, before I came to Islington, to a system which was in effect a levy, or taxation. A demand was made, based upon the actual income of each parish, or, in more sophisticated models, based upon what was judged to be the potential income of each parish. This demand had to be paid.

I was not looking forward to my first Deanery Common Fund Meeting. It was a finance meeting, after all, and I certainly didn't expect 'all the fun of the fair'. I thought it would be boring at best, and probably tense and fractious. I had been told that the churches met in a spirit of mutual co-operation and generosity, giving as much as they could afford to 'the Common Fund', but I'm afraid I put this down to 'spin' or wishful thinking.

In the event I was amazed. It was one of the most Christlike, Christ-centred, faith-filled church meetings I have ever been to (and I include worship services in that comparison). Everyone knew how much the deanery needed to raise in total, and each parish started with a baseline figure assessed according to their previous year's contribution. Those who might struggle to pay explained as much to the meeting, offering reasons that ranged from expensive building repairs to the moving away of some key givers, and others then offered to pay more, sometimes much more, than they had been assessed, in order to plug the gap. The first year that I witnessed it, and most years since, this process produced more than had been asked. It also produced trust (rooted in mutual accountability) and it stimulated prayer and thankfulness for one another. I think it fair to say that there was quite a bit of trust between churches in the deanery that led to the

---

464   In the Church of England a deanery is a cluster of churches that work and relate together under the leadership of an area (or rural) dean.

establishment of this system in the first place, but once established, it certainly built trust further.

In its replacement of coercion with loving accountability and support, its sacrificial generosity, its willingness to believe the best of each other, here was an institutional finance meeting giving clear expression to the character of Jesus. In its willingness to devolve these decisions to the deanery the diocese was giving up direct power and control in a way that empowered us to build the trust to make our own decisions in a face-to-face meeting. If it can happen with finance, it could probably happen with anything.[465]

CHOOSING TRUST OVER LAW: GENERAL SYNOD AND THE CONSECRATION OF WOMEN AS BISHOPS

Rarely can the Church of England's ability to be Christlike have been as severely tested as during debates over the consecration of women bishops. Passions were involved, as deeply owned vocations were called into question on both sides of the debate, leaving many feeling deeply threatened. At its most basic the livelihood and calling of some clergy was at stake. On a slightly more rarefied plane, many genuinely believed that if we 'got it wrong' the Lord would remove His blessing from His church, and we would lose credibility and distinctiveness in our mission. People on all sides of the debate believed this in various ways. To characterise these fears, fears that were mostly rooted in genuine conviction, as 'misogyny' on the one side, or as 'political correctness' or mere 'liberal unbelief' on the

---

465 Since moving to a much wealthier area, I have many times been told that such a scheme doesn't work in rich areas (and indeed there is some evidence that this is the case). This argument has been used as a reason for resisting the implementation of such a scheme. Never have I heard this 'fact' presented as a reason why the rich church needs to learn from the poor. If we cannot behave in a Christlike way in our central councils when dealing with something as important as money, this must raise major questions about the value of what we are trying to go on funding. It shows us part of what Jesus meant when he said, "It is hard for someone who is rich to enter the kingdom of heaven."

other, might be understandable, but appears not only inaccurate, but perilously close to contempt.

I believe politely disguised contempt was not far below the surface at the General Synod debate on 7 July 2008, when the decision in principle was taken to consecrate women as bishops. Witness the following exchange from the 'Thinking Anglicans' website from immediately after the vote.

'In the aftermath of General Synod's decision to kick me out of the C of E, I will refrain from further comment at present—' (posted by AH)

One response to this was,

'It really does sound like children having a temper tantrum because the other children won't play the game according to their rules. It's really very simple. If you can't live with political reality, you can take your ball and leave.' (RL)[466]

In July 2008, the General Synod of the Church of England voted in principle to proceed to the consecration of women as bishops. However, they subsequently refused to legislate for continued provision for those who, in conscience, could not accept this step. Such provision had originally been introduced at the same time as the decision to ordain women priests, and alternative episcopal oversight for opponents of ordained women's ministry, so-called 'flying bishops', were to be allowed to lapse. Many felt this to be a breach of promises that had been made to them. This feeling of betrayal made trust much harder to engender for the decision on female episcopacy.

For many women who supported such consecration, any structural solution that allowed opponents to opt out of the

---

466   www.thinkinganglicans.org.uk/

oversight of a woman bishop meant that all women bishops would exercise forever a second rate or impaired episcopacy and this was unacceptable in principle.

The great difficulty of finding any kind of solution to such a structural and theological impasse was greatly exacerbated by understandably deep passions on each side that for a minority erupted into intemperate anger and contemptuous language.

In 2012 Synod voted down the legislation for women bishops (a two-thirds majority was required, and in one house only,[467] the house of laity, this was not achieved). For many this was a shock result, and one that many of us felt brought discredit upon the church in the eyes of the population at large, who saw this as straightforward gender discrimination. However, though doubtless there were many motives for the opposition in Synod, concern at the lack of alternative provision for opponents of female bishops, seen by some to be in effect a proposal to exclude opponents from the church over an issue of conscience, seems to have been decisive.

The shock, hurt and rejection felt over this vote by many women in the church, particularly ordained women, was palpable.

On 14 July 2014, the same General Synod voted by a substantial majority in each house in favour of the consecration of women bishops. What had changed?

In the build up to the 2014 vote, relating and listening were prioritised and a process of facilitated listening was set up, very similar to the 'indaba' process used during the homosexuality debate at the previous Lambeth Conference.[468]

The aim seemed to shift (at least partly) from winning, to being able to go ahead together. The new Archbishop of Canterbury, Justin Welby, brought in as his director of reconciliation Canon David Porter

---

467   There are three houses, The House of Laity, The House of Clergy, and The House of Bishops. The two latter passed the legislation by the required two-thirds majority.

468   See p.167ff.

from Coventry Cathedral, an expert in facilitating reconciliation with great experience in the Northern Ireland peace process.

One commentator at the time noted 'New, simpler legislation is the result, combined with a noticeable lessening of acrimony.'[469] The new legislation did not try to enshrine complex legal safeguards, but rather was based upon trust, a trust that had been bought by the 'indaba' process.

Canon Simon Killwick, chair of the Catholic Group in General Synod, said: "Following the failure of the previous legislation in November 2012, the Catholic Group immediately called for round-table talks to agree on a new package which could be fast-tracked through the Synod. These talks have been amazingly fruitful in that they have generated a new package which provides a way forward for everyone in the Church of England and the package is being fast-tracked through the Synod with the added bonus in the creation of a much more positive atmosphere of trust, generosity and mutual respect. We look forward to this new atmosphere pervading the debates at the forthcoming Synod and beyond, so that we can all move forward as one."[470]

Notice the key factors in the light of all we have said thus far. Agreement was based on trust more than law, and a process of listening generated an atmosphere of trust, generosity and mutual respect. This new climate enabled the recognition of hurt and fears on both sides and led to the eschewing of 'victim' politics, which always polarises.[471]

---

469 http://www.christiantoday.com/article/general.synod.will.women.bishops. happen.this.time/38749.htm

470 Ibid.

471 The parallels to, and relevance of this approach to trust building and problem solving where legal frameworks alone cannot succeed, are clearly relevant to the current (as I write) impasse over Brexit and the Northern Ireland backstop. Unfortunately, the rest of the world seems not to be paying attention. Beyond the fact of the decision to ordain women bishops, I think few in the general population are aware of what happened at General Synod and how momentous it was. I think it important that we take appropriate pride in what was achieved and how it was achieved, and then move on to share the lessons beyond the church.

In the light of some of the harsh things that have been said on both sides, and some of the actions of both sides that have severely harmed trust, this agreement was a remarkable achievement, based upon risk-taking faith and generosity. As much as the 2012 debate was catastrophic for the church's witness to the world, 2014's debate and decision really does model something that the world needs, namely a way of fostering trust and practical respect in a way that can facilitate loving your enemy even in a polarised institution. In the face of deep fears and deeply held convictions, our General Synod representatives have chosen to 'submit to one another out of reverence for Christ' (Eph 5:21). Surely there was celebration in heaven over that!

HARD DECISIONS

Can institutional leadership imitate Jesus when it has to take hard decisions that are sure to create some losers? We will examine a few contentious areas, namely baptism and marriage policy, and the selection and discipline of church leaders.

The outworkings of policies on remarriage and baptism have often left people feeling bruised and rejected. They may ask, 'if Jesus broke down barriers, and said "come", how can the church put barriers up and say, "don't come"?'

I am not in favour of an indiscriminate baptism policy. However, who is to discriminate? Should it be the clergy person exercising authority, or the candidate? The person on whom the burden of decision making should rest is the candidate for baptism, or the parents of the candidate in the case of infant baptism. The clergy person has the duty of instructing the conscience of the applicant, not of judging it. I have always found it very fruitful to offer parents a choice between a service of baptism and a service of blessing, with careful explanation of the thinking behind each service. Slightly more than a third choose baptism, and slightly fewer than two thirds opt for a blessing and thanksgiving service (though quite a number of those have opted for baptism later). As a result, many have joined a seekers' group and eventually come to faith. In particular, the questions about which promises they can make with integrity often face people for the first time in their lives with the question of whether they are yet disciples of Christ. Surely it is our job to make people aware of the fork in the road but only they can choose which way to take. I am quite sure that few of them would have come to faith if I had simply said 'You are not a Christian' (assuming I could possibly know for sure anyway) or if I had said 'I won't baptise your baby'. We are called to issue Jesus' invitation, not to act coercively and judgmentally.

Marriage after divorce and gay marriage are much trickier and far more contentious issues. If, for the sake of argument, a minister of the Gospel believes that remarriage is *always* contrary to God's will, it is hard to see how they can express God's blessing upon *it*. However, surely God always wants to bless individuals, in the sense of wanting to do them good (as opposed to expressing approval of what they do). These two meanings of 'blessing' often become confused with dire consequences for people's understanding of God.

We have got ourselves into a mess here by taking on the role of the state in solemnising marriages (for good missionary reasons). Those reasons no longer apply. In this post-Christendom situation, why should the church conduct marriages at all? Marriage was given, according to the Old Testament, at the outset, immediately after Creation. It is clearly for everyone, not just for the covenant people. It is for unbelievers as much as for believers. If the state conducted all marriages, and couples could then seek a service of blessing from the church, it would remove a great deal of the human rights baggage associated with any stance the church might take about whom it can appropriately marry, and remove us from being in the place of a moral policeman, or a judge, when considering issues like remarriage. We could explain to people that, whether or not they are starting from the place God (or they) might wish to be starting from, God accepts them as they are, and desires to bless them. On this basis we can then pray for them without passing judgment one way or the other, upon the fact that they are divorced.

When He was asked to rule about the division of an inheritance, 'Jesus replied, "Man, who appointed me a judge or an arbiter between you?"'.[472] In an unholy alliance with the state we have taken on the mantle (or judicial robes) that Jesus specifically rejected. Many damaging things follow from this, not least the tendency to approach Jesus' teaching line by line, looking for applications and loopholes as if it were legislation, rather than an expression of the mind of God. Spoken and written discourse have to be approached according to their genre. You do not read poetry as though it were a football report, or a coroner's report as though it were flat-pack furniture instructions. I used to be a lawyer, and it grates to hear people construing Jesus' teaching on divorce, or even the Sermon on the Mount as though they were extracts from the All England Law Reports. We have already seen[473] how damaging this is, not least because it tends to focus us upon what we can get away with rather than upon trying to please God.

After a long discussion about marriage and divorce, and God's intention, Jesus seems to say quite clearly that this is a matter for individual conscience not legalistic prescription. 'Jesus replied, "Not everyone can accept this word, but only those to whom it has been given. For there are eunuchs who were born that way; and there are eunuchs who have been made eunuchs by others; and there are those who choose to live like eunuchs for the sake of the kingdom of heaven. The one who can accept this should accept it."[474]

In other words, to interpret and paraphrase, 'I'm telling you God's plan and intention; it's the best way, and I invite you to enter the blessing of walking in that direction. It's up to you, no one can

---

472 Luke 12:14
473 P.25ff.
474 Matthew 19:11–12

make this decision but you. What will you choose?' Acting as the state's registrar obscures one of our God-given functions as His church, which is to *instruct* people's consciences, not to act as God's enforcers.

In this respect I believe that we should be glad that there are other denominations with other policies. We do not possess ultimate power in respect of these issues. Individuals have a choice. I believe that this is fully consonant with the fact that Jesus invites to obedience, He does not coerce, and that our role is to instruct consciences, not to police morality. Were we still a state monopoly church this would not practically be possible.

An unavoidable area of institutional discipline is the selection and disciplining of those who will be authorised leaders or representatives of a church. Just as political parties or clubs and societies have a right to insist that their members and officers reflect and support the aims and objectives of the society, so do churches. The requirements for leadership will be different from those for membership. You do not have to be satisfied that someone is no longer attempting to follow Jesus to decide that they should not be a designated leader of a church. Jesus welcomed *all* kinds of sinners and outcasts but only twelve of those sinners and outcasts were chosen to be in the inner circle. Nevertheless, *all* were treated with mercy, grace and generosity. Thus, for example, whether a particular denomination chooses to ordain or not to ordain the divorced and remarried, is a matter for that denomination, and is not of itself an inherently un-Christian decision, whichever decision they take. All that they need to show is that the decision can reasonably be shown to be in accordance with the mind of Jesus Christ as revealed in scripture.

Often, different denominations will come to different decisions. For instance, a Baptist will not normally be ordained if they plan to baptise infants, and in the Church of England a candidate will not normally be ordained if they will never baptise infants. However, for the Baptist

Church to refuse to ordain a paedo-Baptist does not suggest that person is a poor Christian, and a wise Baptist selector would probably steer such a candidate in the direction of the Church of England, grateful for the fact that we have a plurality of denominations. Such refusals are sometimes inevitable, and it will not do just to shout 'coercive' at them as if this settles the matter. However, such policy restrictions need to be as few as possible, and as consistent with the example of Jesus Christ as possible, so that each denomination remains as culturally and temperamentally diverse as possible. We also need to react with the grace and generosity of Jesus by being glad that there are denominations unlike ours, which can embrace those who come to different conclusions, and we need to treat them as equal constituents, with us, of the body of Christ. We can still, like Jesus, act in the spirit that ecumenically crosses boundaries, and reconciles, even when we have to make distinctions and draw lines for the sake of organisational coherence, as long as we do not absolutise our denomination or its policies. This, it seems to me, is the fundamental error of Roman Catholicism, at least in its official teaching, that it does attempt to absolutise a particular contingent manifestation of the church in just this way.

DISCIPLINE OF ERRING MEMBERS

What do we do when a church representative falls seriously short of the expected standards in their conduct? With current scandals concerning abusive priests who have not been disciplined in the past, this is very much a live issue right now.

1 Corinthians Chapter 5 is instructive. A member has committed incest with his stepmother (or possibly, but less likely, his mother). Paul tells them, 'hand this man over to Satan for the destruction of the flesh, so that his spirit may be saved on the day of the Lord.'[475] The

---

475   1 Corinthians 5:4–5

passage is notoriously hard to interpret with any certainty, but seems to mean, treat him as though he were outside the Lord's kingdom. In other words, regard him as an unbeliever or a seeker, not a member, as a sinner loved by God but not yet restored.

That the aim is restoration is clear. Paul refers to the same matter in his Second Letter to the Corinthians when he says, 'The punishment inflicted on him by the majority is sufficient. Now instead, you ought to forgive and comfort him, so that he will not be overwhelmed by excessive sorrow. I urge you, therefore, to reaffirm your love for him.'[476]

The New Testament in fact seems to apply such discipline to any recognised church member, but not to the unbeliever or seeker.[477]

In a church with fluid boundaries, like the Church of England, such discipline presents more problems on the face of it than it does for churches with a more clearly defined boundary. As research seems to suggest that belonging comes first for many people, and then believing, followed by behaving, at least partly as a result of belonging,[478] we should be careful not to expect Christian standards of behaviour and consistency from those who are still wearing their 'L' plates. This is the clear implication of 1 Corinthians 5:9–13, 'What business is it of mine to judge those outside the church?' An over strict application of 1 Corinthians 5:9–13 would wreck the 'belong, [then] believe, [then] behave,' model for evangelism and nurture by demanding Christian behaviour of seekers before they are even converted. Law would then replace grace. A proper application of 1 Corinthians 5:9–13 would, I suggest, seek to maintain standards for those in leadership or recognised positions (ordained or lay, paid or unpaid), would seek to protect the vulnerable from abuse, and beyond that would be more akin to discipling than discipline (though clearly these two are

---

476   2 Corinthians 2:6–8
477   1 Corinthians 5:9–13
478   This was one of the main findings of *Finding Faith Today*, John Finney (Bible Society, 1992).

related). Even when disciplining leaders and those in official positions, it should only be for offences that the denomination judges serious. After all, 'there is no one righteous, not even one'.[479] Were we to follow a policy of zero tolerance of sin we would end up with a perpetual witch hunt, biting and devouring one another endlessly, a direction that the world seems to be pursuing with increasing intolerance, and not one that Christians should follow.

Jesus refers[480] to a disciplinary situation when describing what to do with a fellow Christian who wrongs you. He says talk it out with them, if this doesn't work take some others with you, and 'if they still refuse to listen, tell it to the church; and if they refuse to listen even to the church, treat them as you would a pagan or a tax collector'.[481] This sounds harsh until you remember how Jesus treated pagans and tax collectors. He wasn't called 'friend of sinners' for nothing. If we could continue the conversation and ask Him, "How then should we treat pagans and tax collectors?" I suspect that He would say "Firstly, forgive them, secondly pray for them, and thirdly, try to help them to be reconciled to me." This gives a whole new shape and flavour to the idea of church discipline.

Perhaps Galatians 6:1 sums it up best, 'Brothers and sisters, if someone is caught in a sin, you who live by the Spirit should restore that person gently. But watch yourselves, or you also may be tempted.' In other words, 'deal with it, remember you are a sinner at risk too, aim to restore, not punish, and be gentle.'

So why focus on these passages about discipline, if they are so problematic? Firstly, because they are good examples of those passages, referred to earlier,[482] that are difficult, like a bump in the ground that might yield up hidden treasure. If we grapple with them it might make some of us face the need for some church discipline

---

479   Romans 3:10
480   Matthew 18:15–17
481   Matthew 18:17
482   p.121

a little more squarely and give us a framework for avoiding scandals in the future. However, these verses are excellent examples of the need to interpret the whole Bible through the lens of Jesus Christ. Unless His attitude to sinners and victims shapes our interpretation, and in particular, unless we start from the point of thinking of 'us sinners' not 'those sinners', we will fall into harshness, vengefulness, or scapegoating. We *should* be very reluctant to exercise discipline. If we are eager, we have almost certainly wandered away from Jesus. As it is, I am afraid that these passages have become the preserve of those who by temperament are disciplinarians, or authoritarian, and the rest have tended to ignore them, leading occasionally on both sides of that divide to some interpretations and practice that Jesus might not own.

But why does the New Testament speak of church discipline at all, if, as we saw earlier, holiness is something Jesus *invites* us to? He doesn't dragoon us into it.[483] Why is there a place for moral discipline in the church if, as we maintained in Chapter 2,[484] law cannot make us holy? I suggest that we have here an outworking of the same principle that led Jesus to take stern action against the traders in the temple, and to utter harsh words against the religious leaders. If church members cannot trust each other and wider society cannot therefore trust the church because those who are its mature members and leaders are seriously compromised, then the weak will be dragged down, the lost will not be saved, and the household of God will become a dangerous place for the weak and vulnerable. A generation from now we will be facing a fresh crop of abuse scandals. If we exercise and permit discipline in the church as Jesus did, sparingly, mercifully, and only when power is being abused, we will not go far wrong. However, if we fall for the myth that holiness can be created in individuals by coercion, we will end up trying to play God in other people's lives and thereby doing the Devil's work.

---

483   p.45ff.
484   p.28ff.

DIVISION AND ECUMENICAL FELLOWSHIP

Perhaps at this point we should acknowledge with thanks that there are many different denominations, and therefore many different practices. There is always an alternative in a Christian mixed economy. Whether you marry or bless a couple who have been married before, is not (in a mixed economy) a matter of human rights or coercion because, for them, there always is an alternative.[485]

There are two types of reason for churches to be organisationally separate. Firstly if we feel the 'other group' have so fatally compromised their faith as to be, in our opinion, no longer followers of Jesus Christ, then we must relate to them as to any unbeliever or follower of another religion, that is charitably and humbly, but not as 'members of one body'.[486] However, as we have seen, we should be extremely slow to come to such a conclusion about anyone who claims to be committed to Jesus Christ. Remember, Jesus gave Communion to Judas on the night he was betrayed.

Secondly, in practice, division is often over matters that are not so fundamental, but lead to a different and incompatible polity, such as whether or not to baptise infants. Whether we should divide over such matters is moot, but that, in the economy of God, the resulting mixed economy of churches can be used to His glory, seems self evident.[487] In such circumstances, ecumenical fellowship suggests a way forward.

We recognise each other's genuine Christian faith across boundaries of difference and disagreement, whenever we gather ecumenically. This is the crucial difference between an ecumenical and a multi-faith encounter, however much journalists may confuse the two terms. It has, largely unofficially, become normal to offer

---

485 I will discuss further below whether, in the light of this, institutional unity is normally a worthwhile goal. Monochrome uniformity I suggest would ill serve the church, the Kingdom of God or society.

486 See p.155–157 above for Dietrich Bonhoeffer's approach to this question.

487 See p.219–221

Eucharistic hospitality to all baptised and communicant believers of all Christian denominations, and this is exactly as it should be. Baptists, Pentecostals, Roman Catholics, Anglicans, New Church, Methodists, and many others, pray together and meet together for joint mission, or in ecumenical gatherings, all over the land, and, on the whole, we refrain from bitter criticism (as opposed to civil debate and disagreement) in public. If fellowship is trusting and deep, we will be able to debate vigorously where we disagree because we know our unity is strong enough to take it. Is not this model of ecumenical hospitality a possible way forward in the face of a great deal that is dividing the Anglican Communion at present? Even if, sadly, our Church (whether we are thinking of the Church of England or the Anglican Communion) splits, the tragedy would be greatly ameliorated if we could still treat each other as brothers and sisters in Christ, with ecumenical hospitality. At present though, most of the signs are that if it comes, such a split will be neither amicable nor civil, and the wounds that can then be caused could take generations to heal.

Every Christian church should be able to share table fellowship with every other. If we disagree, it is 'in Christ'. If, very regrettably, anything is allowed to prevent eucharistic fellowship,[488] then we should still be able to meet, pray together and discuss with courtesy and respect.

'THAT THEY MAY BE ONE': WAS JESUS BOTHERED ABOUT ORGANISATIONAL UNITY?

The Reformation has often been portrayed as a tragedy, but one blessing it brought was to de-absolutise the visible and organised church.[489] This leads me to a further thought. We often read Jesus' prayer for unity as though it applied principally to institutional unity. Perhaps this is

---

488   This is why I said earlier that I find the approach of the more 'fundamentalist' opponents of women bishops (boycotting the eucharist at Lambeth, doctrines of episcopal taint, etc.) very problematic. It stabs right at the heart of Eucharistic hospitality and ecumenical fellowship.

489   See p.219–221

partly because it is one of the passages regularly used in 'The Week of Prayer for Christian Unity' with its institutional focus. But what did Jesus mean when he said, "'My prayer is not for them alone. I pray also for those who will believe in me through their message, that all of them may be one, Father, just as you are in me and I am in you. May they also be in us so that the world may believe that you have sent me'"?[490] Was he thinking primarily of institutional or more of relational unity? All I know of Jesus would suggest the latter.

To some extent I concede that this is a false antithesis. If we can have healthy institutional unity, it can greatly help relational unity. However, when institutional unity is preserved at the cost of bitterness, and perhaps the unhealthy exercise of power and coercion, maybe ties need to be loosened to enhance relational unity. Jesus' prayer for unity was 'so that the world may believe'. I do not believe that having a variety of denominations is a great stumbling block to belief in the modern world. People are used to healthy competition in politics and business, and those who are mature know that being competitors does not have to mean being enemies. I'm not sure that in any meaningful sense the various denominations really are competitors, but even if we are I am not sure that this is such a stumbling block.[491] What *is* a stumbling block is bitterness, anger, in-fighting and suspicion between Christians, whether it be monks in Jerusalem, Ian Paisley in Belfast (in the earlier part of his life), factions in Synod, or two pillars of the local church who cannot get on with each other. In our day, such division seems to happen more within denominations than between them. Therefore, if our pursuit of institutional unity is wrecking relational unity, perhaps we have got it wrong? Perhaps we would heed Jesus' prayer better by loosening ties and paying more attention to ecumenical respect and hospitality?

---

490   John 17:20–21

491   In fact I suspect that a monolithic church, given the prevalent alienation from large institutions, and fear of being coerced by them, would prove far more of a stumbling block to belief than do a variety of denominations modelling healthy co-operation and respect, but offering a choice to followers.

So, if the Episcopal Church (in the USA) (TEC) believes that the affirmation of homosexual relationships is a fundamental part of the liberation that Jesus came to bring, and the Church of Nigeria and others strongly disagree, and some other parts of the Anglican Communion are seriously split within themselves, perhaps TEC should be allowed to go its own way, and be independent or semi-independent, with the recognition that we cannot agree and cannot follow, but we can still recognise Christ in one another. Perhaps they will turn out to be pioneers from whom we will all in turn learn. Perhaps they will be making a disastrous mistake that we will all in time learn from. If we could learn to allow such diversity within the one Anglican Communion, without separating, so much the better. We should not separate lightly. But sometimes to separate amicably might be a better witness to Jesus Christ than to remain yoked together while squabbling viciously. If we do separate, we must still recognise each other as brothers and sisters in Christ, although brothers and sisters who no longer live in the same house.

LEARNING TO SEPARATE PEACEFULLY

If there comes a time when we have to walk apart, this should be the last and not the first resort. But sometimes that time does arrive, and *how* we separate becomes very important.

When children reach a certain age, the wise parent allows them to leave home. For many families, the transition to university enables this to happen in a graduated and predictable way. It was a mark of some of the more dysfunctional families that I met in the course of parish ministry in inner London that teenage or adult children often only seemed to leave home after a furious argument and a falling out. Some seemed to have no concept of a mature and peaceful separating. There is perhaps something to be learned from the way the British Empire was allowed, largely peacefully, to dissolve into a Commonwealth of mutual respect and affection. Perhaps allowing the ties of worldwide Anglicanism to loosen would not be such a disaster and would better allow relationships of mutual respect and affection to flourish. There are echoes here of the policy of Henry Venn and the CMS.[492]

JESUS IS THE HEART OF UNITY

Problems arise whenever we make anything or anyone other than Jesus Christ the focus or guarantee of our unity. The limits of episcopacy as a focus of unity are exposed by divisions over the consecration of women bishops in the Church of England. Unity is organic, stemming from our relatedness to Jesus, and maintained by our Holy Spirit-inspired attempts to imitate Him. Attempts to hold together within the same organisation by codes of practice or statutory provision will not be fruitful unless there is a deeper source of unity than episcopacy, or structures, or agreeing on beliefs even.

People and organisations under pressure face a temptation to forget Jesus, to go for quick fixes, to get tough, or to adopt political stratagems and play power games. In the context of an invitation from the Pope to Anglicans disaffected over the consecration of women bishops, *The Times*' religious affairs correspondent, Ruth Gledhill, commented:

'The Archbishop of Canterbury has displayed a munificent turning of the other cheek in response to what many see as a move by the Pope to annex part of his Church. No one doubts his Christian holiness. But a bit more muscular Christianity would not go amiss. In Rome this week he might do better to ask himself not "What would Jesus do?" but "What would Thomas Cromwell do?"'[493]

May God deliver us from such advice. What is the point of 'winning' and forgetting the One who is the goal of the whole 'game'? I

---

492 See p.206–209
493 *The Times,* 19/11/09

seem to remember Jesus asking about the point of winning the whole world and losing your soul.[494]

Jesus is the source, focus and guarantee of unity. I've never experienced unity of heart, mind and spirit like that on interdenominational evangelistic missions (like the 'Walk' missions mentioned on p.90–91). I served for six years on the Council of The Evangelical Alliance, and though there were a multitude of denominations represented, and sometimes we argued determinedly, there was a profound underlying unity, manifested in worship and prayer together, trust and respect, real affection, and common purpose, that exceeded the unity I normally experience within my own denomination. It was a unity that did not come from all thinking the same things (we manifestly did not). It was a unity that, despite our differences, was maintained by an affection for and commitment to Jesus that trumped all disagreements.

The Anglican Communion and the Church of England at the moment feel like families whose unity has been taken for granted for a long time. One day the patriarch or matriarch that held them together dies. Suddenly there is no motivation to get together for family occasions, and the old ties loosen, and eventually warmth is replaced, in some cases by coldness or distance, in others, by squabbles. If we take our eyes off Jesus and focus instead on secondary matters, something very similar soon happens.

Dr Stephen Olford, a participant in a consultation of mission leaders, recalls that 'there were some heated discussions. One afternoon in particular, several men almost lost their tempers in an attempt to sustain their positions. Billy Graham in the chair sought to moderate the debate but there seemed little hope for harmony, let alone progress.

---

494   Mark 8:36

At this point Festo[495] stood up. There was absolute silence. Up to this point I don't believe he had said a word. Appealing to the chair, Festo looked around and said very simply, "Brothers and sisters, I'm not a theologian, and I don't pretend to have the training and experience of these great men around me, but I believe there is a solution to the world's problems and, indeed, to every discussion we're having right now." Then he paused and with exquisite reverence said one word, "JESUS". Every person in that room was smitten with conviction and a spirit of brokenness. At the word from Billy Graham we were all on our knees, and for hours, prayers of repentance, brokenness, confession and restoration poured forth from every person in the room. God had met us under the spell and power of one word, "JESUS".[496]

THE JOURNEY SO FAR

We have seen that Jesus did not coerce obedience, He invited it. He calls us to follow that example, and commands us not to judge. Jesus is thus the answer to post-modern fears of coercive religion and ideology.

This may be fine when Christians are acting as individuals, but what happens when Christians come together as church? Can institutions actually be non-coercive? Clearly many today fear not, which is at least part of the reason why many people will say "Jesus is OK – it's the church I can't stand."

We cannot avoid institutional expression of our faith. We are therefore left with the question, can an institution be Christlike, and if so, how?

I suggest that institutions can be Christlike. This is partly a matter of making sure that the individuals who govern and

---

495 Rt Revd Festo Kivengere, Bishop of Kigezi, Uganda, and renowned international evangelist. I heard him once when he preached in the East End of London in the early 1980s, and it was an unforgettable experience.
496 *Festo Kivengere*, Anne Coomes, p.205 (Monarch, 1990)

serve any institution are as Christlike as possible, and partly a matter of making sure that our systems and culture operate by Christlike values, including being as non-coercive as possible, and enabling Christlike behaviour.

Being as Christlike as possible for a Christian leader means not leading 'like the Gentiles' (out of power and extrinsic authority) but leading by serving. Christian leaders do have real power, which must not be abused despite the many temptations so to do.

Christlike leadership will be empowering, vulnerable, transparent, accountable, and will not bully or manipulate. It will be hugely sensitive to any tendency to play God in the lives of others.

For an institutional culture to be Christlike, that institution must be first and foremost dedicated to Jesus Christ's interests, not to its own. This is harder than it sounds as self-preservation can quickly come to dominate the agenda of any institution. Institutional Christlikeness can be manifested in a willingness to die, what Henry Venn and CMS called 'the euthanasia of mission'.

An institution that is faithful will be willing to embrace weakness, including a willingness to speak from the margins, excluded from the corridors of power. It will practise subsidiarity, making decisions as closely as possible to the people affected. It will keep rules and regulations to a minimum. It will prioritise the poor. It will be culturally diverse. It will practise generosity and mutuality. Jesus should not need to leave the room when church politics is being practised.

There are enough real examples of Christlike institutional practice to suggest that this is not a forlorn hope.

Bitterness and enmity bring Jesus into disrepute. It is doubtful these days whether the disunity of differing denominations existing side by side is seen as a scandal. Indeed, it may even be seen as beneficial. Perhaps we should be more welcoming of the great diversity between churches, and if we must separate as Anglicans, whether in the Anglican Communion or within the Church of England, continue to practise 'ecumenical hospitality' in a way that manifests our ongoing unity in Christ. Sometimes it is better to separate peacefully than to stay together with bitterness and rancour. Unity in Christ cannot be coerced by the denial of choice.

Chapter Ten

The Homosexuality Debate:
Does Jesus Have Anything to Say?

"How can you say to your brother, 'Let me take the speck out of
your eye', when all the time there is a plank in your own eye? You
hypocrite, first take the plank out of your own eye, and then you
will see clearly to remove the speck from your brother's eye."

(Jesus of Nazareth)

Though this book is not about homosexuality, a chapter dealing with
the issue is placed here because:

1) It was processing knowledge of my son's sexual orientation
   that opened for me many of the perspectives that animate
   and guide this book, not least a fresh appreciation of the
   centrality of Jesus and our call to imitate Him.

2) Our response to homosexuality is perhaps one of the most
   contentious issues still threatening to tear the church apart.
   A detailed examination of how the conclusions so far
   might animate that debate is perhaps the best illustrative
   application I can find of what I am trying to say.

I therefore wonder how the fierce argument around homosexuality in
the Anglican Communion might develop if we became more concerned
to be Christlike in the way we deal with difference and dispute.

THE HOMOSEXUALITY DEBATE: DOES JESUS HAVE ANYTHING TO SAY?

Is there anything we can learn about the debate over homosexuality from Jesus? Jesus did not mention or refer to homosexuality once. Of course, this does not mean that the subject does not matter. Jesus accepted the authority of the Old Testament, which does mention homosexuality. We will look at the biblical passages later. However, the absence of any mention by Jesus might suggest to us that His *priorities* are elsewhere, and perhaps we can learn from this.

In much of our church recently it seems to me that gay people have occupied the place that lepers, Gentiles, tax collectors and the unclean did in Jesus' day, and about such people, *and through them*, Jesus had much to teach us. Some may object 'Yes, but homosexuality is a moral issue'. But lepers, Gentiles and the unclean (and by implication tax collectors and prostitutes) were excluded by the Word of God in the Old Testament on religious purity grounds. The issues are not dissimilar.

In this chapter I want to examine some of the implications of what I have argued so far, for how we handle disagreements over homosexuality that are currently dividing the church so painfully. The subject of homosexuality polarises. As soon as it is raised, people within the church frequently take sides, while those on the outside may switch off in frustration or boredom. The biblical, medical and sociological arguments have been rehearsed many times. However, what if, while we were rushing to our trenches, God was saying to us "I'm trying to speak to you about how you treat one another. Please shut up for a minute and listen"? (OK, God *might* not say "shut up", but the general sentiment is exactly what I believe He is saying to his church.) How we hold together 'grace *and* truth'[497] is at stake here, as is our obedience to His command to love one another, and as is the mission of the church.

---

497   John 1:14

FAITHFUL WITNESS OR HOSTILE WITNESS?

Soon after beginning to sketch out this chapter I was encouraged to discover the work of Andrew Marin and 'The Marin Foundation'. From a US perspective Andrew writes,

'Right now the UK has a unique opportunity to potentially model for the rest of the world how to properly address and work within the tensions of faith and sexuality; leading the path of what peaceful and productive systemic relationships look like.

'I believe this because, thus far, neither the GLBT+ *(sic)*[498] nor Christian communities have publicly or sustainably rallied their masses against the other... The UK is not even close to the very vocal, firmly rooted, abhorrence-filled structural disconnect that exists in America between our two communities.

'There was a point where America was at the same place as the UK... At the time, there were no national Christian or GLBT *(sic)* leaders willing to initiate and sustain any amount of conversation in a productive, God-honouring fashion. The only American national leaders that rose up fuelled the fire and dug each community further into their stagnant modes of engagement, unsuccessfully trying to convince the other side they're wrong and need to give up everything they have ever fought for. This aggressive, back-and-forth schism has persisted for the last decade with no reprise *(sic)* in sight... Each community is so strongly opposed and wounded by the other, both are convinced that each will win. In my estimation, even if the culture war lessens to the point where they can talk to the other rather than past the other, the American GLBT *(sic)* and Christian relations will still be about twenty years behind.'[499]

We may not yet be in the same extremely polarised place as the USA, but many non-Christians are distinctly put off by our obsession with this

---

498   Gay, Lesbian, Bisexual or Transgender.
499   'Mission and The Gay Community' an article by Andrew Marin in *Anvil* journal,
      p.283, Vol.26, Nos 3 & 4, 2009.

issue and by the ungraciousness with which the debate is sometimes conducted within the church. They therefore cannot conceive why on earth they should listen to Christians about *anything*. Effectively we are in danger of slanderously misrepresenting the character of Jesus. We do this whenever we caricature our opponents, say untrue things about them, whether deliberately or because we have never got to know them, whenever we act judgmentally as if we were not ourselves sinners, and whenever we give the impression of acting out of fear. It is utterly pointless to tell people that Jesus is the friend of sinners if the public witness of prominent Christians suggests otherwise. At the same time, many Christians, especially younger ones, are becoming alienated from their faith communities over this, even if they still believe in Jesus.

Philip Yancey tells of attending the first gay march in Washington, not as a journalist, nor as a demonstrator (on either side), but to support his gay friend, Mel, who was wrestling painfully with his gay identity. He describes a small group of Christian protesters yelling angrily at the gay marchers:

"'Faggots, go home!" their leader screamed into a microphone, and the others took up the chant: "Faggots go home, faggots go home."

More than a thousand marched under the banner of the Metropolitan Community Church (MCC). (They) had a poignant reply to the beleaguered Christian protesters: they drew even, turned to face them, and sang, "Jesus loves us, this we know, for the Bible tells us so"... The more orthodox group spewed out hate and the other group sang of Jesus' love.'[500]

Who was responding as Jesus would; Philip Yancey, supporting his gay friend, or the demonstrators shouting "Faggots, go home"? The answer seems too obvious to need stating. Yet it *does* need stating. How

---

500   *What's So Amazing About Grace?*, Philip Yancey, p.165–166 (Zondervan, 1997)

many of us from the more conservative wing of the church would have been willing to walk with Mel that day? For much of my ministry I don't think I would. I remember being invited to a conference of the Lesbian and Gay Christian Movement by a gay fellow clergy person and colleague, with whom I was in a developing dialogue. I pleaded that I was too busy, and indeed I was very busy at the time. However, we make time for what is important to us, and I now suspect that I didn't appreciate how much I had to learn, or how important it was to my colleague that people like me stepped out of our comfort zones and learned first-hand. I also suspect that my own unacknowledged discomfort at the thought of going to such a conference made the fact of my busyness extremely convenient.

It was only later, when coming to terms with the knowledge that one of *those* people was my own devoutly Christian son, that I went to 'Courage' and 'Metropolitan Community Church' meetings where, to my surprise I am ashamed to say, I found that Jesus was already there. I met Christlike people, and I was blessed.

WHY HAS HOMOSEXUALITY BECOME SUCH A CAUSE CÉLÈBRE IN THE CHURCH?

Why has resisting the pressure to relax the church's stance on homosexuality become such a polarising cause célèbre? Partly I suggest because many Christians believe that respect for the authority of the Bible is at stake. In a reaction against so-called 'liberalism', conservatives have been looking for a line to draw in the sand in defence of biblical authority, and homosexuality is currently the chosen issue for parts of the church. That much of this pressure to change has come from tides of opinion within secular society makes many Christians all the more suspicious. After all, we are called to be different from the world. There is, therefore, a *prima facie* case to be made that the church is in danger of following currents of fashion and denying biblical revelation. That biblical authority is not *necessarily* at stake I have argued earlier.[501] We will look at this more closely later in this chapter.

Moreover, some celibate gay people, who have struggled at enormous cost and with much pain to be faithful to traditional sexual morality and to their reading of the Bible, feel that their costly sacrifice is being undermined and devalued by a church bent on liberalisation, and for them a lot really is at stake.

But, for the heterosexual majority, why is *this* issue the one on which many Christians have made a decision to take a stand, to draw that line in the sand? The way that homosexuality has been singled out from other issues of biblical interpretation and contention, to stand uniquely as a litmus test for Christian orthodoxy, is not just illegitimate, but distinctly odd. Statements by some that homosexuality is a 'salvation issue'[502] are strange on the lips of those who, claiming to be heirs of the Reformation, should know better than most that we are saved by grace through faith in Christ alone. Furthermore, too much fearful, sometimes hateful and spiteful behaviour, on the part of those who claim to be acting and speaking for Jesus, suggests that there is much more going on here than meets the eye.

Could it be that the debate over homosexuality is a safe argument for Christian legalists who are not gay, as it concerns a temptation they do not feel? Picking on a minority group who are different can give the majority group a sense of superiority, and the illusion of taking control against a threatening tide of moral relativism. By picking on a temptation they are not liable to, it can enable a sense of moral invulnerability, and a way of distinguishing themselves from 'sinners' who are 'out there'.[503] It provides a way of avoiding the challenge of Alexander Solzhenitsyn's remark, "If only there were evil people somewhere insidiously committing evil deeds and it were necessary only to separate them from the rest of us and destroy them. But the

---

501 See p.150–152
502 See p.127–129
503 See p.20–21. 'Those Sinners', or 'We Sinners'.

dividing line between good and evil cuts through the heart of every human being…"[504]

James Alison,[505] in an illuminating study of the reactions to Jesus' healing of the man born blind,[506] exposes the dynamics at work here in the tendency to pick on and exclude someone else to establish your own righteousness. He goes on to show how Jesus subverts this tendency in His challenges to the Pharisees. The religion of sacrifice looks for a scapegoat to ensure the stability or purity of what remains. Jesus has been that scapegoat once and for all and declared an end to that whole game. 'I desire mercy, not sacrifice.'[507] Note that this is not an argument about the rights and wrongs of homosexual behaviour, any more than the way that Jesus treated the accusers of the woman caught in adultery[508] was an attempt to argue that Moses' law on adultery was superseded. The accusers were technically right about the issue of Moses' law at stake here, but their hearts, their motives and their perception of the situation were deeply wrong.

As soon as any group of believers starts demanding that members become 'like us' as a condition of belonging, they have taken the focus off Jesus. They have made something else the way to salvation. Alison comments, 'Many of us have participated actively in groups whose idea of religious conversion is that we should become like them, for whom the standard of righteousness and soundness is being "like us", behaving like them, sharing their worldview, their politics, their bad guys.'[509] This always operates together with a silent blackmail. As we have seen earlier, this is not the way of the Kingdom of God,

---

504   *The Gulag Archipelago*, Alexander Solzhenitsyn, Ch.1. See p.21 above.

505   *Faith Beyond Resentment*, James Alison (Darton Longman and Todd, 2001), Ch.1, 'The Man Born Blind and the Creator's Subversion of Sin.'

506   John 9

507   Matthew 9:13

508   John 8:1–11. 'The teachers of the law and the Pharisees brought to Jesus a woman who had been caught in adultery. They proposed to stone her, and sought to trap Jesus by asking what he thought. He said, "Let he who is without sin cast the first stone", and they slunk away, ashamed.'

509   *Faith Beyond Resentment*, James Alison, p.129 (Darton Longman and Todd, 2001)

which delights in diversity and is led by a King who never blackmails, manipulates or coerces in any way.

I observe that many of those who are fiercest opponents of gay liberalisation seem not to really know any gay people. By 'know' I mean as friends, not as superficial acquaintances. Partly this is because of fear, partly because friendship can only flourish in the absence of judgmentalism. Friends do not have to agree, even on quite fundamental things, but they do need to suspend hostilities, and that means suspending judgment.

A pre-condition of graciousness and of being able to deal gently with those who sin seems to be knowing our own fallenness, our own deep complicity in sin, and our own danger of falling further at every step. It also means knowing that we are still deeply loved by God, accepted and acceptable because of Jesus, and thus we are all in the same boat. Thus Galatians 6:1, after saying 'Brothers and sisters, if someone is caught in a sin, you who live by the Spirit should restore that person gently', continues 'but watch yourselves, or you also may be tempted'.

Because homosexuality does not tempt the majority, I believe that as an issue it attracts a disproportionate number of those who struggle to live with the fact that they too are sinners dependent upon grace. Here is an issue that, if we let it, can foster the illusion that we are morally superior, and allows us to approach the sinners in question without any empathy. "They must be profoundly warped and sinful, after all, to find anything so disgusting attractive." I remember the first time this came home to me. I was in conversation with a deeply Christlike person whom I admired greatly, who turned out to be a celibate gay. I dismissively said, about gay sex, "but it is repellent". He simply said, "but not to me", thereby coming out, and challenging my self-righteousness all in one sentence. As I reflected, that remark had a huge impact on me.

A final reason, I believe, why this issue has become such a 'cause célèbre' in Britain and the USA is that in the West, as we discussed in Chapters 2 and 4, we have so little that is distinctive about our discipleship and so little focus on 'the imitation of Christ'. If we have opted for a therapy model of discipleship or for the 'prosperity gospel', having perverted or sidelined the greater part of Jesus' teaching and example, we are going to have to pick something else to make us seem holy and distinctive. What better than to be rigorous about an issue that is not directly going to affect the vast majority of our members, that enables us to focus on 'dying to self', but at someone else's expense? Those who want to appear holy without a costly investment in real holiness have always had a disproportionate investment in shibboleths and in scapegoating. Wasn't this often what was at the root of the conflict between the religious authorities and Jesus?

WRONG IN GOOD FAITH?

As an issue with which to draw a line in the sand regarding biblical authority, homosexuality only makes sense if the range of possible interpretations of Scripture cannot reasonably be held to embrace the point of view of those we are opposing (whichever side we stand on). My own conclusions are that the biblical teaching on homosexuality is, on a balance of probabilities, best interpreted in a 'conservative' way. I cannot say however that those who take a more liberal view have necessarily disregarded the authority of the Bible. Which side of the homosexuality debate we might come down on, and whether we are persuaded by a more or less conservative interpretation of the biblical texts, is very much secondary to my main argument here. All that is necessary for the argument of this book, that Jesus Christ is the heart and definition of our faith, is to accept that some of those who take a different line from us on a scriptural issue may do so in good faith, seeking conscientiously to be biblical and to be faithful to Jesus, but coming to different conclusions. It is not necessary that we are persuaded by their arguments, only that we are sufficiently persuaded that in good (even if, in our opinion, mistaken) faith, they are seeking to serve Jesus Christ and to work out their beliefs from the Bible in a way that is not manifestly absurd, dishonest or unbelieving.

Of course, not *all* who disagree with us are even trying to be biblical in any sense we would recognise. We have all come across those who profess to be Christians, but when the Bible that bears witness to Jesus appears to disagree with them, are content to think, 'so much the worse for the Bible'.[510] That must raise questions about the seriousness of their Christian commitment. However, we must beware of coming to this harsh conclusion too readily. 'To their own master, servants stand or fall.' I have found many of those who stand on the other side of the debate about homosexuality from me to be at least as serious about discovering and heeding what the Bible says and about following Jesus, as I try to be. Once I realise this, if I am a follower of Jesus, I must respectfully and affectionately engage with them as brothers and sisters in Christ, *not* as 'enemies of the cross of Christ'.

IS HOMOSEXUALITY GIVEN, ACQUIRED, OR CHOSEN?

We will now examine some of the issues and experiences around homosexuality that might explain why there has been an impulse towards re-examining our interpretation of the Bible on this issue.

What if you or I had been born homosexual (assuming you were not)? Some Christians seem to deny the validity of such a question from the outset. They assert, in the face of the evidence, that there is a choice in this matter. Surely, however, there is a choice about actions, but

---

510   They are the flip side of, and betray a similar attitude to, some 'certainty merchants' who say, "The Bible says, and I agree with it". Often the latter are just more dishonest about what they disagree with. They just ignore what the Bible says about social justice, or the Holy Spirit, or whatever their particular bug bear or blind spot happens to be.

not usually about orientation. There is no choice about the terrible dilemmas that being gay leaves you with.

The same testimony is given by most gay people I have known at all well (and I have known a number in each of the churches in which I have served). Nearly every one wished to be 'healed' at one time or another, and not a single one was so 'healed'[511] in any sense that could be described as a change of basic orientation and desires.[512]

There are some who are bisexual, and a few who choose to experiment with gay sex. Such people might have some element of choice.[513] However, this should not cloud the issue. These are not truly homosexual in the sense that I am discussing here. For the homosexual person, *homosexuality is not a chosen orientation.*

When we consider truly homosexually oriented people who, try as they might, cannot find attraction to the opposite sex, and cannot lose their attraction to their own sex, there has been no choice of orientation, therefore no turning aside, literally no perversion.

George Hopper, a heterosexual evangelical Methodist, who wrote of his journey from a hard line, to a different view, commented on the pain and cost to those like our son, who discover in adolescence that they are gay. 'Young people on television spoke of how they had come to realise – sometimes with fear bordering on horror – that they were different from their peers: they were gay. Some of them spoke about the pain they had experienced upon telling their parents, who often

---

511   I am referring here to homosexuals, not lesbians. I know lesbians who do claim such healing, and I suspect that female homosexuality is not an identical phenomenon to male homosexuality. Research is needed here by a brave soul willing to enter the minefield not only of same-sex sexual attraction, but also of innate differences between men and women.

512   Each of them wished their homosexuality to remain secret from the congregation. This fact alone disturbed me, not that they would not be open, but that the church of Jesus Christ was not a safe place for these faithful Christians to be real. I therefore have not felt it right to approach them to tell their stories, and instead have chosen already published stories that reflect what I know to be true from pastoral experience.

513   Though many who are intersex were also born that way and face equally unavoidable pressures and dilemmas.

found it hard to understand and were sometimes unsupportive. Some young people had even been thrown out of their family home.

Others had grown up within a church community, only to discover that they belonged to the very group that is condemned and rejected by many church people for something over which they (and we) have no control – our sexual orientation."[514]

The phrase 'sexual preference' is, therefore, pernicious and ignorant. THERE IS NO CHOICE FOR MOST. Again, to be quite clear, I am not at this point talking about choice concerning behaviour, but about choice concerning orientation.

Let's allow the last word in this section to a gay guy who came to one of George Hopper's study groups and said, "Do you think I would *choose* to be homosexual with all the pain and heartache that goes with it?"[515]

CAN HOMOSEXUALITY BE 'HEALED'?

Courage (UK) was a Christian ministry founded to bring about change of sexual orientation for homosexual and lesbian people through healing, counselling and deliverance, and to support those who took the road of celibacy. Twelve years later in 2000, Jeremy Marks, Courage's founder and director, repudiated the so-called 'ex-gay' movement, proclaiming that it did more harm than good. This led to expulsion from 'Exodus International'[516] and 'The Evangelical Alliance.'[517]

Hugely significantly, thirteen years later on 19 June 2013, *Christianity Today* reported that 'Exodus International' had changed

---

514 *Reluctant Journey*, George Hopper, Ch.1 www.reluctantjourney.co.uk
515 Ibid.
516 At that time a movement offering 'healing' to gay people to which 'Courage' were affiliated.
517 Recounted in *Exchanging the Truth of God for a Lie* by Jeremy Marks, Introduction p.viii (Courage UK, 2008)

their stance to mirror that of 'Courage'. Their president forswore ex-gay therapy and apologised to the gay community for the hurt and damage they had caused. This was for the same reasons as Courage's change, namely lack of evidence over many years that 'ex-gay' therapy works, and a huge amount of evidence of the harm it causes, meaning that the leaders felt that they could no longer in conscience continue.

Jeremy Marks commented: 'In reality, the long-term consequences for many who took part in our discipleship programmes were pretty depressing – near disastrous for some. The long-term damage to all of us has been incalculable. A strategy that had largely been inspired by hyped-up charismatic expectations of change proved spiritually catastrophic. Many people gave up their faith altogether.'[518]

Jeremy Marks' pastoral experience chimes with mine. Not only have I never yet personally come across a gay man whose basic sexual orientation has been changed, but also, despite many times asking those who assert that such change is possible, I have never been presented with one example of such 'healing' that has endured.

I have watched my own son's repeated and persistent attempts to find 'healing' with increasing anguish. I have witnessed his failure to find any deep-seated change of orientation, and the increasingly desperate attempts of well-meaning Christians to say "if you only try this therapy, or that prayer ministry or the other approach, you will find healing". I have also seen the greater peace that has come through self-acceptance, and the acceptance that this kind of healing was not required or offered by God.

It's not enough to say, 'just try deliverance ministry, you never know', if we know full well that it is most unlikely to produce any lasting change in orientation. That way lies disillusionment and despair. It lacks integrity to keep insisting that God can do anything when all the evidence suggests that this is not a way He normally chooses to act.

---

518   Ibid. p.7–8

The evidence seems to be that 'healing' or 'cure' in the sense of a change of orientation doesn't normally happen. By 'cure' I mean a change of basic orientation, so that one is able to desire the opposite sex and be set substantially or entirely free from same-sex erotic desires. It is important to be absolutely clear about this. I am not saying that God cannot 'heal' a homosexual orientation, or even that He never does. That would be silly. God is almighty and can do anything, but as a rule He clearly does not do *this*. If God does change sexual orientation, then the numbers involved are vanishingly small, far too small to build a pastoral strategy upon with any shred of integrity.

Jeremy Marks lays it on the line after years doing as much as anyone in the Christian community to bring about such change: 'To those who claim that "healing from homosexuality" is possible, we have to say that after more than ten years of working in "ex-gay" ministry, we cannot with integrity uphold a message that God plainly does not support. The evidence is that it just does not work. Give them five years and their apparent change breaks down.'[519]

This matters because not only does it often lead to disillusionment, loss of faith, and despair, not uncommonly it leads to suicide.[520]

Once you admit that 'healing' does not usually happen for homosexual people, a whole host of further questions then follow about what a Christian should do to include and support their fellow sinners in the same way as was modelled by the one who was known as 'a friend of sinners'. How would Jesus have us behave towards those who have been treated as outcasts by the 'holy people'? What does Jesus want us to do in relation to those who often find difficulty accepting themselves, let alone believing that other believers, or even God, can accept them? A false promise of healing has been a cop-out from these questions. Now

---

519   Ibid. p.66
520   See for example, the story of Simon Harvey in *Reluctant Journey* by George Hopper, Ch.1, www.reluctantjourney.co.uk or of 'Robert', in *Exchanging the Truth of God for a Lie* by Jeremy Marks, p.1–3 (Courage UK, 2008), just two of many examples.

is the time to face a more demanding love that doesn't leave it all up to God but demands a little more of us. This will be a love that seeks to listen, understand and walk with, rather than judging, proscribing and prescribing. It will be a love that sees *people*, not just 'homosexuals', and is willing to be a friend and not just a case worker. Otherwise we are like those of whom James says, 'Someone will say "Go in peace; keep warm and well fed" but does nothing about their physical needs, what good is it? In the same way, faith by itself, if it is not accompanied by action, is dead.'[521]

WHAT IS IT LIKE TO BE GAY?

To really answer the question 'what is it like to be gay?' I would refer you to accounts by gay people themselves.[522] Only they can speak authentically about their own experience. Of course the answer will be different for every person who answers it. There is no one gay experience.

Better still, befriend gay people and learn. To avoid the many pitfalls and the many unwitting ways of causing offence, I strongly recommend reading *Love is an Orientation* by Andrew Marin.[523] This is an account of how Andrew was shocked when three of his closest friends came out to him as gay in successive months, and of the journey of learning and loving that this started for him. As a conservative evangelical believer, who has not changed his conservative biblical beliefs, he faced the dilemma of how he could still love his friends as Jesus wished.

Perhaps I should leave this section at that and leave gay people to speak for themselves. However, given the inability of many churches

---

521   James 2:16b–17

522   I would recommend *Exchanging the Truth of God for a Lie* by Jeremy Marks, p.1–3 (Courage UK, 2008), *The Other Way? Anglican Gay and Lesbian Journeys*, edited by Colin Coward (Changing Attitude, 1998), *Undivided* by Vicky Beeching (HarperCollins, 2018) & *Living Out*, www.livingout.org/

523   *Love Is An Orientation*, Andrew Marin (IVP Illinois, 2009)

to allow gay people any safe space to speak honestly, or to give them any credibility if they do speak, and given that many gay people will find it hard to allow Christians (especially conservative Christians) to get too close, perhaps I do need to say a little more, with the proviso that nothing I say can be definitive, and will only be useful if it gets the reader into an open and gracious conversation with gay people, not as a 'project' but as friends, or as brothers or sisters in Christ.

We need to hear all shades of gay experience, and especially from the many gay Christians; from those in relationships, on the one hand, to the celibate gay person who believes he or she is called to abstinence on the other, from the 'out and proud' to those who are silent about being gay, too afraid of rejection to speak up. Too often we do not hear from celibate gay people, as, somehow, we have created a church where they dare not speak, and which often prefers to have it that way. If they had met Jesus in the flesh, sitting by a well perhaps, one suspects that everything would be open for discussion very quickly. Too often the celibate gay person feels undermined on the one hand by the cry for liberalisation, as if some Christians are making light of their sacrifice and saying it was unnecessary after all, and on the other, feels permanently on probation in their church, and therefore dares not be open.

This silence from celibate gay people may be changing in recent years since the publication of 'Living Out',[524] a website started by five leading conservative evangelical clergy who are gay and celibate. The site is notable for a willingness to be vulnerable on the part of its contributors and for introducing a new level of reality and honesty into the conservative side of the debate. Contributors are clear that healing of orientation does not normally happen, and that church support for gay people has been sadly lacking. They call for celibacy, acknowledging the toughness as well as the blessings of this challenge, and for gay-friendly, very much more supportive churches. At last the

---

524   http://www.livingout.org/

call to abstinence comes from the only ones with the credentials to make it, those who are walking that road. This has the potential to change the nature of the debate and to introduce some of the honesty and compassion into it that Andrew Marin calls for.[525]

Once we start speaking with gay Christians stereotypes begin to evaporate. One of the first to go might be that gay people are lustful, only interested in sex. This issue is not only, or even primarily, about lust, and sexual desire. For many it is about belonging and companionship, particularly in old age (many civil partnerships seem to have been contracted by older people), about having someone to go home to in the evening, having someone to care for you when you are ill. I'll never forget the wistful sadness of one celibate Christian gay friend who said to me, "You know, it's not mainly about sex. I just wish there were someone to come home to at the end of a day's work." Being homosexual is often about no kids, no grandchildren, about self-identity, and about belonging in a hostile world. It is not only or even mainly about sex.

So, you might think, if you are gay why not form deep friendships, take in a lodger, form a community? You do not have to be alone. However, these solutions do not fully meet the need for most, mainly because, unless you become a monk or a nun, there is no permanence, no covenanted relationship, and therefore no security. You might find companionship for a while but are likely to be left bereft in old age if not long before. If a relationship is more long-lasting or permanent, that is likely to be seen by some as problematic. In the current climate in many parts of the church, close gay friends are likely to be the cause of gossip and speculation, if not outright rejection. Then again, how do you have a close, long-term and intimate friendship with someone you are deeply sexually attracted to without falling into sexual sin? It is not easy. Neither is it helped by the constant prospect of falling victim to a witch hunt. Of course, single people, who are single not through their

---

525   See p.236

own choice, face similar issues. However, no one has told them at the outset of their young adult lives that there is no hope for them of *ever* marrying. There is a lot of truth in the saying that 'it is better to travel hopefully than to arrive'. Unless we try to understand what exactly it is like for a celibate gay Christian, we cannot love him or her with the love of Jesus Christ, and our fellowship and support will be glib and uncaring at best, and at worst harsh and cruel.

The relative absence of the extended family or household (assumed by much of the Bible), with numerous generations, and all kinds of relatives, under the same roof or at least in the same neighbourhood, can be problematic. Our modern Western not-so-biblical focus on the nuclear family has made the situation very much worse. It is now much harder to belong anywhere if you are gay, single, bereaved or elderly.

The option of civil partnership seems to be part of the solution here. It offers a way to relink friendship and covenant, to recover stability and permanence, faithfulness and unconditional commitment. If we all have to work out our own salvation with fear and trembling, and it is primarily for gay people themselves to respond to Jesus' invitation by discerning whether their path demands celibacy or not, then civil partnerships offer a better path, surely, than a path of casual sex or short-term relationships and insecurity. For those called to celibacy and for those who choose a sexual relationship, civil partnerships offer the legal and institutional backing for the development of a culture of permanence, fidelity and stability. In a wider culture that has seen heterosexual marriage increasingly marginalised and often denigrated, we have in the gay community a movement towards the rediscovery of the value of covenant and faithfulness. Surely the whole Christian community should be able to either welcome this, or, if they cannot agree, at least respect the motivations of those involved.

Though we now have state provision for same-sex marriage, I do not personally believe that this is the best solution for the church. I believe that marriage and civil partnerships are ontologically different and that they are best not confused, though there are many obvious parallels. I think the church would be wise to continue to maintain the distinction but I would hope that this was in the context of a greater celebration, rather than mere toleration, of diversity. In such a context difference does not have to be seen as second class. This would particularly be true in the light of my earlier proposal for the church to no longer act as registrar or judge by no longer conducting (as opposed to blessing) weddings.[526] This would remove much of the sting of the church's current position.

If it is hard to have a sense of secure belonging at home or in society for some gay people, it is often even harder in church. Where is the gay Christian, or the gay seeker after Jesus, to go? In my experience many of them come to our churches, often to the more conservative churches. Given the risk of rejection involved, that is remarkable, and speaks volumes about spiritual hunger and spiritual courage in the gay community. The truth is, as we have already seen, that as often as not gay people have encountered rejection, or only very qualified acceptance in the church.

Philip Yancey writes of a conversation with a gay believer. "'I still believe," one told me. "I would love to go to church, but whenever I've tried someone spreads a rumour about me and suddenly everyone withdraws." He added a chilling remark, "As a gay man, I've found it's easier for me to get sex on the streets than to get a hug in church.'"[527]

How many evangelical churches are safe even for celibate gays?

George Hopper tells us of one gay man who, after a brief search, met God and decided to live for Christ. 'His sexuality was still the same, although now he lived for Christ. He felt it was time to find a church to share in the worship of the God who had called and blessed him.

But this is when his problems began!

"It would be better if you went elsewhere", was the rejoinder

---

526 See p.218, 219
527 *What's So Amazing About Grace?*, Philip Yancey, p.168 (Zondervan, 1997)

when he finally told his story to his pastor because when preparing for baptism he thought he should share who he was and remove any deceit.'[528]

If Christian fellowship is not a safe place for the vulnerable and for those truly seeking God something VERY fundamental is wrong. James Alison speaks tellingly of 'voices of accusation and expulsion dressed up in the language of grace.'[529]

How then should we behave, especially if we have a conservative theology on this issue as I do? An article on the Courage website gives some apt advice. The author is a gay Christian in a conservative church, who has reluctantly decided to leave because he no longer feels welcome: 'If you are going to say "celibacy for life", then you had better make absolutely certain that as a church you make that bearable – what sort of a family will you be to the gay Christian? Will you bear with his or her frustrations, emotional ups and downs, with the unpredictability of those deepest feelings? Do not talk about change. I say that primarily because the "change concept" is unscriptural. But it is also a cop-out. When you seek to impose the yoke of celibacy upon a gay Christian, you are saying something very severe and very profound.

'If a gay person tells you something then you are privileged because you may well be the first person that he or she has ever spoken to. Do not be shocked by what you hear. Do not suggest "quick-fit" solutions or be quick to speak. Instead, listen and start praying for that brother or sister whose pain and hurt has been bottled up for so long. You will do the greatest service by ministering the love of Jesus to someone who knows that love for themselves, but rarely experiences it through the church body of which they are a part... It may well be your view that the Bible is absolutely clear on this issue... Maybe you are right, but will you dare to give your gay friend the space to consider and question? To

---

528 *Reluctant Journey*, George Hopper, Ch.3, www.reluctantjourney.co.uk, 1996
529 *Faith Beyond Resentment*, James Alison, p.142 (Darton Longman and Todd, 2001)

reject your view, even? Will you give them the opportunity to come to terms, or not, with hard sayings that really are hard?'[530]

Tragically, without meaning to, many Christians have convinced gay people that God hates them. Dave Tomlinson wrote about Brian. 'He couldn't escape the feeling that God hated him. And it was driving him crazy. I assured him that God did not hate him and tried to offer him a different interpretation of Christianity that accepted and affirmed gay people. He thanked me for this.'[531]

Before Dave could visit again, Brian had committed suicide.

Even the most conservative interpretation of the biblical teaching about sexuality does not change the fact that we are all sinners invited into God's mercy, and therefore anything that even suggests that some are especially sinful, or even beyond the pale, is a perversion of the Gospel. Furthermore, any approach that leaves fellow sinners experiencing rejection rather than loving acceptance is not faithful to Jesus Christ. If we believe gay people are called to celibacy this places a great onus upon us to model to them the love and acceptance of God, and to be the kind of individuals and the kind of community where masks can safely be permitted to come down.

However, I have become convinced that it is not just one-way traffic. It is not just that gay people need healthy Christlike churches. Churches need the fellowship and testimony of gay Christians.

There are many gay Christians, and for reasons we will analyse, they have a particularly powerful and rich testimony. However, their voices are rarely heard, and when heard, not really taken seriously. We meet and listen to all kinds of Christians with whom we disagree on quite fundamental issues, but not, it seems, on this issue. There seems

---

530 Courage UK Website. 'No Longer Welcome? A plea from a young, gay, evangelical Christian.' http://www.courage.org.uk

531 *Exchanging the Truth of God for a Lie*, Jeremy Marks. 'Afterword' by Dave Tomlinson, p.78 (Courage UK, 2008).

to be some kind of visceral fear operating. To what other group of Christians and fellow sinners do we say, "first get yourself sorted out, and then we will speak to you, then we will allow you in our churches, then we can tell you that God loves you."

Did God treat *us* like that? All too often the demand for repentance first and the insistence on offering 'healing' are ways of avoiding real befriending and relationship, and real listening. Furthermore, do we really believe that because we might disagree with our gay Christian brother or sister, they have everything to learn and nothing to share with us, nothing to teach?

The Testimony of Gay Christians

We need to understand that there are many gay Christians who are sincerely committed to Jesus, often more deeply committed than many of those who condemn them. In each church I have served in there have been a number of gay people, who have kept their sexual orientation secret from nearly everyone. There have probably been others who have not told me. In addition, many gay Christians will be found in more gay affirming churches, whether explicitly gay affirming, like the Metropolitan Community Church, or unofficially gay affirming, like some Anglican churches. It takes considerable courage to pursue Jesus Christ and explore faith when churches have such a reputation for hostility towards gay people. The perseverance of many gay people in their faith, and the resultant quality of that faith, reminds me of those whose faith has been forged in arenas of persecution. There is often a courage, a perseverance, a willingness to pay the price and an awareness of and love for Jesus that the rest of us could learn from. Unfortunately, when heterosexual Christians are urged to listen to the experience of gay people, if we heed the call at all, we often assume that all we have to learn about are gay issues and gay sexuality. We are in danger of failing to see the whole person, due to an obsession with sex. This easily leads to a diminishment of our grasp that before us is a person, a child of God. What if, by listening to gay Christians, we all have a great deal to learn about God, about faith and about our own discipleship?

When I learn from my Iranian Christian friends, or from my former colleague who was imprisoned for his faith in Eritrea, I do not need to feel that I agree with them on everything. Nor do I have to believe that they are perfect and sinless in order for me to learn about God from them, or in order to be inspired by their example. I learn because they have worked out their discipleship in fear and trembling in situations of weakness and in the face of challenges I have not known. Because of this I can see in them manifestations of Jesus Christ that are very special. I find it to be the same with many gay Christians. Can we not treat gay Christians as we would treat any other brother or sister in Christ?

I think of a gay friend who long ago decided to live a celibate life, and who sublimates his need for intimacy into loving care for and service of others. I think of his wonderful Christian example, but also of the pain that lies beneath it and the cost to him, borne cheerfully, of living like this. I think of the sense of dependence upon Jesus Christ that he radiates, though few know the burden he carries. Sometimes he is irascible. He is flawed. He is one of the most Christlike people I know. He is an inspiration.

I think of a different friend who is in a civil partnership, though ordained, and who, far from thinking of himself as a libertine, regards himself as a pioneer, bringing Christian standards of faithfulness, chastity, love and permanence into a culture that has been insufficiently aware of such examples and witness. For this he faces ostracism by some, and the constant risk of losing his licence as an ordained clergyman. Can we not honour such courage, and recognise that it is inspired by faith in Jesus Christ, whether we agree with his path or not?

Some years ago, with my son, I attended a fellowship meal followed by worship and Bible study at a meeting organised by 'Courage'. I was nervous and ill at ease for a while. Once the worship began, this uneasiness rapidly evaporated. People around me were singing familiar worship songs with rapt attention centred on Jesus. The focus of the evening was Jesus, not 'being gay'. The teaching was biblical and inspired, focused on discipleship and holiness. It was blindingly obvious that here were devout and genuine Christians. God did not reject them. That did not mean that God approved of everything they did or said, any more than knowing that God does not reject me means that He approves of everything I say and do. This experience led me to seriously wonder how many of those who claim that homosexuality is a 'salvation issue' are really secure in their own salvation. Surely it is not possible to fully understand the extent to which one is a sinner and still loved by God, and then turn around and deny someone else the same grace?

Jeremy Marks describes the ethos and purpose of 'Courage' when he says 'It is the story of a group of Christians who came to realise that God calls us to more than repentance and more than dutiful obedience to a set of rules. As we follow Christ, God calls us to become imitators of the one we worship (Ephesians 5:1–2). This calling will mean transformation at every level. And those who embark on this pilgrimage have Good News to share – the greatest imaginable news and the greatest possible cause for rejoicing – for the whole of mankind.'[532]

What I saw that evening while worshipping with 'Courage', the seriousness about discipleship and transformation and the infectious joy in Christ, were so obviously real and profound that it left an indelible impression upon me. These were not cynical dissectors of the Bible, looking for 'get-out clauses', and seeking for God to bless their sinful ways. They were serious seekers after God and serious (and joyful) disciples.

Therefore, though I believe on balance that the scriptural witness

---

532   *Exchanging the Truth of God for a Lie*, Jeremy Marks, p.4 (Courage UK, 2008)

invites gay people to celibacy, I am glad that 'Courage' exists following a different interpretation, and I recognise Jesus Christ among and in them. In fact, *accepting* each other despite these differences in policy is something we do all the time with other churches and denominations, so why do we find it so hard concerning homosexuality? We can recognise Christ in our brothers and sisters when we disagree about infant baptism, or pacifism, or how to handle money, or the role of the priest in the Eucharist, or marriage and divorce, and we are all the richer for such Christ-centred diversity. Why is it so much harder to recognise Christ in each other when we disagree about sexuality?

George Hopper noticed something special about the faith of gay Christians. 'I find their faith amazing. To hold to faith when many (though not all) find the church is spiteful to them, shows a true faith.' 'When I am with these friends, I feel close to Christ! Perhaps that is because they, like Him, know what it is to be despised and rejected and yet show patient love and understanding in return.'[533]

As I have said, I find a similar quality of faith in many gay Christians (both celibate and partnered) to that I find in Christians who have been persecuted. I noticed also, when I attended the 'Courage' meeting, that the organisation had to be circumspect about publicising the venue where they were meeting. The danger was of attracting Christian demonstrators and pickets, or of being evicted from the church premises they used. The atmosphere felt very similar to what I experienced in the Iranian church during the final years of the Shah's regime. There too, whilst not actively persecuted by the state, Christians experienced much unofficial persecution and restriction, and real dangers from fanatical Moslems, and had to be circumspect. I experienced an uncanny feeling of déjà vu at the Courage meeting. This pressure seems to produce an automatic quality control for many gay Christians that the rest of the church in the West currently seems

---

533   *Reluctant Journey*, George Hopper, Ch.1 (www.reluctantjourney.co.uk)

to lack. You do not put up with that kind of thing, as a rule, unless you are deeply committed.

Jeremy Marks expresses it this way:

'As gay Christians who have grappled with these difficult issues and paid a heavy price for seeking to live with integrity, we have found our hope in Christ alone. Through our relationship with Jesus Christ, we have found peace with ourselves and a sense of God's acceptance of committed same-sex partnerships. We realised that expressing our convictions would cost us our reputation and that we would lose credibility with most of our fellow evangelical Christians. Some of us have felt a bit like those early disciples who, on hearing Jesus' radical and unpalatable message about eating his flesh and drinking his blood, wanted to leave. But we have had to say, along with the few who stayed with Jesus, "Lord, to whom shall we go? You have the words of eternal life." (John 6:68)'[534]

I do not have to agree with Jeremy Marks about what God thinks of same-sex partnerships, to recognise that, in him, I have encountered a brother in Christ. I can argue vigorously with a brother in Christ. We can disagree profoundly, but we are still brothers in Christ, and this changes everything. Once I admit that here is a brother in Christ, from whom I have much to learn and receive, this will enormously change the nature of the argument and the debate. It may still be a vigorous argument, but it will have the tone of a profound conversation, not of a battle. It will be marked by mutual acceptance, not by a tone of rejection. It will be a conversation of hope, not of anxiety or despair.

We noted in Chapter 7 how we need to be in fellowship with people different from ourselves if we are to rightly understand scripture. One does not have to explore in any great depth with gay Christians in our culture to discover for ourselves how true this is.

---

534   *Exchanging the Truth of God for a Lie*, Jeremy Marks, p.70–71 (Courage UK, 2008)

WHAT OF THOSE WHO CANNOT IN CONSCIENCE AGREE?

If such a tone of gracious mutual respect, love, and fellowship is to mark our approach to gay people, should it not also, as far as possible, mark our approach to those whose beliefs sometimes put them at odds with the gay community, and increasingly with mainstream society?

I think immediately of Lilian Ladele, a registrar in what was then my home borough of Islington, who lost her job because of her refusal, on grounds of Christian belief, to conduct civil partnership ceremonies. There is a failure here to understand the nature of conscience. We live in a society in which consumer choice has become so much a guiding principle for all action that the idea that conscience can constrain, is, I believe, genuinely alien to many people, including many policymakers.

I am here, at this point, neither attacking nor defending Lilian Ladele's beliefs. There is a long and widely held tradition, until comparatively recently, of belief that the recognition of homosexual partnerships in law is wrong and contrary to both Christian conviction and government policy. It should be a matter of the utmost importance to the justice of her case that the law operated on this assumption when Lilian Ladele took up her post as registrar. Since then the goalposts have moved. Surely it is only a matter of justice that she should not be forced out of her job because of this. Now that the goalposts have moved, and the law has been changed, anyone applying for a job as a registrar would have to submit to the conditions that the job demands. However, there seems to be something deeply illiberal and intolerant about trashing the career of someone who came into their post on profoundly different assumptions. What is sauce for the goose has to be sauce for the gander. There must be respect and tolerance in both directions if we are not to continue poisoning the whole debate about homosexuality in society and in the church. If Lilian Ladele had kept her post, civil partnerships would have continued to be celebrated by other registrars. There would have been no diminishment of service to gay people, and Islington Council would have demonstrated a *genuine* commitment to diversity, tolerance and multiculturalism.

There is a similar case to be made about Catholic adoption agencies. Regulations promulgated under the 2007 Equality Act meant that adoption agencies could not refuse to place children for adoption with homosexual couples. Despite appeals from most of the main Christian denominational leaders, the Charity Commission, Parliament and the courts refused to grant any exception for religious organisations in order to take account of ethical beliefs held in good conscience. In the current climate of opinion, it is vanishingly unlikely that gay couples would find it difficult to find an adoption agency willing to consider them. The argument has been repeatedly put forward that religious organisations can hold any beliefs they wish, but when they are acting in the public sphere, they are not allowed to discriminate in a way that affects anyone else. Accusations of bigotry, ignorance and blind prejudice have been freely thrown at the Catholic Church. All of this assumes that the argument that children ideally need a parental role model of each gender is so stupid as not to be worth consideration. It is fairly unreasonable to argue this. A perfectly reasonable and evidence-based argument can be put forward on both sides of this particular debate. Once again, we seem to be losing the ability to live with opinions and decisions that we do not like, within a mixed economy of belief and practice. Surely, we do not live in the Soviet Union where the state had a single policy on everything and was the sole provider of goods and services.

More recently the case of Christian bakers in Northern Ireland who refused to bake a wedding cake containing the message 'Support gay marriage' has hit the headlines. At a lower court and then again on appeal they were found guilty of breaching the Equalities Act. It was only at their final appeal, to the Supreme Court, that they were acquitted. Lady Hale, the president of the court, said in her judgment that if the bakery firm had refused the order on the grounds that the purchaser was gay, this would be illegal discrimination, "but that is not what happened in this case". She pointed out that their refusal was to bake a cake with whose message they disagreed. It is astonishing to me that initially the courts were willing to force people to publish[535] opinions with which they profoundly disagreed. This is even more surprising given that at that time Northern Ireland was the one part of the United Kingdom where same-sex marriage was not yet legal. We may or may not think that this is a good thing, but how can it be right to stifle and coerce expression of opinions in an ongoing debate? The shocking fact that this could not be perceived in the two lower courts reveals the extent of contempt and disdain for legitimate Christian conscience that can exist around this issue. Contempt and disdain produce polarisation. This is not the way to avoid 'the very vocal, firmly rooted, abhorrence-filled structural disconnect that exists in America between our two communities' of which Andrew Marin warned us.[536]

The analogy is often drawn with racial discrimination, but it is a poor analogy. It is manifestly obvious that it is not *necessarily* the case that having two parents of the same gender has no effect upon the children being brought up. Whether this is *actually* the case will doubtless require much research and long debate. However, it is a matter of common observation that we are particularly intolerant of the values of the generation that went before ours. Thus, for much of the twentieth century, the term 'Victorian' became a term of abuse, and 'Victorian values' were assumed by many to be ridiculous. Now, with a little more perspective, the Victorian age is receiving a more discriminating hearing. We are able to admire some values and practices, while rejecting others. It is dangerous and unjust, as soon as values begin to shift, to start treating those who still hold to the old values as though they were knaves or idiots. I suspect that we tend to do this because they often remind us of our parents, against whose values most of us have reacted in one way or another.

---

535 The fact that this was icing on a cake should not obscure the point that people were being forced to *publish* opinions contrary to their conscience.

536 See p.236

Unless we recognise this, we are hardly likely to respond with mature judgement.

It seems to me that much of the polarisation in current debates is created by fear, on both sides, of the thin end of the wedge. Thus, when legislation opened the possibility of permitting churches to conduct civil partnership ceremonies on their premises, it was opposed by the mainstream denominations because of the fear that such permission very soon becomes a requirement. Given what we have seen in the case of the Catholic adoption agencies, such a fear is not unreasonable. However, a number of denominations, among them the Quakers and the Unitarians, have requested permission to conduct such services. They should not be denied by law, in order to accommodate the consciences of Anglicans and others who fear the thin end of the wedge. This is manifestly unjust. If they are to be denied, it should be on broader grounds of social policy, which is hard to argue when the state has already decided to allow civil partnerships, and when these denominations are asking for it. Fear of the 'thin end of the wedge' on the part of other denominations is a poor argument for denying someone else freedom of conscience. We need to forswear 'thin end of the wedgery' as a way of stifling change, and we need to forswear the practice, once a social 'victory' is won and a law or prevailing opinion is changed, of assuming that those on the defeated side are fools or knaves, and must be bludgeoned into falling in line. This kind of illiberal intolerance restricts social change, by creating a climate of fear and distrust. No one dares make a concession lest it is used against them to restrict their liberty of conscience, lest, in other words, it turns out to be the thin end of the wedge.

Liberty of conscience should be an important Christian value and the law should coerce conscience as little as realistically possible. Each individual is answerable to God for their actions and attitudes. The law should therefore be cautious about intervening in matters of personal conscience, and should, wherever possible, seek to allow latitude for such conscience. The extreme reluctance to coerce demonstrated by Jesus should particularly make Christians respectful of the individual conscience and of the dangers of coercing the consciences of others. Where there are overriding reasons why respect for such conscience would cause undesirable social results and harm to others, then coercion may well be appropriate. We have seen that even Jesus would act coercively in such cases. It is not enough to say that because of my religious beliefs I wish to exterminate Jews, or practise female circumcision. Where this boundary line falls will always be contentious. However, a few general principles can be adduced. Among them might be that we should presume against coercing conscientious beliefs that until very recently have been mainstream and recognised by law. We should be cautious about prohibiting views and actions that, because we operate in a mixed economy, would not actually cause hardship if allowed to operate because there are other providers of services who would step in (as in the Ladele or the bakery case). Actions stemming from views, however conscientiously held, that are individualistic, quirky, or not represented by a substantial tradition or body of opinion, should face a heavier burden of proof in resisting legislative control if proven to cause any harm. It is not beyond human ingenuity to work out such principles through unfolding case law.

Bigotry is unacceptable. It is unacceptable when it comes from a supposedly Christian conservative voice who cannot admit that there is any interpretation of the faith but their own. It is equally bigotry and equally unacceptable when it comes from supposed liberals who denounce anyone who disagrees with them as bigots. 'Bigot' has become such an unthinking term of abuse that our society would be a great deal better if we simply excised the word from our vocabulary. Quite often I feel that one of the surest signs of a bigot is when anyone uses the term to castigate their opponent.

EXPERIENCE SHOULD TAKE US BACK TO THE BIBLE FOR A FRESH LOOK

I have been made to think afresh about faith and homosexual people partly because of the experience of my son. Some would say that I'm falling into the trap of being led by experience, and not by the Bible.

However, whether we admit it or not, we all interpret the Bible in the light of our experience and in the light of all kinds of assumptions. We dealt with this to some extent in Chapter 7. Unless we pause to reflect, it is too easy to remain unconscious of what are the experiences and assumptions that shape our frame of reference. Fresh experience, by raising fresh questions, can alert us to all kinds of issues in the Bible that we might not have seen before. I have already argued that this is one of the reasons why I find it helpful to read through the whole Bible annually. A principled approach to Christian faith and revelation demands not that we allow experience to dictate our beliefs and practices at the expense of the Bible, but that experience should drive us back to re-examine the Bible and the conclusions that we draw from it.[537] If we are wise we will not limit ourselves only to taking account of our own experience, which is necessarily partial and culturally limited. As we saw earlier,[538] we need the input of those of other cultures if we are to understand Scripture aright. This must include the voice of gay Christians just as much as it must include any other Christian subculture.

As usual, Jeremy Marks puts it very well. 'Gay Christians... follow the same path to Christ as their straight brothers and sisters. So when they, with sincere conviction, take a view that challenges the traditional understanding of homosexuality, then... if we believe in our own core values, we should give them an honest hearing.

Since we must all stand to give account before God, who dares

---

537 We examined the interaction of scripture and experience more fully on pp.145–148.
538 P.138ff.

presume that their interpretation of the Bible on a point of doctrine has greater validity because they are heterosexual?'[539]

A Look at the Biblical Evidence

Though the interpretation of the Bible on this subject is well-ploughed ground, I am going to run quickly over a few of the contending interpretations once again in order to establish that the range of possible legitimate and honest Christian interpretations is quite wide.

As I said earlier, all that is strictly necessary for my argument is to establish that whichever side of this debate we are on, at least some of those who disagree are sincerely committed to discovering God's will even if we are convinced that they are mistaken. Once we acknowledge this much, we must treat each other as fellow members of the body of Christ. However, I am, in a rather delicate exercise, going to try to go further, namely to attempt to demonstrate, in the case of homosexuality, that the biblical case is a good deal more ambiguous than most of us (on either side) would like. It is a delicate exercise because, having weighed the evidence, I still believe, on balance, that the Bible invites the homosexually oriented to celibacy. However, understanding better the reasoning of those who believe otherwise has helped me to perceive that this is not such a straightforward argument as I once believed. I no longer believe that my conclusion is the only conceivably correct one.

On the face of it, the Bible prohibits homosexual behaviour. As George Hopper says, 'it is the contention of those who see condemnation of homosexuality in the Bible that the word *(homosexuality)* is plain and unambiguous.'[540]

Hopper argues that some passages previously (mis)translated

---

539   *Exchanging the Truth of God for a Lie*, Jeremy Marks, p.55 (Courage UK, 2008)

540   *Reluctant Journey*, George Hopper, Ch.5, www.reluctantjourney.co.uk

as 'sodomite' in fact refer to, and are now translated as, 'shrine prostitutes', e.g. Deuteronomy 23:17-18; 1 Kings 14:24, 15:12, 22:46; 2 Kings 23:7. This can easily be verified by comparing modern translations with the King James version of the Bible. These passages are all about cult prostitution, rather than sexual orientation, and reflected God's and Israel's detestation of the pagan practices of the tribes that occupied the land before them, and do not refer to sexual orientation as such.[541]

He then examines Genesis 19:1-11, an account of attempted homosexual rape at Sodom. That this passage cannot possibly justify a blanket condemnation of homosexuality is so obvious that it should not need stating. Perhaps it is a reflection of just how much this debate has become rooted in visceral feelings at the expense of logic that I still hear Genesis 19 used in this way. If the homosexual rape described here is a condemnation of all homosexuality, then the very similar passage at Judges 19:22-30, describing a heterosexual rape, is a condemnation of all heterosexuality.

In the Old Testament this leaves Leviticus 18:22 and 20:13 as the key passages.[542] Hopper argues that they refer to sexual experimenters, heterosexuals who wilfully turn aside. He bases his argument upon the ignorance of the Old Testament authors.

'When rereading the Bible in the light of this issue, my overriding

---

541 Unless otherwise cited, this, and subsequent references to Hopper in this section come from George Hopper, *Reluctant Journey*, Ch.6. www.reluctantjourney. co.uk.

542 'Do not have sexual relations with a man as one does with a woman; that is detestable.' (Leviticus 18:22) 'If a man has sexual relations with a man as one does with a woman, both of them have done what is detestable. They are to be put to death; their blood will be on their own heads.' (Leviticus 20:13) I do not propose to deal here with the requirement of the death penalty, repugnant though it is to modern sensibilities. It is not particularly relevant to the arguments at issue. The death penalty is prescribed for many things in the Old Testament, as in many older societies, often reflecting the weaknesses of methods for detecting and punishing crimes, and the need therefore to have exemplary deterrents. Among those many things are theft, adultery and murder, but our repugnance at the death penalty does not mean that these things should not be discouraged or prohibited. In the current context therefore the provision to 'put to death' is a red herring.

impression was that the writers knew nothing of homosexuality as we know and understand it today.[543]

I am instinctively suspicious of arguments that treat those of former times as if they were somehow less aware, not as observant as we enlightened moderns are. I simply do not believe that nothing was known of homosexuality, as we know it, in Old Testament times. Surely there were priests, and others then, with sons and daughters who had a gay orientation, or who struggled with their own sexuality?

I think that Roy Clements gets us closer to a possible truth when he focuses on vocabulary. 'It is clear that within the human population there is a substantial minority who develop erotic feelings for the same sex. To use vocabulary that was not available to the biblical authors, such individuals have a homosexual orientation.'[544]

Surely the key point is that they did not have the language for a permanent, unchanging and unchangeable homosexual orientation, or at least if they did, we are not aware of it. This raises questions about what exactly the author of Leviticus is referring to. Without the vocabulary it is not possible for us to be completely certain.

Hopper then goes on to argue that, on the basis of his interpretation of Leviticus 18:22 and 20:13, that Romans 1:21–27,[545] and 1 Corinthians

---

543 *Reluctant Journey*, George Hopper, Ch.7, www.reluctantjourney.co.uk
544 *Why Evangelicals Must Think Again About Homosexuality*, Roy Clements, http://www.courage.org.uk/articles/thinkagain.shtml
545 'For although they knew God, they neither glorified him as God nor gave thanks to him, but their thinking became futile and their foolish hearts were darkened. Although they claimed to be wise, they became fools and exchanged the glory of the immortal God for images made to look like a mortal human being and birds and animals and reptiles.
   Therefore God gave them over in the sinful desires of their hearts to sexual impurity for the degrading of their bodies with one another. They exchanged the truth about God for a lie, and worshipped and served created things rather than the Creator – who is for ever praised. Amen.
   Because of this, God gave them over to shameful lusts. Even their women exchanged natural sexual relations for unnatural ones. In the same way the men also abandoned natural relations with women and were inflamed with lust for one another. Men committed shameful acts with other men, and received in themselves the due penalty for their error.'

6:9 (which probably had Leviticus in mind)[546] do not apply to non-abusive homosexuality. It seems to me that this conclusion is by no means obvious or inevitable, but it is possible.

Furthermore, Roy Clements argues, 'The Pauline references in I Corinthians 6 and I Timothy 1 hinge on the meaning of two disputed words: "malachoi" and "arsenokoitai". The first, meaning literally "soft ones", does not necessarily relate to sexual behaviour at all. It could, for instance, refer to effeminacy in dress or manner. The second may well be a deliberate echoing in Greek of the Hebrew text of Leviticus 18:21. It is a very rare word, but seems always to be associated with sins of exploitation and abuse rather than sexual immorality per se.

There are strong grounds, then, for believing that these two words are heavily laden with cultural connotations specific to the first-century pagan world where, for instance, male prostitution and pederasty were widespread. Certainly, to translate them "homosexuals" begs an enormous number of questions and is in any case thoroughly anachronistic since the notion of sexual orientation did not exist before modern times.'[547]

Dan O. Via[548] and others deal with the Leviticus passages in a more summary way, arguing that many of the Levitical laws are uncleanness and purity laws that Jesus specifically abolished when he said, '"Nothing outside a person can defile them."'[549]

One of the better cases for a more permissive interpretation of the Bible on this issue is made by Keith Runcorn in an appendix to the Church of

---

546 'Do you not know that wrongdoers will not inherit the kingdom of God? Do not be deceived: neither the sexually immoral nor idolaters nor adulterers nor men who have sex with men nor thieves nor the greedy nor drunkards nor slanderers nor swindlers will inherit the kingdom of God.'

547 *Why Evangelicals Must Think Again About Homosexuality*, Roy Clements, http://www.courage.org.uk/articles/thinkagain.shtml

548 *Homosexuality and the Bible: Two Views*, by Robert A. J. Gagnon and Dan O. Via, Location 113ff. (Fortress Press, Minneapolis digital edition, 2003)

549 Mark 7:15

England's Pilling report. Quoting Dick France, he says, 'A truly biblical hermeneutic must not confine itself to the overt pronouncements... but must be open to the biblical evidence as a whole, including its narrative and incidental parts.'... This... 'may lead us to re-examine the way we have interpreted the more "obvious" texts.'[550]

Among the wider readings he suggests we should take into account are 'it is not good for the man to be alone',[551] Paul's recognition that celibacy is not possible for all to sustain and therefore must be freely chosen (in 1 Corinthians 7),[552] and Jesus' habit of 'scandalous inclusions.'[553]

Dan O. Via argues that, because of the mounting evidence of harm to gay people from a more restrictive interpretation, more weight should be given to such texts as these. 'The burden of proof in the last twenty years has shifted.'[554] This is a classic example of experience leading us not to put the Bible aside, but to return to it with renewed vigour to re-evaluate what it says.

Not all of the arguments put forward in defence of a more permissive opinion about homosexuality seem to me to hold water. For example, Hopper's argument that, 'Therefore there is now no condemnation for those who are in Christ Jesus',[555] means that we should not condemn homosexual acts. However, it is surely illegitimate to extrapolate from a statement about the justification of sinners and the forgiveness of sins, to saying that we cannot therefore make a judgement about ethical issues. That way lies the end of all ethical discernment.

The advocates for a conservative case tend to argue that the meaning

---

550 Report of The House of Bishops Working Group on Human Sexuality, p. 179 (Church House Publishing, 2013)
551 Ibid. p.183 referring to Genesis 2:18
552 Ibid. p.189
553 Ibid. p.191 (citing R. Burridge, *Imitating Jesus: An Inclusive Approach to New Testament Ethics*, p.78 (Eerdmans, 2007))
554 Gagnon and Via, Location 465
555 Romans 8:1

of the key texts (especially Leviticus 18:22 and 20:13, Romans 1:21–27, and 1 Corinthians 6:9) have been rightly translated and traditionally rightly understood.

This case has been clearly and compellingly made in a minority report within the Pilling Report, by Keith Sinclair, Bishop of Birkenhead. Dealing with the contested word 'arsenokoites' in 1 Corinthians 6:9, he argues that 'there is an overwhelming case, well documented in the literature, that the word means someone who sleeps (i.e. has sex) with other men.'[556] It adds powerfully to his argument here that a number of those who argue for liberalisation concede this point, among them Dan O. Via.[557]

Via argues that the Old Testament does proscribe homosexuality, but that this proscription in Leviticus is simply another example of the kind of ritual cleanliness laws that Jesus abrogated, or fulfilled. However, this argument is seriously undermined, as Via admits, by the fact that in the New Testament Paul 'reinterprets homosexuality as sin rather than as uncleanness'.

Furthermore, what of Jesus' teaching about self-denial? Does this not apply to gay people? Sinclair argues 'In today's culture, it is not easy to insist on self-denial. We have been seduced by popular philosophies spinning the illusion that the uninhibited expression of our desires ("being who you are") is the key to human flourishing.'[558]

This is given added force by the witness of contributors to the 'Living Out'[559] website who testify to the liberty of a life of celibacy. The most prominent among them is Vaughan Roberts, Rector of St Ebbe's in Oxford. Though one of the five has married a woman, they bear witness to the fact that God does not normally change orientation, but that He does give grace to live a chaste and celibate life.

---

556   Report of The House of Bishops Working Group on Human Sexuality, p. 135
       (Church House Publishing, 2013)
557   Gagnon and Via, (op. cit.) Location 192
558   Report of The House of Bishops Working Group on Human Sexuality, p. 124
559   http://www.livingout.org/

In conclusion, I would argue that a possible and plausible case has been made for a more permissive interpretation of what the Bible has to say on homosexuality. Because none of the arguments seemed to me to be conclusive, this brief summary of some of them might seem confusing. I hope however that I have established that the range of potential Christian conclusions on this issue is quite wide. It was not my aim to persuade anyone to change their mind on the issue. I hope however that I have demonstrated clearly why I can no longer say that those who are more permissive on this issue are necessarily unbiblical. This is despite the fact that I am not myself fully convinced that a sufficiently strong case has been made for reinterpreting either the Leviticus passages, or the Pauline Epistles. I remain, therefore, inclined towards the traditional interpretation, but respectful of the Christian stance of those who disagree.

WHAT THEN SHOULD WE DO?

However, whatever our interpretation there remains a further question: what do we do about it?

In the light of what we said in Chapter 2 about Jesus choosing to invite, not coerce, surely it should be for gay Christians to decide their own discipline. Furthermore, given the contentious nature of the biblical evidence, it is particularly inappropriate for the church to maintain a hard line on this issue.

But I would also appeal to those who stress liberty to remember that dying to self is at the heart of the Gospel, is the road to life and freedom, and is deeply countercultural. Given the place of dying to self in Jesus' message it would be rather odd not to consider that this also might be what God is saying to gay people, as he says it about many issues to all people.

If the call to celibacy must not, on the one hand, be coercive, on the other hand neither must it be drowned out. It is for gay people themselves to decide. Why should we single out those who are gay for harsh discipline, while allowing the rich (for example), who often will not deny themselves, to self-regulate?

I would appeal to those who maintain the conservative view to take full account of what a heavy thing it is to embrace a call to celibacy, and according to Jesus, not all can accept it. For those who do accept it the church needs to be a family in a much more real and thorough sense than is at all common in the Western world. Church needs to really be family, not just a once-a-week club.[560]

We have absolutely no warrant for denying that those who disagree with us are fellow Christians any more than we do if we disagree about other biblically contentious issues like war and peace, or infant baptism. Our debate can be, possibly needs to be, robust, and our disagreements honestly faced. We must not refuse to argue, but must do so with respect, affection, charity and within the bonds of peace, as brothers and sisters in Christ. Probably the most helpful thing we can do for the world is to model a truly Christian way of disagreeing. Few things have given me as much hope that this can happen as the tone of the 'Living Out' website. At last a group of conservative evangelicals are talking about 'us' not just 'them'. I cannot over emphasise the importance of this. When to this are added the use of 'indaba' type dialogues in the debates over homosexuality and women bishops, and the way the decision over women bishops was eventually taken, I have more hope than I did. However, there is still much cause for concern. As we seek to disagree and debate in a Christlike way and for Jesus Christ's sake, it is not easy to steer a path between strident shouty nastiness and coercion on one side, and unprincipled fudge for the sake of institutional survival on the other.

Signs of hope have been long overdue. The way the homosexuality debate has been conducted at times has been deeply damaging to many gay people, damaging to the faith of many, both heterosexual

---

560 Those who convert from some other faiths often have need of the same sort of support.

and homosexual, and has been deeply damaging to the church's witness. Christians are perceived as being nasty and unloving. The vast amount of evidence to the contrary is ignored, or not even noticed. It seems to matter little how much Christians are involved in voluntary work looking after the vulnerable in their neighbourhood as long as the public perception is that we are the people conducting a vendetta against homosexuals.

Jesus invites us to self-discipline, not to coercing and policing each other. This means I have every right to argue my case from Scripture, no right to characterise those who take a different view as non-Christians, no excuse for not being in fellowship with different churches from mine who might practise a different discipline, and no right to coerce, reject or judge.

I suggest that we allow each other the kind of liberty St Paul evinced when he said 'All of us who are mature should take such a view of things. And if on some point you think differently, that too God will make clear to you. Only let us live up to what we have already attained.'[561]

WHAT IS GOOD NEWS FOR GAY PEOPLE?

Jesus reintegrated the scapegoated and the excluded. He restored them all, the demoniac, the man born blind, the lepers, the woman caught in adultery, the tax collectors, the Gentiles and the sinners. Surely, historically, gay people have been among the excluded, and the scapegoated. How does Jesus restore and include them? He certainly is not doing it through changing their orientation.[562] What, then, is good news for gay people? Surely it is the same as good news for the rest of us. That good news is Jesus, God among us, who died for our

---

561   Philippians 3:15
562   See p.245–248

sins and invites us into fellowship with Him. If, instead of the message that Jesus is good news for gay people, we convey the message that gay people are bad news for the church, we do not just betray gay people, we betray Jesus himself.

Homosexuality is NOT a salvation issue. Jesus is the only salvation issue. Moreover, if we believe that we are Bible people, we must trust the Bible to speak to gay people also, and if we believe that the church is the community of the reconciled and redeemed that crosses every boundary, we need to hear the voice of gay people interpreting the Bible if we are to stand a chance of letting the Bible speak through our own cultural prejudices and blinkers (just as gay people need to hear the voices of those who differ from them). I do not here for a moment imagine that gay people speak with a single voice.

We seem able to uphold the teaching that marriage is sacred, and is between one man and one woman, for life, without making the divorced and remarried feel that they are a cancer in the church. Can we not achieve the same with gay people, whether partnered or not? If not, why not? Perhaps because gay people are a small enough minority to either ignore, avoid or bully as seems most expedient?

Wouldn't it be better, as far as institutional discipline can conceivably allow, to leave gay people to choose their discipline, their biblical interpretation, for themselves? Don't we trust them? Are they not adults? Why do they have to be legislated for? Remember, self-denial cannot be imposed.

Some seem instinctively to react to anything but the most extreme literalism in interpreting the Bible, with the suspicion that someone is trying to 'get away' with something. This betrays a lack of confidence in God's law as gift, as blessing. It betrays a lack of understanding of the call to self-denial as invitation, not imposition. Once we see 'the law' as a gracious gift, it becomes something to be shared rather than imposed, and those without it become those to be pitied, rather than those to be angry with, except to the extent that they are harming others.

To what extent are non-celibate gay people harming others? Are they undermining marriage? A good case could be made for saying that at present, in British society, it is gay people who are arguing for recognition of permanent and stable relationships who are doing most publicly to defend the covenantal permanence of relationships.

A rediscovery of an understanding of God's law as gracious gift will free us to really appreciate, honour, and understand the Bible, because it takes the fear and anxiety away from our discipleship.

We must treat our gay brothers and sisters as just that, brothers and sisters in Christ, whether they are abstinent or not. In order to treat each other as brothers and sisters in Christ in this way, friendship, dialogue, fellowship and worship with one another is essential. Jesus made friends with anyone who would be open to Him, with tax collectors, prostitutes, Samaritans, Romans. Who are we to be exclusive, to be not just holier than thou, but, apparently, holier than Jesus?

Gay people can read the Bible for themselves, and gay Christians are no less able to respond to God's leading than the rest of us (perhaps more so). The majority need to put down our weapons, forswear coercion, and trust them. After all, singleness and celibacy are gifts to be freely received from God. You don't impose gifts with rules and sanctions. Jesus, while discussing divorce and remarriage, said:

"'Not everyone can accept this word, but only those to whom it has been given. For there are eunuchs who were born that way, and there are eunuchs who have been made eunuchs by others – and there are those who choose to live like eunuchs for the sake of the kingdom of heaven. The one who can accept this should accept it.'"[563]

In the light of this I do not believe that celibacy can normally be imposed, any more than the call or invitation to celibacy should be stifled. God's will for us is a gracious gift to be freely embraced by willing disciples. In place of this we have too often opted for therapeutic

---

563   Matthew 19:11–12

or consumerist models of fulfilment, and turned Jesus into the great therapist, or the great provider of material blessings and comfort, or we have opted for a totalitarian vision of faith, with Jesus as Big Brother and us as His not so secret policemen. Thus the religion of therapy that promises to deliver from homosexual orientation, fulfilment religion with its assumption that we can find happiness only through the fulfilment of our desires, and the religion of coercive conformity that seeks to nail others to the cross, the three positions around which much of the controversy swirls, may all be equally false alternatives, as un-Christlike as each other, and a bypassing of Jesus' joyful invitation to follow as His disciples.

Could it be that in a more Christlike atmosphere, where gay people were, and felt, loved in the household of Christ, that the testimony of many fulfilled celibate gay Christians could be heard again, that the challenge to die to self could be heard from the only ones who have a right to issue it, namely those who have walked that road? I believe that would happen. And if not? Well, it could be that our conservative interpretation of scripture could turn out to be wrong. I don't believe it will, but it could. As long as so many questions are left unasked, let alone un-answered, as long as an atmosphere of ungrace makes most of the church a no-go area for gay people, I don't see how we can really progress in our understanding of the Bible, and of discipleship. Truth does not thrive in an atmosphere of intimidation and fear. The Bible can only be understood aright when it is lived. We *need* those who are working out their discipleship in a way we may not agree with. Only God, in His good time, can show us what is right and what is wrong.

And if we turn out to have made a mistake?... That is the risk that faith has to take.

The church might take a wrong road, and not for the first time. It's the same risk that the Reformers took when the Bible was put into the hands of every believer. It was the same risk Jesus took when He came to earth and made Himself vulnerable.

Or we may end up understanding the Bible and the ways of God more profoundly.

'The main hindrance to the use of scripture lies in the notion that you are already acquainted with its contents.'[564]

THE JOURNEY SO FAR

What can we learn from Jesus that is relevant to the church's debate around homosexuality? The fact that Jesus never mentioned it does rather suggest that, whatever His conclusions, His priorities are elsewhere.

In many ways homosexual people have been treated as outcasts in church and society. Jesus has a very great deal to teach us about, and through the outcasts of His day.

Moreover, Jesus' teaching and example may have a great deal to say to us about how we conduct the current debate and disputes in this contested area. Too often this debate has been characterised by lack of grace and love.

Whenever the discussion takes on the tone of 'us righteous against those sinners' we find ourselves in a dangerous and deeply un-Christian place.

Homosexuality only makes any sense as an issue with which to draw a line in the sand regarding biblical authority if the range of possible interpretations of Scripture cannot reasonably be held to embrace the point of view of those we are opposing.

I am now convinced that:
1) *For most gay people theirs was not a chosen orientation.*
2) *'Healing' of homosexuality does not normally happen.*
3) *This has huge implications for the acceptance of people as they are.*

564　*A Statesman's Manual*, Samuel Taylor Coleridge, p.30 (1816 edition, http://openlibrary.org/b/OL7193406M/statesman's_manual)

Any approach that leaves fellow sinners experiencing rejection rather than loving acceptance is not faithful to Jesus Christ.

The church too is greatly impoverished when we do not fully include gay Christians who often have a particularly powerful and rich testimony. Their testimony and sacrificial commitment is, in many ways, parallel to that of the persecuted Christians who have so often enriched and challenged me.

As we concluded in Chapter 7, fresh experience should prompt us to take a fresh look at our interpretations of scripture, and for that task we need the input of those whose experience of life is different from ours. We lose immeasurably when we only regard gay Christian voices as a problem and not a resource.

Bigotry can be two-edged. Just as the exclusion of gay people has been unacceptable, so is discrimination against those who hold to a conscience-driven view that they cannot, for example, celebrate a gay marriage or partnership.

Whatever conclusion we come to on this issue, I believe that it is hard to argue that our conclusion is the only possible one for a Christian of integrity.

- *It is for gay Christians themselves to decide which path to follow as they work out their own discipleship.*
- *It is important that the call to die to self is seriously considered in this issue as in every other discipleship issue.*
- *If some are to take seriously the call to celibacy the church needs to be far more of a true community than is commonly found in the West.*
- *We have no warrant for denying that those who disagree with us on this issue are fellow Christians.*
- *Faithfulness demands that we disagree honestly, even robustly sometimes, but graciously, affectionately and within the bonds of peace.*

- *The world needs us to model a Christian way of living with and handling deep disagreement.*

We all need to be able to answer the question 'What is good news for gay people?' Gay people need to have a key part in answering that question.

God's will is good news. It is a gift to mankind. Gifts are usually offered, not imposed.

The religion of therapy that promises to deliver from homosexual orientation, fulfilment religion with its assumption that we can find happiness only through the fulfilment of our desires, and the religion of coercive conformity that seeks to nail others to the cross, the three positions around which much of the controversy swirls, may all be equally false alternatives, as un-Christlike as each other, and a bypassing of Jesus' joyful invitation to follow as His disciples.

CHAPTER ELEVEN

CONCLUSION

The Son is the image of the invisible God, the firstborn over all creation.[565]

THE IMAGE OF THE INVISIBLE GOD

We go wrong in all kinds of ways if we lose our focus on Jesus. Our unity suffers as we each choose secondary things to centre upon, our discipleship suffers as we focus on issues or dogmas, often at the expense of character. All sorts of idolatries take over as He ceases to be our Lord and saviour. A plea to keep Jesus central can sound rather simple-minded, but I hope I have done enough to show in detail how such an approach might be worked through in a disciplined and thoughtful way.

It is not that Jesus is the most important person of the Trinity, but as the climax of God's self-revelation it is through the person of Jesus that we understand God the Father and God the Holy Spirit. God was not in disguise in Jesus. His humanity revealed His divinity. Whenever at Christmas I sing the lines *'veiled in flesh the Godhead see'* I want to say "No! No! No!" The vulnerability, the humility, the empathy, the love thereby revealed illuminate the nature of God, they do not veil it. We tend to think otherwise however when we start

---

565   Colossians 1:15

with the God of the philosophers, and then allow Jesus to modify that picture somewhat, which is what Western theology has often done.

In its attempt to reach the then predominantly Greek world, the early church adopted much of the thinking of classical philosophers, and as the known world was Christianised, so was the church Hellenised.

This has had advantages and disadvantages, but to the extent that the person of Jesus ceases to be normative for our understanding of God, serious consequences can result, not least in the implications of our understanding of God the Father for the exercise of power. Jesus shows us that God is vulnerable and suffers all the pain of love. The philosophers taught us that God is 'impassible', that is, He cannot suffer. The philosophers taught us that God is omnipotent, whilst Jesus has taught us that God has limited His power voluntarily. He does not throw His weight around. The philosophers taught us that God is unchanging, but Jesus grew in wisdom and stature. Given this background it is no surprise that discipleship is often modelled on the God of the philosophers, who so often appears to sanctify our worldly approach to power, rather than on the God who said 'not by might, nor by power, but by my spirit'.[566]

'In a note discovered after his death, Blaise Pascal, the seventeenth-century scientist and philosopher, recorded an intense religious experience that changed his life. He provided few details of what happened other than to say it was like "fire". In this experience Pascal became completely certain of the reality of God. While Pascal was far from being a despiser of reason and philosophy, the God whom he knew with certainty in his fiery experience was "God of Abraham, God of Isaac, God of Jacob, not of the philosophers and scholars". For Pascal, the living God is the God of the biblical witness: "God of Jesus

---

566   Zechariah 4:6

Christ... He is to be found only by the ways taught in the gospel... We keep hold of him only by the ways taught in the gospel".[567]

What is at stake is our image of God. We must choose between the image God has revealed, supremely in Jesus Christ, or idolatrous self-constructed images. Our image of God will shape our personalities and our culture. If we see God as a man with a big stick always forcibly straightening others out, then we will justify bullying and intolerance. Idolatry is the hidden root of many evils.

THE LIVING LORD JESUS – OR IDEOLOGY

Jesus is real and He is alive. He is not just a symbol that stands for our moral opinions, or a cipher that provides a particular way into heaven. He is alive and will have the last word, and everything we think we believe must be provisional before His final judgment. It is easy, however, to make our conclusions about Jesus more absolute, more important, than Jesus himself. That way lies mere ideology. Then we may come to Him because He seems to agree with some of the things we already think important, whether it is justice and peace, or family values or any one of many other values. This way we never seem to move on to be transformed by Him, but instead His image becomes conformed to what we already believe. At this point we particularly need the companionship of Christians who are significantly different from us, who will challenge us and stimulate us as they understand aspects of Jesus to which we are blind.

'Ideology is what you have when you don't have faith. When you are not aware that there is Another, bigger than us, who is holding all of us in his hand through the upheaval and that ultimately we are safe, there is room, we can be wrong, and we can learn to get it right; when

---

567 Quoted in *The Power of God and the gods of Power*, Daniel L. Migliore, p.60 (Westminster John Knox, 2008)

you are not aware of that, then you are frightened of disagreement and what you need to do is to produce a unanimity of opinion, of ideology, you need to get everyone to agree, and have those who are in, in, and those who are out, out.

'But this is the classic sign of people who have a compulsion for certainty, a compulsion for being right, and a compulsion for being considered to be good, and so who grasp onto a fake certainty, a resolved righteousness, too small a togetherness. If we react like this, then it means that our anchor isn't in the rock beyond the veil. If it were then we would be happy to know that we can all be wrong together, all learn together, and that our squabbling about what is right is a necessary part of the process of all of us learning.'[568]

Confidence in Jesus Christ as God's last word frees *us* from having to have the last word. It makes it possible to hold clear convictions with some degree of provisionality and humility.

We can say with Paul, 'My conscience is clear, but that does not make me innocent. It is the Lord who judges me.'[569] We can take our opinions and conclusions seriously, but without absolutising them. This might go a long way towards defusing the growing secular opinion that Christians are arrogant.

What if in some of our current debates within the church, particularly over homosexuality, God is more interested in the *way* we handle this issue and treat each other than in which side wins? If so, then it is quite likely that He will not one day simply vindicate one side or the other.

Abraham Lincoln famously wrote, 'In the present civil war it is quite possible that God's purpose is something different from the purpose of either party.'[570] This was in the context of people on either

---

568   James Alison quoted in *Exchanging the Truth of God for a Lie,* Jeremy Marks, p.9 (Courage UK, 2008)
569   1 Corinthians 4:4
570   *Meditation on the Divine Will,* Abraham Lincoln, 1862

side claiming the divine will for themselves. To argue as Lincoln did was not to argue that He didn't care about the outcome, or that the preservation of the Union and the abolition of slavery were not causes He believed right.

This doesn't mean that the so-called substantive issues don't matter, just that something else matters even more.

FINALLY...

We are not primarily called to be the inspector who regulates the proper manufacture of the loaf. We are called to be the salt and the yeast that gives the loaf its quality and flavour. We need to have the flavour of Jesus Christ.

So, when we contend for truth we do so not to win, but to bless, and with the hope that both we and our opponents grow closer to the truth. 'Humility asserts truth not to bolster the ego with control or with triumphs in debate, but as service to Christ and love to the adversary.'[571]

Christian faith is about gracious invitation, not law enforcement. We are not meant to be the Taleban, but messengers from a king with an unexpected invitation to a banquet.

This, to me, is summed up in a story told by Philip Yancey about his gay friend Mel coming out.

'Mel's parents, conservative Christians and respected pillars of the community (Mel's father had been his city's mayor), had a tougher time accepting the situation. After Mel broke the news to them, they went through various stages of shock and denial. At one point, a TV interviewer asked Mel's parents on camera, "You know what other Christians are saying about your son. They say he's an abomination. What do you think about that?" "Well," the mother answered in a

---

571 *Brothers, We Are Not Professionals*, by John Piper, p.163 (Broadman and Holman, 2001)

sweet, quavery voice, "he may be an abomination, but he's still our pride and joy.'"[572]

Yancey goes on to point out that this is a heart-rending definition of grace. We are all of us, in one sense, abominations to God, yet He loves us anyhow.

To care passionately and remain gracious and humble is a rare and winsome combination. Sometimes our church debates are best characterised by the words of W. B. Yeats: 'The best lack all conviction, while the worst are full of passionate intensity.'[573]

The voice of God in such circumstances might not be that obvious. When Elisha needed to hear God, he found that God's voice was not in the earthquake, the wind or the fire, but came as a still, small voice.[574] Such a voice demands attentiveness. If we are in love with the sound of our own voice, we are likely to miss it.

In a self-portrait that reverberates with the character of Jesus, God says through Isaiah to a contentious and quarrelsome people:

> 'For this is what the high and exalted One says –
> he who lives for ever, whose name is holy:
> "I live in a high and holy place,
> but also with the one who is contrite and lowly in spirit,
> to revive the spirit of the lowly
> and to revive the heart of the contrite."'[575]

---

572   *What's So Amazing About Grace?*, Philip Yancey, p.170–1 (Zondervan, 1997)
573   *The Second Coming*, W. B. Yeats
574   1 Kings 19:11–13
575   Isaiah 57:15

REFERENCES

THE HOLY BIBLE, NEW INTERNATIONAL VERSION®, NIV®
Copyright © 1973, 1978, 1984, 2011 by Biblica, Inc.™ Used by
permission. All rights reserved worldwide.

JESUS AND POWER, by David Prior, 1987, Hodder and Stoughton.
Extracts used by permission.

EXCHANGING THE TRUTH OF GOD FOR A LIE, by Jeremy Marks,
2008, published by the author. Extracts used by permission.

WHAT'S SO AMAZING ABOUT GRACE? by Philip Yancey, 1997,
Zondervan www.zondervan.com. Extracts used by permission.

THE JESUS I NEVER KNEW by Philip Yancey, 1995, Zondervan
www.zondervan.com. Extracts used by permission.

Extracts from THE TIMES and THE SUNDAY TIMES © News UK.
Used by permission.

ABOUT THE AUTHOR

Until recently, the author was Mission Advisor to Guildford Diocese.

After serving in Iran, then as vicar in multi-racial inner London, he learned that Jesus illuminates and is illuminated by cultural diversity and complexity. Lately those insights have been enriched by exploring with his son "what does it mean to be gay and Christian?"